Palm Beach

Visual Arts

Palm Beach

Visual Arts

Deborah C. Pollack

PELICAN PUBLISHING COMPANY

GRETNA 2016

The word "Pelican" and the depiction of a pelican are trademarks of Pelican Publishing Company, Inc., and are registered in the U.S. Patent and Trademark Office.

Library of Congress Cataloging-in-Publication Data

Names: Pollack, Deborah C., author.
Title: Palm Beach visual arts / by Deborah C. Pollack.
Description: Gretna : Pelican Publishing Company, 2016. | Includes
   bibliographical references and index.
Identifiers: LCCN 2016010414| ISBN 9781455622221 (hardcover :
alk. paper) |
   ISBN 9781455622238 (e-book)
Subjects: LCSH: Art and society—Florida—Palm Beach—History. | Art,
   American—Florida—Palm Beach.
Classification: LCC N72.S6 P65 2016 | DDC 701/.03—dc23 LC
record available at http://lccn.loc.gov/2016010414

Printed in South Korea
Published by Pelican Publishing Company, Inc.
1000 Burmaster Street, Gretna, Louisiana 70053

Contents

Acknowledgments

I could not have accomplished this without the cooperation of the Historical Society of Palm Beach County (HSPBC) and the magnanimous generosity of Debi Murray, its chief curator, and Jeremy W. Johnson, CAE, president and chief executive officer. Aside from Debi's graciousness and support for the project, she made many helpful suggestions after reading the manuscript's first draft. Nick Golubov, the society's research and curatorial assistant, was a tremendous help in finding their hidden archival treasures and never complained once about my numerous requests, which were enough to exhaust anyone else.

My husband, Edward Pollack, deserves credit for his patience during the many hours each day I spent devoted to research, writing, and photographing. I want to acknowledge and thank The Society of the Four Arts and the Norton Museum of Art, whose generosity overwhelmed me. Editor in chief of Pelican Publishing Company, Nina Kooij, deserves my sincere thanks as well, for taking on this project. I also want to thank associate editor Erin Classen, executive secretary Sally Boitnott, and the editorial and design team.

More specifically, I am also very grateful to Mel Abfier; Margaret Acton, volunteer archivist, Historical Society of Palm Beach County; Aleesha Nissen Ast, assistant registrar, Norton Museum of Art; Margaret Z. Atkins, reference services, Archives of American Art, Smithsonian Institution; Barridoff Galleries; George Bolge, Museum of Art, Deland, Florida; Kimberly Botelho, graphic designer, Kaminski Auctions; Rachel Bradshaw, registrar, Henry Morrison Flagler Museum; Ruth Bryan, CA, director of archives and university archivist, University of Kentucky Libraries, Special Collections; Mary Ellen Budney, public services assistant, Beinecke Rare Book and Manuscript Library; William Bunch Auctioneers; Melissa M. Caldwell, chief curator, Philadelphia Art Alliance; Molly Charland, director of education, The Society of the Four Arts; Thomas Clarie; Cottone Auctions; Phyllis Brinkman Craig; Babe Davidoff; Daryl Davidoff; Olympia Devine; Nicole C. Dittrich, reading room supervisor, Special Collections Research Center, Syracuse University Libraries; Margaret Greer Edmiston, Edmiston & Edmiston, St. Augustine, Florida; Katie Edwards, director of marketing, The Society of the Four Arts; Catherine Patterson Fleischner, who like other family members was so gracious to me; Alfred Frankel, MD; John W. Fraser; Mignon Roscher Gardener; Amanda Gaspari, senior account manager, Bridgeman Images; Susan Gillis, Boca Raton Historical Society; Joy Goodwin, archivist, Archives of American Art; Betse Gori, librarian, The King Library, The Society of the Four Arts; John S. Gray (Jack Lorimer Gray's son), whose cooperation and information was of great assistance; Barbara Grygutis; John Guinee; Robert Harper, executive director, Lightner Museum; Matthew A. Harris, research and reference, Collections Library, University of Kentucky; Bruce Helander, who so generously shared memories; Historic Map Works; John Stephen Hockensmith, Fine Art Editions; David Hoffman; Elizabeth

Hoffman; Julia and Lawrence Holofcener; Allison Ioli, VAGA; Tracy Kamerer, chief curator, Henry Morrison Flagler Museum; Paul Kaufman; Detra and Howard Kay; Corby Kaye; Curtis Kelly, whose knowledge was essential; Bruce Kirby, reference librarian, Manuscript Division, Library of Congress; Jim Koebel, assistant general counsel, University of North Carolina Wilmington; Michael Kondratov, Aspire Auctions, Inc.; Joanna Ling, Sotheby's Picture Library / Cecil Beaton Studio Archive; Iva Lisikewycz, manager, curatorial affairs, Detroit Institute of Arts; Robert Livingstone; Audrey Lorberfeld, reference associate, Frick Art Reference Library; Cindy and Ted Mandes; Phil, Shannon, and Taylor Materio, McMow Glass Studios; Pamela Nash Mathews, who couldn't have been more generous; Nancy Mato, executive vice president and curator, The Society of the Four Arts; Katie McCann, Studio Manager, Barbara Grygutis Sculpture LLC; McMow Art Glass; Jana Meyer, Filson Historical Society; Jordan Mitchell; Seeley G. Mudd, Manuscript Library at Princeton University; Julia Murphy (who also was very generous), digital asset manager, Hirshhorn Museum and Sculpture Garden; Lisa Oakes, graphic designer, James D. Julia, Inc.; Amy Petit, creative service manager, Keeneland Association Inc; William Rayner, who shared much of his time and recollections with me; Chamisa Redmond Sr., information and reference specialist, Library of Congress; Regine Reimann, Church of Bethesda-by-the-Sea; Hannah Rhadigan, rights administrator, Artists Rights Society; Adina Riggins, university archivist, Randall Library, University of North Carolina Wilmington; Heidi Roth, executive assistant, arts programming, The Society of the Four Arts; Cathy Schenck, librarian, Keeneland Association Inc.; Peter W. Schweitzer; Bobbye Smith and Susan Mathews Sperandeo, who were also extremely gracious; Fred E. Staley Jr., Church of Bethesda-by-the-Sea; Robin Starr, Skinner, Inc.; Karen Steele, interim executive director, Ann Norton Sculpture Gardens; Lorrey Stewart, Published Materials, South Caroliniana Library; Matthew Suhre; Kyle Tannler, manager, licensing, Condé Nast; Sandra Thompson; Maria Antonia Salom de Tord, administrator, Federico Beltrán-Masses estate; Jean Wagner Troemel; David H. Turner; Edgar Vickers; Sam and Robbie Vickers; Richard Waterhouse, director, Cahoon Museum of American Art; Dianne Weaver, Kaminsky Auctions; Louis LeB. Webre, senior vice president, marketing and media, Doyle Auctioneers and Appraisers, New York; Mary Ellen Whitford, Preservation Foundation of Palm Beach; and Jasminn L. Winters, Library of Congress, Office of Business Enterprises.

Introduction

A history of Palm Beach visual arts is like a history of art itself and equally as fascinating. The thin strip of island paradise became a southern resort in the late nineteenth century, and blessed with the combination of tremendous wealth, glamour, talent, and taste, it has hosted the most affluent art supporters and remains a trove of artistry. A culmination of Palm Beach style and the quest for a tropical artistic civilization has created a heritage and legacy of excellence that continues to attract universal attention. This is the first study of the area's overall and relevant visual arts history and seeks to inform, entertain, and clear up some lingering misconceptions.

Fine art, illustration, crafts, and photography have been embraced in Palm Beach like no other international resort. Visual artists and art supporters have intertwined themselves with the island due to its beauty. Art lover Henry Morrison Flagler developed it into a resort. Queen Victoria's photographer, Ernest Walter Histed, established a studio in town, and he and other photographers, painters, and sculptors depicted notables during winter visits. Joseph Jefferson, Sir Cecil Beaton, Constantin Alajalov, Salvador Dali, and Sir John Lavery were among the many popular artists who created works reflecting their time in Palm Beach. Beaton often expressed opinions about its allure, as did Marcel Duchamp while lounging poolside. Significant art collectors such as Jules Bache, Otto Kahn, and Chester Dale wintered on the island, and well-known socialites such as Jayne Wrightsman, Mona Williams, sculptor Gertrude Vanderbilt Whitney, and Audrey Chadwick Berdeau enhanced the roster of Palm Beach art patrons. Formidable yet generous society doyennes, including Eva Stotesbury, Amy Phipps Guest, Mary Woodhouse, and Maud Howe Elliott, helped found and sustain art organizations. The Medici-like culture supporter Alice De Lamar funded the visual arts in several ways. Influential art dealers such as Lord Joseph Duveen and Mary Duggett Benson were as remarkable as the artists they handled. Benson's sublime persona and soulfulness can be contrasted with David Stein, who allegedly sold fake paintings to a few unsuspecting millionaires before he was caught.

While numerous books explore the architecture of Palm Beach, this will uncover, emphasize, and at times analyze the significant art painted, sculpted, crafted, photographed, exhibited, collected, and/or maintained in town, some embedded in its architecture. It will delve into the visual artists, art lovers and philanthropists, art dealers, art centers, and exhibitions that burgeoned along with the growth of the resort during the "season," that heady period of felicity and nonstop culture. Since West Palm Beach is just over the bridge, its art and artists will be explored as well.

Palm Beach

Visual Arts

Chapter One

1880-1893: The Pioneer Years

Nestled between the Atlantic Ocean and Lake Worth, the remote, tropical island later called Palm Beach consisted of wild jungles and pockets of swampland ruled by bears, panthers, alligators, and snakes in 1880. A handful of stalwart settlers had already discovered this paradise when its only opulence was natural beauty, its primary wealth in balmy breezes, its sole glamour from colorful blossoms, and its jewels as sunlit and moonlit glints sparkling on waterways like spilled diamonds.

One of the first artists Palm Beach attracted was illustrator George Wells Potter (1851-1924), who arrived by 1881 when the island's artistic design, aside from a couple of inns, could be found in neat rows of coconut palms planted by pioneers from a wrecked ship's hoard. A former Cincinnati newspaper cartoonist and engineering/art student, Potter had taken instruction at the Ohio Mechanics Institute with Henry F. Farny, a renowned painter of the American West. Potter took advantage of inexpensive land prices and homesteaded a large (150 acres) ocean-to-lake property just south of where Southern Boulevard is today. He named it Figulus, meaning "Place of the Potter." Employed as a surveyor, Potter provided topographical illustrations of the lush area.[1]

The first artist to promote the Lake Worth region, Potter had good reason as he also owned a real estate firm with Owen Sylvester Porter in the early 1880s. Potter illustrated their pamphlet, *Under the Cocoanuts* (fig. 1), which described the delights of South Florida and included sporting activities on both sides of Lake Worth. He also illustrated *Camping and Cruising in Florida* (by James Alexander Henshall) in 1884. When Palm Beach was located in Dade County and the entire region along the lake was known as Lake Worth, Potter continued chronicling early South Florida civilization.[2]

Potter depicted members of the Seminole tribe (see fig. 2) who visited Palm Beach often and traded and interacted affably with pioneers. Anna Fremd (Mrs. Percy) Hadley recalled that some tribe members sold venison to the settlers and that although her house had a "high fence with a locked gate," the Seminoles simply "came right in."[3]

In 1893 Potter married Ella Dimick, the niece of Cocoanut

Fig. 1. George Wells Potter, *Under the Cocoanuts*. (Courtesy HSPBC)

Grove House owner/future Palm Beach mayor Elisha Newton Dimick. After Potter sold his Palm Beach property, he and his bride set up housekeeping at 606 Olive Avenue in West Palm Beach. He surveyed and plotted out the town and, with George W. Lainhart, founded the Lainhart & Potter Building Supply Company, a business which would last for several generations. Civically contributing to West Palm Beach, Potter served as president of the city council, mayor of West Palm Beach, and president of the Pioneer Bank; yet he never gave up his love for art. He had more of an opportunity to paint after he retired from business and exhibited with the Palm Beach County Art Club as late as March 1924, just prior to his death in July of that year.[4]

The first art collector to winter in Palm Beach was pioneer Charles John Clarke, a significant art supporter and friend to artists. Clarke, who spent his first winter in Palm Beach as early as 1890-91, held an enlightened opinion about women's art education and helped establish the finest opportunities for their study while president of the Pittsburgh School of Design and vice president of the art department at the Pennsylvania College for Women. He established the

Palm Beach Yacht Club and became its commodore.[5]

Clarke and his family maintained a close friendship with the island's first professionally exhibiting artist, Hudson River School painter Laura Woodward (1834-1926), who relied solely on her artistry to earn a living. Born in Mt. Hope, Orange County, New York, she exhibited extensively throughout the Northeast and Midwest.[6]

Woodward and her younger sister Libbie, in delicate health, spent the spring, summer, and early fall in Palm Beach in 1890, staying at Elisha Newton Dimick's Cocoanut Grove House, a small inn. As noted in Woodward's biography, she indicated in an interview that she had made an earlier visit to Palm Beach without her sister, traveling to the island along an arduous three-day route, taking three trains, a steamboat, and a mail boat. Although Woodward said she didn't paint very much on that trip, at least two Palm Beach watercolors from 1889 confirm her previous visit.[7]

Woodward explored the island when it was largely a hammock- and swamp-filled jungle. Falling in love with its natural beauty and undeterred from the heat, humidity, mosquitoes, and sand flies, she painted happily *en plein air*. Although she later admitted that some of the wild animals lurking in the jungles and on the beach frequently interrupted her sketching, she was determined to catch every nuance of tropical splendor around her (see figs. 3, 5, and 6).[8]

Woodward returned to St. Augustine toting her watercolors and exhibited larger works in her studio at Henry Morrison Flagler's Hotel Ponce de Leon, where the art-loving mogul visited her. She also displayed them at Flagler's newspaper's headquarters amid fountains and statuary. Woodward and mutual friend, society leader Frances Cragin (who had first visited Palm Beach by 1887), helped influence Flagler to establish a hotel in Palm Beach, utilizing Woodward's paintings as evidence of its potential as a resort. According to Woodward's cousin Myra Mapes Corwin, who later disclosed this family secret, Woodward "saw immediately" Palm Beach's "promise as a winter playground, and through

Fig. 2. George W. Potter, *Seminole Canoe* and *Willy and Little Tiger*. (Courtesy HSPBC)

works correspond to historical photographs (see figs. 4 and 5); however, unlike photographs, Woodward's portrayals of Palm Beach were true to nature in full color, not in photographic use until the twentieth century. And in direct opposition to the Barbizon or American tonalist schools in which detail and color become secondary to a muted, atmospheric style, Woodward relied on her Hudson River School training as well as her familiarity with Pre-Raphaelite techniques to precisely capture Palm Beach's splendor. She thusly conveyed its lush beauty and potential as a resort more vividly than any verbal description or recollection.

In St. Augustine, Woodward quickly became well-known for her renderings of the royal poinciana trees bursting with vermillion blossoms throughout Palm Beach during the late spring and into the summer months (see fig. 7). Winter residents and tourists in the Ancient City called these paintings

Fig. 3. Laura Woodward, *Palm Beach Trail,* ca. 1890, watercolor, collection of Edward and Deborah Pollack.

Fig. 4. John S. Clarke on a bridge on the Barton property, ca. 1890s. (Courtesy HSPBC)

her eyes and paintings, Henry Flagler immediately saw it."[9]

Woodward depicted Palm Beach pioneers' properties, including one belonging to Cornelius Vanderbilt Barton, who first wintered on the island in the mid 1880s. Many of her

"curious" as they had never seen the tree in bloom. Flagler admired these royal poinciana works to such an extent that he soon purchased one for Kirkside, his St. Augustine home. He bought at least one other painting by Woodward as well. In the meantime, publications credited Woodward for boosting Florida tourism, which she accomplished from prints of her work dispersed throughout the nation and by visitors bringing originals back to their homes and clubs.[10]

Woodward returned to Palm Beach in the spring of 1891 and continued painting in the area including the Robert McCormick property. She and Libbie left Palm Beach in early July and headed back to St. Augustine after stopping at the Indian River Hotel. Two years later Flagler would build his aptly named Hotel Royal Poinciana in Palm Beach, fulfilling Laura Woodward's dream of a grand hotel in which she could exhibit and sell her works in the place she loved. The birth of the nineteenth century's most magnificent resort in the world was about to occur.[11]

Fig. 6. Laura Woodward, *Lake Trail, Palm Beach,* ca. 1890, collection of Edward and Deborah Pollack.

Fig. 5. Laura Woodward, *Bridge on the Barton Property,* private collection. (Courtesy Edward and Deborah Pollack Fine Art, Palm Beach)

Fig. 7. Laura Woodward, *Royal Poinciana Tree along Lake Worth,* ca. 1890, oil on canvas, Sam and Robbie Vickers Florida Collection. (Photograph by James Quine)

Chapter Two
1893-1913: The Flagler Era

Laura Woodward returned to Palm Beach by the spring of 1893 and, according to local artist Daisy Erb, in her data for a history of Palm Beach County, "Woodward came with Mr. Flagler." He bought several large plots of land, including the Robert McCormick property on which Flagler built Hotel Royal Poinciana. At Woodward's insistence, Flagler established a studio for her during the hotel's construction, and knowing how important art was to a resort community, he made certain it was one of the first finished rooms. He became Woodward's benefactor and sponsored a temporary home (after the Cocoanut Grove House burned down in 1893) for Laura and Libbie at the hotel—a generous statement of his support and gratitude.[1]

After the hotel opened in 1894, Woodward continued painting studies of tropical blossoms and her other favorite subjects—the lush trails, ocean surf, Seminoles, and the Styx (the African American settlement of workmen and hotel employees in Palm Beach). She led by her example, taught numerous South Florida painters to venture outside and paint the landscape *en plein air,* and inspired her friend Winifred Clarke Anthony in her floral work. In a 1918 letter to Anthony, Woodward summed up her feelings about her favorite island when she wrote succinctly, "I love Palm Beach." By then she had established herself as the pioneer of a Palm Beach art association that would continue to honor her well beyond her death in 1926. In 2013 the State of Florida would also acknowledge Woodward's significance by inducting her into the Florida Artists Hall of Fame, the highest accolade given to a creative individual.[2]

In the meantime, Enoch Root, an artist and teacher from Chicago, settled in Palm Beach in 1892. Like many other pioneers, Root purchased land from the ocean to the lake, part of which is called Root Trail. Root supported the visual arts in all its tendencies. He had been educated at the Chicago Academy of Design and later led the art school, serving as president in 1881. Writing an article in 1888 propounding photography as fine art, he urged amateur photographers to read up on the aesthetic writings of John Ruskin and to familiarize themselves with all the nuances of painting, including light, shade, and perspective. Civically involved with the Palm Beach pioneer settlement, he relinquished painting professionally and by the turn of the twentieth century served as a justice of the peace. He was also an early postmaster of Palm Beach and in 1911 became one of the first town councilmen under the leadership of Mayor Elisha Newton Dimick.[3]

The first photographer at Hotel Royal Poinciana, Edward Ledyard Russell, had been wintering on the island since 1892 and established a studio by 1894 next to Laura Woodward's. Like Woodward, Russell promoted Palm Beach for Flagler but with photogravures depicting the island's visiting Seminoles and sporting amenities (see figs. 8 and 9). Russell's winter studio lasted until he died in 1902 at the age of forty-seven. Besides being an accomplished photographer, he was a remarkably well-liked gentleman and his death saddened many people in Palm Beach and West Palm Beach.[4]

Fig. 8. Edward L. Russell, *A Day's Fishing at Palm Beach,* 1896, collection of Edward and Deborah Pollack.

Fig. 9. Edward L. Russell, *Billy Bow-legs* [visiting Palm Beach]. *A Seminole of Lake Okeechobee, Florida,* 1896, collection of Edward and Deborah Pollack.

Another early visual artist in Palm Beach was Hermann Herzog (1832-1932), a master of the Florida landscape who rendered over three hundred lush visions of the state (see fig. 10). The acclaimed Düsseldorf landscapist, who immigrated to Philadelphia in 1871 and became an American citizen in 1876, explored many Florida locales, including east coast hammocks and waterways. Attracted to Palm Beach's inherent beauty and ample fishing opportunities, Herzog arrived by the mid-to-late 1890s and depicted the jungles and swamps with particular relish. Using his Düsseldorf training of painting *en plein air* and revering nature, he captured every detail of the island's tropical foliage. Herzog enjoyed Palm Beach so much that he established a winter residence there for a brief time by the turn of the twentieth century.[5]

Herzog's student, Pennsylvania artist George Cope (1855-1929), joined his teacher in Palm Beach in 1898 and painted a scene of the *Lake Work Post Office* abutting the lake (fig. 11). Situated on the north end of Palm Beach, it consisted of not much more than a dock and shack.

One of the earliest examples of American outdoor public sculpture in Palm Beach was modeled by Frederick William MacMonnies (1863-1937). His piping, mischievous *Pan of Rohallion* (fig. 12), standing on a fish-supported sphere, is beautifully situated in a pool at the entrance of Pan's

Fig. 10. Hermann Herzog, *Hunter and Dog in a Palmetto Grove*, collection of Edward and Deborah Pollack.

Fig. 11. George Cope, *Lake Worth Post Office,* 1898, Sam and Robbie Vickers Florida Collection.

Garden, maintained by the Garden Club of Palm Beach and the Preservation Foundation of Palm Beach. MacMonnies studied with American master Augustus Saint-Gaudens and at the École des Beaux-Arts, and later earned fame at the World's Columbian Exposition in 1893. He completed an eight-foot-high Pan in 1890 for financier Edward Dean Adams's country estate, Rohallion, in New Jersey. (A collector later loaned it to the Metropolitan Museum of Art.)[6]

Period critics for the most part raved about *Pan of Rohallion,* calling it a "charming work of fancy" and "full of gamesome grace." Many decades later, Palm Beach's Lydia B. Mann owned the illustrated, approximately four-foot version of the *Pan of Rohallion* and generously donated it to the Preservation Foundation of Palm Beach garden. So popular a piece, the *Pan of Rohallion* was produced in smaller statuettes; one was purchased by the novelist Edith Wharton.[7]

Around 1894, Joseph Jefferson (1829-1905), born in Philadelphia to a family of actor-painters and renowned for his portrayal of Rip Van Winkle and the title role of *Our American Cousin,* wintered in Palm Beach, living at "The Reefs" (a.k.a. Reef Cottage) on Breakers Row. Jefferson had been a Broadway star on the same lofty tier as Edwin Booth. As a working thespian, Jefferson's sayings were legendary. He purportedly quipped, "There are no small parts, only small actors." When a New York church refused to bury a friend simply because he was an actor but the Church of the Transfiguration around the corner would, Jefferson coined its famous nickname by declaring, "God bless the little church around the corner."[8]

Similar to Herzog, Jefferson was an ardent fisherman; and like Herzog and Woodward, Jefferson loved nature and revered South Florida's environment. Infinitely better known in Palm Beach as an orator than a painter, Jefferson nevertheless kept an active studio on the island where he rendered Barbizon-inspired scenes of Louisiana bayous or Florida swampland with delicate, wind-swept palms beneath a silvery sky (see fig. 13). While he was self-taught and

Fig. 12. Frederick MacMonnies, *Pan of Rohallion,* Pan's Garden, Preservation Foundation of Palm Beach. (Photograph by author)

Fig. 13. Joseph Jefferson, *Swamp Landscape,* 1894. (Courtesy HSPBC)

painted for relaxation, his canvasses reached a professional level. Jefferson also became the island's first *bona fide* superstar—even when he fished it made the papers.

Jefferson also contributed to the development of West Palm Beach; in fact, his beneficial accomplishments in building the city were multitudinous and surpassed only by his good friend Henry Flagler. When Jefferson died in 1905, his family received thousands of condolence cards, former president Grover Cleveland mourned publically, black crepe draped the city of West Palm Beach, and flags were lowered to half-mast.[9]

Ernest Walter Histed's portrait of Joseph Jefferson in his Palm Beach studio in early 1905 (see fig. 14) is a perfect example of a photographer using the medium as an art form. Histed (1862-1947) brought Jefferson's distinct features and buoyant personality to life as if the photographer had painted Jefferson's portrait in oils.

Histed, who added platinum to his cabinet card photographs to keep them from fading, was born in Lord Byron's former

Fig. 14. Joseph Jefferson in his Palm Beach studio, 1905, shortly before his fatal illness. (Photograph by Ernest W. Histed, from *The Critic,* June 1905, 482)

house in Brighton, England. He later worked with famed photographer Louis-Jacques-Mandé Daguerre in Europe and obtained clients in British aristocracy, the theater, and royalty, including Queen Victoria, Queen Mary, Empress Frederick of Germany, and Grand Duchess Serge of Russia.[10]

Histed planned to move to Florida by the 1880s but became discouraged after hearing tales of predatory alligators and instead relocated to Chicago and then Pittsburgh. Summering in Newport, Rhode Island, he became accustomed to taking pictures of the mega-wealthy displaying their perfect pearls and pleasing the Vanderbilts, Wideners, and Drexels with his work. Coming to Palm Beach around 1898, he opened his "Jungle Studio," south of the Hotel Royal Poinciana on a palm-tree lined dirt trail later known as County Road. Throughout the years he purchased and sold several Palm Beach properties and chronicled the island's affluent residents and visitors while whistling as he worked.[11]

In 1895 Histed took a breathtaking society portrait of Cordelia Rundell Bradley Drexel Biddle (1876-1947) in her wedding dress (see fig. 15) and years later a version was exhibited in Histed's studio in Palm Beach. The Pittsburgh beauty married wealthy Philadelphia financier Anthony Drexel Biddle Sr., who gave her $90,000 and the heirloom necklace she wears in the portrait. After the wedding, the Drexel Biddles often wintered in Palm Beach; by 1902 they regularly stayed at The Breakers. Cordelia's son, Anthony Drexel Biddle Jr., a noted ambassador, later built a home in Palm Beach and would help found the Oasis Club and the Bath and Tennis Club.[12]

Upon viewing the portrait one can readily see why critics compared Histed with the cream of society portraitists, John Singer Sargent and John White Alexander. The photographer captures the personality of his subject as she gazes with a knowing, patient look, apparently unaffected by her extraordinarily tight corset resulting in one of the tiniest waists of the Gilded Age.

Photographer Richard Resler (1865-1946) also made his

Fig. 15. Ernest W. Histed, *Cordelia Rundell Bradley Drexel Biddle,* inscribed "For Jamie, With love and best wishes for the New Year, Cordelia Drexel-Biddle, January 1896," collection of Edward and Deborah Pollack.

way to South Florida but took an arduous route before arriving at West Palm Beach in 1897. Born in Austria, he immigrated to Baltimore and later moved to Brooklyn, where he became an American citizen. He then relocated to Mexico after aligning himself with socialists. Keeping an active studio on Myrtle Street in West Palm Beach, he photographed several people, homes, and neighborhoods.[13]

His photograph *The Styx in 1900: Looking North on County Road in Palm Beach, Florida* (fig. 16), not only conveys the artistry of the moment, but is also a significant historical chronicle of a period in time in which inequality was in force because of Jim Crow laws of segregation. The residents are appealing in their poses; one gentleman, sporting a tilted hat, appears rather proud of it. Another rests on a downed tree and yet another, wearing an officer's cap, sits on a decrepit wooden crate. All the men's trousers are rolled up so as not to soil them from the dusty road on which they live.

The Styx—perhaps deriving its name from a swamp lining the entire eastern side of it, bringing to mind the River Styx—was located where today Sunset and Sunrise Avenues intersect County Road. The neighborhood was poorly run and ironically a tourist attraction, which lasted until real estate developers moved the families to West Palm Beach and cleared the area to build a posh new neighborhood. Notables from the Styx included the first African American doctor in West Palm Beach, Thomas Leroy Jefferson, who was born in Mississippi, taught and practiced medicine in Louisiana, and according to family history was a relative of Thomas Jefferson through Sally Hemings.[14]

Richard Resler and Ernest Histed made a profitable living from photographing famous locals; Histed especially did well portraying his client Henry M. Flagler (see fig. 17) in at least two versions. In 1902, Flagler, remaining a friend and patron to artists, moved into his Beaux-Arts mansion, Whitehall (now the Henry Morrison Flagler Museum), which comprises a trove of paintings and sculpture, including some of the finest examples by Pennsylvania native Martin Johnson Heade (1819-1904). As soon as Flagler built Whitehall, he decorated it with Heade's Jamaican *View from Fern Tree Walk* (currently at the Minnesota Marine Art Museum).[15]

Fig. 16. Richard Resler, *The Styx in 1900: Looking North on County Road in Palm Beach, Florida.* (Courtesy HSPBC and State Archives of Florida)

Fig. 17. Ernest W. Histed, *Henry Flagler,* 1909. (Courtesy HSPBC)

Heade, who learned the art of portraiture from Thomas Hicks, later became a Hudson River School landscapist influenced by colleagues such as Frederic Edwin Church. He moved to St. Augustine in 1883, became part of a colony of painters there, and met his most generous patron, Henry Flagler, who changed the artist's life. In 1886 Heade sold Flagler a portrayal of an extensive *Great Florida Marsh* (fig. 18), wherein Heade revealed a primeval wilderness by implementing his Hudson River School training in reverence of nature and Pre-Raphaelite attention to nature's detail. Unlike Laura Woodward, Heade never relocated to Palm Beach, but his paintings, including the *Great Florida Marsh,* still thrill visitors at the Henry Morrison Flagler Museum.[16]

In Whitehall's music room, Flagler and his wife, Mary Lily, displayed a magnificent painting by William-Adolphe Bouguereau (1825-1905), *Young Girl Defending Herself Against Eros (Jeûne Fille Se Défendant Contre L'Amour)* (fig. 19), which received much acclaim when exhibited at the Paris Salon in 1880. In 1882 a critic in the *Art Journal* wrote,

Fig. 18. Martin Johnson Heade (American, 1819-1904), *The Great Florida Marsh,* 1886, oil on canvas, Flagler System, Inc. (Courtesy Flagler Museum, Palm Beach, Florida, photograph © North Carolina Museum of Art)

Fig. 19. William-Adolphe Bouguereau, *Young Girl Defending Herself Against Eros (Jeûne Fille Se Défendant Contre L'Amour),* 1880, in Whitehall's music room until 1925 when its contents were dispersed, now at the University of North Carolina Wilmington. (Courtesy University of North Carolina Wilmington)

concerning a loan exhibition at New York's Union League "Ladies Reception," that "the collection was also notable for a large Bouguereau, 'Contending with Love,' property of H. M. Flagler—which shows Bouguereau in all his delicacy and sweetness without any of his insipidity."[17]

The mythological theme of Eros (Cupid) trying to impale young, beautiful women with an arrow of love was well utilized by several nineteenth-century painters and sculptors. Bouguereau, a master of rendering the nude and semi-nude, expressed this playful confrontation with his usual panache in well rounded figures and smooth, softly shadowed flesh tones. A smaller version of the work is located at the Getty Museum.[18]

Once displayed in a drawing room at Flagler's Hotel Ponce de Leon and currently featured at The Breakers in Palm Beach, *The Sultan's Favorite* (fig. 20), 1886, by Juan Gimenez y Martin (1858-1901) is indicative of Flagler's penchant for the Gilded Age's pervading aesthetic taste in Orientalism, or subjects primarily of the Middle East but also of Asia.[19] The daydreaming harem girl awaits her master after a busy day of music making. She has been smoking a hookah and reclines languorously on a leopard-skin rug, which is draped over a divan. Animal-skin rugs were often utilized in aesthetic period paintings, and in this instance, as in others that include women resting upon them, perhaps signifies feminine power in conquering the sexual beast in man. The carpet leads the viewer's eye toward the sultan, who, bearing a scimitar, the iconographical image of authority, approaches while musicians accompany the imminent scene of lovemaking. Fragrant roses are scattered about the floor leading to the divan and freshening air made stale from the smoke emanating from a brass samovar. Gimenez y Martin, also known for his Venetian canals and piazzas, painted at least one other version of this exotic genre scene.

Flagler also implemented Gilded Age taste in collecting European belle époque representations of elegant women at leisure. The painting *En Voiture* (fig. 21) by Italian artist Eduardo Tofano (1838-1920), who exhibited at the Paris

Fig. 20. Juan Gimenez y Martin, *The Sultan's Favorite,* 1886, The Breakers, Flagler System, Inc.

Fig. 21. Eduardo Tofano (1838-1920) *En Voiture,* late nineteenth century, oil on canvas, Flagler System, Inc. (Courtesy Flagler Museum, Palm Beach, Florida)

Salon, is the perfect example of the period's opulence complementing Whitehall's grand atmosphere. Purchased in 1888, *En Voiture* is one of many that Flagler acquired from M. Knoedler & Co. in New York and is currently at the Flagler Museum in Palm Beach.[20]

The two chic women, one accessorized in pink and the other in aqua, are the epitome of the upper class as they ride in an open-air carriage and carry parasols that shield their perfect complexions from the sun. The play of light and detail on the lace and tassel of the parasol in the foreground rival the beauty of the women and their decorative bonnets. One may ponder exactly what has captured their attention, but it is certainly not something dangerous. If anything, the women appear mildly curious as to what lies ahead of them.

When not actively purchasing fine paintings, Henry Flagler joined other powerful men of history—such as Adm. George Dewey—along with artists, musicians, and writers—including Mark Twain—who visited the Cragins' home, Reve d'Ete (Garden of Eden). In fact, some have stated that Palm Beach society stemmed from the Garden of Eden. The Fortnightly Club, the first cultural group in Palm Beach, began there and featured poetry readings and musical concerts, but it appeared that support for the visual arts was largely not included in the club's agenda. This would change dramatically some two decades later when socialites became a major force in promoting the visual arts in Palm Beach.[21]

In the meantime, art decorated a popular Palm Beach gathering place, Col. Edward R. Bradley's Beach Club, a private supper club and gambling casino established in 1898. Dressed in the finest evening clothes, men and women socialized and participated in games of chance before a large painting by Harry Finney entitled *Longchamp Racecourse* (fig. 22). Finney, a Philadelphian who studied in Paris with Bouguereau and Joseph-Nicolas Robert-Fleury, exhibited at the Paris Salon, the National Academy of Design, and the Pennsylvania Academy of the Fine Arts.[22]

Bradley's penchant for horseracing prompted him to

Fig. 22. Harry Finney, *Longchamp Racecourse,* ca. 1899, once at E. R. Bradley's Beach Club, now at Keeneland Clubhouse, Lexington, Kentucky. (Courtesy Keeneland Association, Lexington, Kentucky)

Fig. 23. Joseph J. Hollenbeck, *Royal Poinciana, Palm Beach.* (Courtesy Alfred Frankel)

purchase this colorful painting. He owned a Kentucky horse farm and reportedly once named a horse Bad News because "bad news travels fast." Later Bradley, who was a generous supporter of the visual arts, gave *Longchamp Racecourse* to Dr. Fred Rankin, who in turn presented it to Keeneland Racecourse in Lexington, Kentucky.[23]

By 1908 Ohio-born artist Daisy Erin Erb (1875-1959) began to regularly winter in Palm Beach. Erb, who had studied in England, Germany, and at the Académie Julian in Paris, took the lead of Laura Woodward and set up her studio at Hotel Royal Poinciana, where she too sold paintings of the jungle trails to the well-heeled tourists.[24]

Other artists joined them, such as Joseph J. Hollenbeck after arriving in Palm Beach from Jersey City in 1910. In New York, Hollenbeck had studied privately with renowned American painters William Merritt Chase and Robert Henri, as well as with other instructors at the Art Students League. Inspired by the tropical beauty of Palm Beach and following Laura Woodward, Hollenbeck depicted the blossoms on the island, including its royal poinciana trees in bloom (see fig 23). Besides maintaining a studio at Hotel Royal Poinciana, Hollenbeck also kept one at The Breakers and later at Whitehall when it became a hotel. Hollenbeck along with Woodward and Erb would soon join others to form Palm Beach's first art association and further the promise of a tropical artistic civilization.[25]

Chapter Three
1913-1922: The Artistic Rise of a Resort

After Henry Flagler's death in 1913, the cause of art endured in the resort he created. Palm Beach artists painted as an informal art colony in small studios on Enoch Root's property (Root Trail), later purchased by Daisy Erb (see fig. 24). An artist inspired by aestheticism's message to women to earn a living through arts and crafts, Erb explored many areas of handicrafts by 1913. While a competent painter, she shone brightly in jewelry design, which she actively pursued. She sold many of her pieces to the silver-spoon set both in Palm Beach and San Francisco. According to one society doyenne, Erb's rings were "quite the thing to wear when playing bridge."[1]

In her Palm Beach studio, Erb designed the illustrated pendant (fig. 25) made of

Fig. 24. Daisy Erb, "Individuality—A Keynote to a Young Woman's Success," *California's Magazine, Edition Deluxe,* vol. 2 (San Francisco: California's Magazine Co., 1916), 187.

hand-wrought silver and moonstones that helped earn her a gold medal at San Francisco's Panama-Pacific Exposition in 1915. She also created furniture and tooled leather objects and became a Palm Beach real estate baroness, purchasing and selling several properties from Root Trail to Oleander Avenue.[2]

Around 1913-1914, Ben Austrian (1870-1921) from Reading, Pennsylvania, joined Joseph Hollenbeck, Daisy Erb, and Laura Woodward at the Royal Poinciana. Skilled yet self-taught, Austrian earned a stable income by providing images of chicks for the Bon Ami Company and selling paintings of that subject (see fig. 26) along with South Florida landscapes

Fig. 25. Daisy Erb, pendant, 1915, "Individuality—A Keynote to a Young Woman's Success," *California's Magazine, Edition Deluxe,* vol. 2 (San Francisco: California's Magazine Co., 1916), 188.

to tourists, like the other hotel artists who emulated Laura Woodward. In 1920 Austrian built a residence at Bradley Place and Sunset Avenue, a year before his sudden death from a stroke in Reading.[3]

Also in the 1910s, society photographer William Louis Koehne kept a studio south of The Breakers in the Royal Park neighborhood. After studying at the Fine Arts Academy in Munich, Germany, he became well-known in Chicago as a commercial photographer and brought his expertise to Palm Beach each season. He advertised that "The wonderful lighting effects obtainable in Palm Beach cannot be equaled anywhere in the world." An avid golfer and ballroom dancer, Koehne named his modern oceanfront home Villa Zila after his wife, Zila.[4]

Fig. 26. Ben Austrian, *Chicks in a Straw Hat,* private collection. (Courtesy Edward and Deborah Pollack Fine Art, Palm Beach)

California-born artist, architect, and graphic designer (see fig. 27) Addison Mizner came to Palm Beach in 1918 and was so financially challenged when he arrived that he could only afford to rent an old mule shed belonging to photographer Ernest Histed. Mizner's luck changed when sewing machine heir Paris Singer commissioned him to build the Everglades Club. Mizner then settled into an enviable niche, becoming a leader of society and an innovative architect. He continued to build houses for the privileged class; in Palm Beach alone he designed sixty-seven buildings, including the famous Via Mizner on Worth Avenue, where he eventually resided. Mizner would change the island's profile into one reflecting Florida's Spanish heritage and provide numerous job opportunities to talented artists and artisans.[5]

In the interim, the outdoor sketching group who painted along Root Trail became structured in 1918, led by Daisy Erb, Jane Peterson (1876-1965), and artist Isabel Vernon Cook. Laura Woodward also helped in organizing the sketch group, although dimming vision had largely stopped her from painting by that time. Peterson and Cook were both members of New York's Professional Woman's League (later the National Association of Women Painters and Sculptors), but Peterson was the far more successful artist. Born Jennie Christine on November 28, 1876, in Elgin, Illinois, Peterson drew from nature and supplemented her education with art courses at

Fig. 27. Addison Mizner, *Copyright,* from Addison Mizner, Oliver Herford, and Ethel Watts Mumford Grant, *The Altogether New Cynic's Calendar of Revised Wisdom for 1907* (San Francisco and New York: Paul Elder, 1907), copyright page (un-paginated).

the Elgin Public Schools. In 1895 she traveled to New York City to study art at the Pratt Institute. After completing her instruction she combed the world in pursuit of vibrant subjects, venturing into exotic areas such as the Sultana of Turkey's garden and a Bedouin encampment in the Sahara. Astronomer and writer Percival Lowell exhibited Peterson's work in Paris and arranged for "her first one-woman exhibition in Boston, which led to a near sell-out exhibition in New York City." By 1912, Peterson had many wealthy patrons and traveled and painted with her teacher, the great Joaquín Sorolla y Bastida, and esteemed American artists Louis Comfort Tiffany, John Singer Sargent, Childe Hassam, and Maurice Prendergast. Due to the fact that she could paint with the best of the men, the art world took notice and she won several awards and international acclaim. Her works have been included in the collection of the Hirshhorn Museum and Sculpture Garden, Brooklyn Museum of Art, Metropolitan Museum of Art, New Orleans Museum of Art, and several other important institutions.[6]

In Peterson's rendering of *Palm Beach* (fig. 28), one can see Sorolla's influence in color application with crisp white brushstrokes juxtaposed against dark, creating a lively beach scene. Until Peterson arrived in town, this strong yet painterly postimpressionist technique had not been utilized by any other artist on the island. Indeed, Peterson brought an artistic sophistication to Palm Beach previously unseen; therefore her participation with local artists no doubt helped raise the esteem and credibility of the loosely formed group.

With no indoor venue large enough to display their paintings in Palm Beach, the art colony's first formal art exhibition occurred in 1918 in West Palm Beach under the auspices of the Woman's Club. It was not unusual for a woman's club to uphold the cause of art; women's organizations in Miami, New Orleans, Atlanta, and other southern cities also supported artists. Besides, Daisy Erb, Laura Woodward, and their female colleagues were already members of the Woman's Club and had formed an

Fig. 28. Jane Peterson, *Palm Beach*, Hirshhorn Museum and Sculpture Garden, Smithsonian Institution, The Joseph H. Hirshhorn Bequest, 1981. (Courtesy Hirshhorn Museum and Sculpture Garden Collection, photograph by Lee Stalsworth)

art committee within that organization. According to Erb, their exhibition, appropriately called "Art Day," occurred for one day only and was so popular it seemed that practically the entire citizenry of the Palm Beaches attended. This encouraged the group to strive for more exhibits, which would soon occur.[7]

Meanwhile, pioneer Charles John Clarke's son, Palm Beach winter resident Thomas Shields Clarke, an internationally renowned painter and sculptor who studied in Paris and New York and exhibited at the Pennsylvania Academy of the Fine Arts among other venues, enjoyed Palm Beach so much that he wanted to share it with the affluent world. He thusly publicized the resort by writing a lavishly illustrated article about Palm Beach for *Country Life* magazine, a popular periodical read by the highest realms of society. Published in 1911 and entitled "An Artist's Florida," Clarke's article was accompanied by gorgeous color photographs of sunsets and foliage. He wrote: "At ten o'clock every morning the family assembles in the garden, each one with a basket containing a bathing suit and some fresh-picked oranges and guavas, and walk in a straggling line through the Cocoanut Trail to the beach, half a mile away; some to bathe in the mild Gulf Stream and some to sit in the shade and enjoy sweet idleness. Both ocean and lake offer a great variety of sport for the fisherman—from amberjacks to pompano, not to mention sharks and tarpon and other big game."[8]

Local papers acknowledged Clarke's help in enticing tourists. He also sent a copy to his friend Daniel Chester French, one of the most accomplished sculptors in America. French was so taken with Palm Beach that he wrote, "The pictures are beautiful! We are properly impressed not only with the beauty of the pictures, but with the charm and magnificence of your home in Florida. Think of our nursing an opportunity of visiting in a place like that." In 1919, so proud of his Palm Beach residence, Primavera, Clarke offered to loan it to fellow Princeton alumnus Pres. Woodrow Wilson as a vacation home. Wilson declined to take up Clarke's offer, however, as he was obligated to remain in Washington, DC.[9]

During World War I Clarke modeled a popular statue, *The Future* (fig. 29). The war's stress and uncertainty made America's future appear tenuous to some, but Clarke's lovely fortune teller in the midst of predicting what would occur nonetheless captivates the viewer. And as the seer wears a laurel wreath symbolizing victory, the future appears very optimistic indeed. Clarke sent a version of *The Future* to the National Academy of Design's winter exhibition, where it received rave reviews; one critic called it "an exquisitely finished bronze figure holding a crystal ball."[10]

The sculptor created many forms of art in Palm Beach; for

Fig. 29. Thomas Shields Clarke, *The Future,* private collection. (Courtesy Edward and Deborah Pollack Fine Art, Palm Beach)

instance, in 1920 along with Florenz Ziegfeld and Addison Mizner, Clarke assisted in designing costumes for tableaux vivants, in which participants dressed as those in famous artworks and remained as motionless as the painting. The festivities were held at Pennsylvania industrialist Joseph Riter's lakefront estate and benefited a British charity.[11]

Clarke no doubt supported one of the first formal group art exhibitions occurring in Palm Beach. It took place thanks to Jane Peterson and H. Grant Kingore, a Palm Beach winter resident and owner of Kingore Galleries in New York at 668 Fifth Avenue. In 1919 Kingore arranged for several artists to add to Peterson's work at an exhibition on New York/Miami designer Paul Chalfin's houseboat, *La Singerie,* moored at the Beaux Arts docks on Lake Trail. Chalfin had studied art with James Abbott McNeill Whistler but relinquished painting for designing because of poor eyesight. Between 1914 and 1916 he was instrumental in creating James Deering's Miami palace, Villa Vizcaya, and in the 1920s would help build Coral Gables. The Palm Beach exhibition Chalfin hosted benefited a local African American hospital by raising funds to abolish its debt and also to supplement patients who could not afford medical care. An array of the finest New York painters and sculptors contributed, including John Singer Sargent, George Bellows, Cecilia Beaux, Gertrude Vanderbilt Whitney, and Jo Davidson (a close friend of Whitney's). The opening, attended by the reigning tier of Palm Beach socialites, was an enormous success and a noted event of the season. More importantly, the expected total of raised money doubled from admission fees and profits from sold paintings.[12]

News of the exhibition reached the prestigious *International Studio* and *American Art News* published in New York. In March the *Art News* commented, "Except for some architecture on old Spanish and Moorish lines, Palm Beach is not associated in the public mind with art save that form of art in dress and adornment practiced by the fair butterflies who have been flitting through the now

waning winter season at the Florida resort. It is, therefore, surprising to learn that . . . a most credible art exhibition was recently organized. . . ."[13] With this report it appeared that Palm Beach had earned a bit of respect from northern art circles.

The cause of art continued to flourish when in 1920 Daisy Erb heard that the National Association of Women Painters and Sculptors planned to exhibit in Virginia and suggested the group go a bit farther south and join the Palm Beach artists in South Florida. Thus in February local artists provided works along with the New York association, who contributed several paintings to the show at the Woman's Club.[14]

Subsequently, male painters and sculptors such as Joseph J. Hollenbeck, Clarence Percival Dietsch (1881-1961), and muralist Reginald Sherman Kidd Winton (1877-1952) wished to exhibit; therefore the Florida alliance quickly evolved into the Palm Beach County Art Club, officially established in 1920 with Laura Woodward as an honorary member. Daisy Erb became the first president, followed by Augustus Goodyear Heaton (1844-1930), the acting critic of the group. Born in Philadelphia as Augustus George Heaton, he trained at the Pennsylvania Academy of the Fine Arts and became one of the first Americans accepted in Alexandre Cabanel's Paris studio. In the 1880s Heaton achieved international acclaim for his *Recall of Columbus* in the United States Capitol (later engraved on a stamp), as well as other historical paintings.[15]

Aside from his talent in historical painting, Heaton was an author and famed numismatist as well as a noted portraitist in New Orleans. A delightful and rather unusual fellow, he changed his middle name from George to Goodyear later on in life because, as he explained, it held more meaning for him. He also expressed that artists feel the world while laymen merely see it.[16]

Heaton settled in West Palm Beach in 1919 (aside from spending summers in the Northeast). He immediately became a member of the Everglades Club and purchased a home called Crane's Nest, situated on a large property extending from 1400 South Olive Avenue to the lakefront, which he renamed Lake Breeze Lodge. The beauty of the property's jungle-like, tropical nature inspired Heaton to paint a large canvas in 1921 depicting Juan Ponce de León dreaming of the Fountain of Youth, a popular subject at the time (see fig. 30). The only semblance of wildlife within the lush foliage is evidenced by a few cardinals on the right hand side, perhaps signifying the church's support of Ponce de León's voyage. In 1928 Heaton sold the work for five hundred dollars to Walter Fraser, director of the Fountain of Youth Archaeological Park in St. Augustine, Florida. It is still in St. Augustine and has remained with the Fraser family.[17]

Meanwhile, by 1920, with art exhibitions having taken place in Palm Beach and West Palm Beach courtesy the Woman's Club, the area began to bud as an art center and simultaneously gained more attention from New York and more support from its prominent townspeople. One of them

Fig. 30. Augustus G. Heaton, *Ponce de León Dreaming he has Found the Fountain of Youth,* 1921, painted in West Palm Beach, Fraser family collection. (Photograph by author)

was Alice De Lamar, who would become Palm Beach's Medici and bring to town Mary Duggett Benson, one of Palm Beach's most influential and gracious art dealers.

Later called "an American legend," Alice Antoinette De Lamar, born on Madison Avenue in New York City on April 23, 1895, was the privileged daughter of Joseph Raphael De Lamar, a financier born in Amsterdam, Holland, in 1843. In 1893 he and Nellie Virginia Sands were married when Nellie was seventeen and Joseph was fifty. Unfortunately, the couple divorced in Paris when Alice was only two years old, leaving the child to spend weekends at her mother's Parisian home and the rest of the time with her father. At the age of five (see fig. 31), Alice's father returned to the United States, where they lived in his grand New York City mansion. The house was filled with exquisite British academic works by such artists as Sir Lawrence Alma-Tadema; French masterpieces by Jean-Léon Gérôme and William-Adolphe Bouguereau (*L'Aurore,* now in the Birmingham Museum of Art); important oils by Barbizon and Hudson River School artists; and antiques, including the most ornate ormolu French furniture. Among such grandeur De Lamar lived a rather lonely childhood, somewhat neglected by her father, who was absent from the house for long periods of time. She did not see her mother again until the age of fifteen and in the interim became rebellious. When she was twelve years old her loving godfather, William Nelson Cromwell, stepped in and enrolled her in the Spence School, where she at last found solace and felt secure under Cromwell's solicitous eye and that of the headmistress. They each took care of her, supported her emotionally, and arranged for her to visit her mother during school vacations.[18]

After Joseph De Lamar's death in 1918, Alice inherited over $10 million dollars in cash and real estate, including the contents of her father's New York residences. But after volunteering as a Red Cross ambulance driver (see fig. 32) in World War I along with Gertrude Stein and Ernest Hemingway, who later visited Alice in Palm Beach, she had matured and developed her own taste, which shunned the grandiose in art and decoration.[19]

By 1920, nineteenth-century heavily ormolu furniture and classic French paintings were not necessarily *en vogue* to those who preferred more modern art. In consequence of this and of her finding herself, that year De Lamar (see fig.

Fig. 31. Jan Van Veers, chromolithograph after his painting *Alice De Lamar about the Age of 5,* ca. 1900.

33) sold almost all of her inherited art and furnishings at auction.

By then she had come to admire old master paintings after fellow Red Cross volunteer Carl Hamilton showed her his collection. Hamilton, who courted De Lamar to no avail, introduced her to renowned collector Bernard Berenson, whose cache of old master paintings rivaled most museums. Hamilton took De Lamar and Berenson to view Isabella Stewart Gardner's collection of old masters in Boston. De Lamar then developed more of an educated eye through her visits to Berenson's house in Europe, studying in his art library for hours and also learning about fine art via various artistic friends. De Lamar soon devoted herself to art and artists completely. She would keep many of them afloat but remain mysteriously anonymous in her philanthropic activities. She felt a need to constantly surround herself with the finest creative people and in the 1920s counted Florenz Ziegfeld, Addison Mizner, and actress Eva Le Gallienne as close friends. The fascinating De Lamar became the intimate companion and financial angel to equally fascinating women, such

Fig. 32. Alice De Lamar, 1918. (Courtesy HSPBC and William Rayner)

as art deco artist and designer Eyre de Lanux and aviatrix and frequent Palm Beach visitor Lucia Davidova.[20]

Alice De Lamar first came to Palm Beach when she was five years old for only a few days before her father headed to Miami in pursuit of even better fishing opportunities. She returned in 1916, began regularly wintering on the island during the 1919-1920 "season," and bought a property at 1425 South Ocean Boulevard in 1921. Two years later Addison Mizner built her mansion. A great admirer of Mizner, De Lamar felt like he was part of her family. They knew each other from years before when, as an artist in California, he had maintained a close friendship with one of her uncles, also an artist. The two gentlemen were mutually devoted and had bequeathed everything they owned to each

other. But after her uncle's untimely death in an auto accident, De Lamar's mother rummaged through his desk, found the gentlemen's wills, and burned them.[21]

De Lamar adored Palm Beach, especially in November before the frenzied social whirl and when the weather was perfect. She swam in her pool and in the ocean, became a recreational boater and an avid fisherwoman, and would sometimes surprise party hostesses with gifts of fish she had just caught. Along with her close friend Mary Duggett Benson, De Lamar would remain an integral part of Palm Beach visual arts.[22]

By 1920 many artists had flocked to Palm Beach,

Fig. 33. Paul Thèvenaz, *Alice De Lamar,* ca. 1920, photographer unknown. (Courtesy HSPBC)

including Caroline Van Hook Bean (1879-1980) (see fig. 34), who studied with some of the greatest American impressionists. As soon as she arrived she found much to inspire her and immersed herself in the budding Palm Beach County Art Club. With her refined personality, ease

Fig. 34. Caroline Van Hook Bean at Addison Mizner's fountain, Palm Beach. (Courtesy Robert Livingstone, *Caroline van Hook Bean: The Last of the Impressionists*)

PALM BEACH VISUAL ARTS

with foreign languages, and cultured upbringing, including education at Smith College and European travel, Bean easily joined the ranks of Palm Beach society and sold her paintings from her studio/home, Villa Carola, on Worth Avenue and at the few galleries in town. A friend of Addison Mizner, Bean helped him by providing sketches of his architectural accomplishments, which he utilized for promotional purposes. She also rendered Mizner's library; Marjorie Merriweather Post and E. F. Hutton's house, Hogarcito; and Paris Singer's apartment at the Everglades Club. She soon became a sought-after Palm Beach portraitist and earned the approval of *American Art News.* She believed that portraiture should reflect the sitter's vision of themselves—not the artist's—which made her even more popular among Palm Beach society. She also had the knack for completing a portrait within two or three sittings. Her notable subjects included her friend Marjorie Merriweather Post, art collector and philanthropist Eva Stotesbury, and Florenz Ziegfeld's actress-wife Billie Burke.[23]

The promotion of Palm Beach through art continued with the combined efforts of real estate developer and former mayor of West Palm Beach George Graham Currie (1867-1926) and artist Josephine Lindley. The duo published a winter greeting card/souvenir in 1921 entitled appropriately "The Season's Greetings from Palm Beach." Lindley's delicate vignettes of coconut-palm lined trails, flowers, and the ocean accompanied Currie's poem "The Gulf Stream Boulevard," extolling the benefits of wintering on the coast from Palm Beach to Delray Beach:

All you who dread Winter with what it implies
In the far away realms of Jack Frost;
And you who are stricken when Dame Nature dies
And would fly from her snows at all cost . . .
Then come! Oh do come! To our city of Flowers,
And partake of our bliss we beseech!
In the North leave Earth's storms and exchange them for showers
Of the Heaven that you'll find at Palm Beach.

Fig. 35. George Graham Currie and Josephine Lindley, *The Season's Greetings from Palm Beach*, 1921. (Courtesy HSPBC)

A successful marketing campaign, the booklet enticed many tourists to visit the area (see fig. 35).[24]

Lindley had moved from Indiana to Deland, Florida, by the late 1890s and relocated to South Florida by the 1910s. Primarily a watercolorist of flowers, she lived in West Palm Beach and, like other local artists, was inspired by Laura Woodward to paint *en plein air* and depict the Palm Beach pathways and ocean. Lindley also joined Woodward and Daisy Erb as active members of the Woman's Club. Remaining politically and civically involved throughout her life, Lindley was not shy about expressing her opinions, especially in support of the downtrodden.[25]

Currie also helped promote the cause of art when he befriended African American sculptor Augusta Christine Savage (1892-1962) (see fig. 36), who had moved to West Palm Beach in 1915 from Jacksonville. After Savage found clay from a local potter, she modeled a figure of the Virgin Mary and one of a horse; when her school principal noticed her adept work, he asked her to teach clay modeling for one dollar per day. Later, Currie commissioned her to model his portrait bust, and in 1919, as superintendent of the Palm Beach County Fair, he fulfilled her request for a booth at the fair to sell her sculptures. Her small figures of animals, extremely popular with visiting tourists, earned her $175 from sales alone. Additionally, the fair officials awarded her a prize of $25 and a ribbon of honor. In 1921 Savage's likeness of Currie was displayed at the county fair and deemed "so natural you could see the glasses on his nose."[26]

So impressed with Savage's talent, Currie wrote a poem about her in his book, *Songs of Florida*, published in 1922, which read in part:

Augusta is a sculptress fine
A poetess as well
Her coal black hair and eyes that shine
A soulful story tell . . .
With steady eye she looks on me
Then takes a lump of clay
When lo another self I see
With all my faults away.[27]

Savage provided at least five poems for *Songs of Florida*. In one entitled "Compensation," she reflected on her love of nature and being African American:

I've spent hours in deep communion
With the humming birds and bees.
I've exchanged loves deepest secrets
With the softly sighing trees . . .
And upon life's harsh alarms
I've turned my back . . . And my heart is filled with song,
As I wend my way along,
For my soul's attuned to nature,
Tho I'm black."[28]

Currie noted in *Songs of Florida* that Savage's literary and artistic talent showed "conclusively that this girl brought up

Fig. 36. Augusta Christine Savage modeling an animal figure, by Everett, WPA still image from a film.

PALM BEACH VISUAL ARTS

under the most adverse circumstances has succeeded in the finer arts in a remarkable degree." He then entreated the community: "Any assistance that readers can render to enable her to perfect herself along the lines she has so fondly chosen will indeed be appreciated by her and be of unquestionable value to her whole race in America."[29]

Along with Florida senator Thomas Campbell, Currie encouraged Savage to pursue greater horizons with study in New York. Consequently, with a letter of recommendation from Currie to sculptor Solon Borglum, who headed a school of sculpture in New York City, Savage moved out of South Florida to become a noted member of the Harlem Renaissance and the first African American accepted by the National Association of Women Painters and Sculptors.[30]

Newspaperman Joe Earman also played a role in art boosting when in 1921 he, along with thirty friends of Palm Beach's first mayor, Elisha Newton "Cap" Dimick (1849-1919), planned a statue to commemorate the great pioneer townsman. Small in height yet towering in his achievements, Dimick certainly deserved a lasting memorial. He had been essential in developing the town, and Palm Beach County as well.

Earman provided the bulk of the funding and called for a competition of twelve prominent American sculptors to submit sketches for the statue. Ohio native Burt William Johnson (1890-1927), who maintained a studio in Flushing, New York, won the commission. With tutelage from his sister, Annetta Saint-Gaudens (married to one of America's greatest sculptors, Augustus Saint-Gaudens), Louis Saint-Gaudens (Augustus's brother), and James Earle Fraser, and with further studies at the Art Students League, Johnson was the perfect choice to portray Dimick in a realistic fashion. After all, some of his instructors took part in the American Renaissance, a movement beginning in 1876, when painters, sculptors, actors, and writers adhered to the classical ideal.[31]

Dimick had died in 1919, so to achieve a realistic result Johnson relied on photographs as well as Earman's descriptions of Dimick's character. Earman also traveled to

Fig. 37. Burt William Johnson, *Elisha "Cap" Newton Dimick,* Palm Beach. (Photograph by author)

New York on several occasions to critique Johnson's work.[32]

The sculptor finally completed the superb, life-sized work of polished realism revealing Dimick's warm personality and visionary outlook (see fig. 37). Dimick is shown as relaxed, one hand holding his customary cap, which gave him his nickname, and the other clasping a pocket watch, a symbol of temperance and moderation. The plaque beneath the statue reads, "In honor and memory of Elisha Newton Dimick who served his community well 1849-1919. Legislator Developer and Friend" A laurel branch (a symbol of victory and peace) serves as the dash between Dimick's birth and death dates. Hestia, the virgin goddess of the hearth, home, and municipality, keeps Dimick's flame (or legacy) alive on the left side of the plaque. On the right side, the goddess Columbia wears a laurel wreath as a crown and holds a wreath as well, a symbol of victory and honor.

Cast in bronze by the Gorham foundry, the statue of Elisha N. Dimick was unveiled in February 1922 in front of the State Board of Health Building in West Palm Beach. (Earman chose that location as he was the board's president.) The work received enthusiastic and unanimous praise; the press congratulated Johnson for his fine workmanship, and influential Palm Beach and West Palm Beach leaders celebrated the sculptor. Over two decades later it would be relocated to Royal Palm Way in Palm Beach and cause a great amount of controversy.[33]

Daisy Erb also helped the cause of art in 1922 when she made an impassioned statement in an article entitled "Art in Palm Beach County." Her entreaty, published by the *Palm Beach Post* on December 3, expressed that the Palm Beaches needed more art and, most importantly, an art museum, "a gallery where annual exhibitions might be held and perhaps a permanent exhibition, as pictures would gradually be acquired. Cities smaller than West Palm Beach have their own galleries and such have never failed to be a source of great pride to the community." Erb hoped that "some day will see a gallery that will house works of art

both from our own artists . . . and exhibits sent here from the northern art centers." It would take many years for this quest to become reality.

In 1921, sculptor Gertrude Vanderbilt Whitney (1875-1942) (see fig. 38) returned to town aboard her and her husband's yacht *Captiva.* As the wealthy daughter of Cornelius Vanderbilt and wife to the heir (Harry Payne Whitney) of an estate worth over thirty-five million dollars, by the turn of the twentieth century she could afford ample time to study the art of sculpting. And study she did—at the Art Students League with James Earle Fraser and in Paris with Auguste Rodin. Influenced by the Ashcan School in the early 1900s, she devoted herself to collecting their works and other progressive art, as well as promoting artists in general. She would later found the Whitney Museum of American Art after the Metropolitan Museum of Art declined an endowment of her impressive collection. Along with her influential friends, she would also assist in bringing the cause of art to Palm Beach. Indeed, from 1923 to 1930 the area's art reputation would continue to blossom and reach higher national renown thanks to its principal art boosters, an array of some of the most fascinating people in American history.

Fig. 38. Paul Helleu, *Gertrude Vanderbilt Whitney.* (Courtesy HSPBC, photograph by Bert and Richard Morgan)

Chapter Four
1923-1930: Art Blossoms and Booms

Palm Beach attracted a wealth of artists and celebrities during the regime of Paris Singer, creator of the exclusive Everglades Club, and architect Addison Mizner, innovative builder of the Spanish-inspired Palm Beach we think of today. These men, especially Mizner, did their share of utilizing artists and artisans and importing fine art; however, they were not the only cultural boosters in town. Other art supporters included leading socialite Eva Stotesbury (called "Queen Eva"); her husband, Drexel & Co./J. P. Morgan partner Edward Townsend Stotesbury; art dealer Velma Glenn Hodges; the sculptor Gertrude Vanderbilt Whitney; aviation promoter Amy Phipps (Mrs. Frederick) Guest; heiress extraordinaire Marjorie Merriweather Post; Edith and Henry Rea; architect Marion Sims Wyeth; Mizner's client Nell Cosden; and, of course, Alice De Lamar.

In 1923 Edward Stotesbury headed the second cultural boosting group on the island, the Society of Arts. Eva Stotesbury promoted the visual arts portion and helped organize exhibitions at Flagler's former home, Whitehall.

Addison Mizner had designed the Stotesburys' expansive residence, El Mirasol, and in 1923 he built another splendid Palm Beach mansion, Playa Riente. He employed his friend, painter/sculptor C. Percival Dietsch, to enhance the Spanish-inspired home. Dietsch, who maintained a studio at 238 Peruvian Avenue in the 1920s and in Old Saybrook, Connecticut, in the off season, had studied at the American Academy in Rome and enjoyed the tutelage of William Merritt Chase and Attilio Piccirilli in the United States. An international prize winner, Dietsch became an honored member of the National Sculpture Society and the Architectural League in New York.[1]

Dietsch began to winter in Palm Beach for health reasons after serving in World War I. The island offered not only mild, curative weather but also creative employment opportunities, since Dietsch's aesthetic was perfectly in line with Addison Mizner's. One of the first members of the Everglades Club, Dietsch provided murals, sculpted many Palm Beach stone fountains, and worked at Mizner

Fig. 39. Mizner Industries plaques. (Courtesy HSPBC)

41

Industries, creating designs for the various craftsmen to copy (see fig. 39). He also modeled a relief portrait of Mizner for art collector Dr. Preston Pope Satterwhite and his wife, which adorned the façade of the couple's Mizner-built mansion.[2]

In keeping with Playa Riente's Spanish heritage theme, Dietsch decorated the exterior and interior of the home with portrayals (in bas-, mid-, and high-relief sculpture) of the myth of Juan Ponce de León's search for the Fountain of Youth, during which he discovered Florida. In an outdoor panel placed above an entranceway, Dietsch carved a scene of Ponce de León flanked by his conquistadors, having landed on the shores of Florida (see fig. 40). He brandishes his sword, symbolizing powerful authority, and claims the land for Spain while Native Americans look on curiously.

In figure 41, Ponce De León, a priest, and others watch in awe as an old man has been transformed into a youth after bathing in the magical fountain. In figure 42, Ponce de León, mortally wounded by a Native American arrow, lies in the foreground amid Florida vegetation. One of his conquistadors raises Ponce de León's sword to heaven in an effort to save him. Behind him, a rising female spirit holds a sunflower, the

Fig. 40. C. Percival Dietsch, *Ponce de León Claiming Florida for Spain,* once at Playa Riente, now on the grounds of the Driftwood Resort, Vero Beach, Florida. (Courtesy Driftwood Resort, photograph by author)

Fig. 41. C. Percival Dietsch, *Rejuvenation,* once at Playa Riente, now on the grounds of the Driftwood Resort, Vero Beach, Florida. (Courtesy Driftwood Resort, photograph by author)

Native American symbol of a solar deity. The conquistadors' ship waits in the harbor to sail to Cuba, where Ponce de León will die.

Playa Riente's owner was an Oklahoma-born beauty named Nell Cosden (see fig. 43), whose husband, Joshua, earned his fortune in oil. A prominent socialite featured in *Vogue*, Cosden had extraordinary taste. When Addison Mizner met her she was so attractive he thought her unintelligent, but she soon proved him incorrect. Shortly after their first encounter, Cosden and a young woman accompanied the architect on a

Fig. 42. C. Percival Dietsch, *The Fatally Wounded Juan Ponce de León is Comforted by his Men,* once at Playa Riente, now at the Driftwood Resort, Vero Beach, Florida. (Courtesy Driftwood Resort, photograph by author)

lively, fun-filled voyage to Spain and France. Mizner relished the women's company and was deeply saddened when they abandoned him in Nice for Florence, Italy, to investigate the newly restored Palazzo Davanzati.[3]

Upon viewing palazzo's interior design, Nell Cosden couldn't help but appreciate the work of Florentine copyists Federigo (sometimes spelled Federico), Alberto, and Achille Angeli—who, under the directorship of the palazzo's owner, Elia Volpi, and painter, Silvio Zanchi—had uncovered its original mural decorations buried beneath a layer of whitewashed rough cast. She admired the brothers' restoration so much that she had Mizner hire them to decorate Playa Riente. Cosden wished to duplicate the Florence palazzo's dining salon in her dining room (see fig. 44); therefore the Angeli brothers precisely copied the Palazzo Davanzati's Sala dei Pappagalli (The Parrot Room, set up like a dining salon) (see fig. 45). Federigo (the most accomplished of the brothers, who would later exhibit professionally), Alberto, and Achille also decorated Nell Cosden's bedroom and loggia as well as other areas in the house. Benozzo Gozzoli's *Procession of the Maji* (1450-1460, Palazzo Medici-Riccardi, Florence) inspired the hallway (or dressing room) adjacent to one of the master bedrooms (see fig. 46).[4]

Fig. 43. *Nell Cosden Wearing her Famous $600,000 Fletcher String of Pearls* (*Tulsa Daily World,* May 21, 1922)

Achille Angeli remained in Palm Beach and soon earned the commission of painting murals in the Everglades Club. He also decorated the South Ocean Boulevard residences of Alice De Lamar and Edith and Henry Rea (Lagomar). De Lamar further implemented her Medici-like philanthropy in supporting Palm Beach artists by hiring Angeli to paint her New York apartment and helped him obtain other Palm Beach clients as well as those in New York, California, and Connecticut.[5]

While working on the Everglades Club murals, the twenty-three-year-old, exceedingly handsome Achille Angeli commanded the attention of Florence Mizner, the new wife of Addison's brother, Wilson. Mizner's nephew, Horace Chase, warned Angeli not to respond to Florence's advances lest he risk a probable murderous attack by Wilson or the loss of further jobs through a scandal. Luckily Angeli took Chase's advice and avoided any romantic contact with Florence. Achille also attracted male decorators in town, but the painter fended off any advances with affable humor and remained interested only in women, especially Addison

Fig. 44. Detail, Playa Riente, dining room, Angeli brothers. (Courtesy HSPBC, photograph by Frank E. Geisler)

Fig. 45. Detail, Sala dei Pappagalli, Palazzo Davanzati, Florence, Italy. (Courtesy Wikimedia Commons, photograph by Saiko)

Mizner's niece, Ysabel, whom Angeli courted. Hoping that Ysabel and Angeli would wed, Mizner furthered Angeli's career; however, the marriage did not occur.[6]

Addison and Wilson Mizner delighted in teaching Achille Angeli, who spoke poor English, the saltiest of words, and the three often amused themselves with this irreverent game. Alice De Lamar recalled that one day Eva Stotesbury, whom Angeli called "Mrs. Strawberry," spoke of taking some "sun on the beach." Angeli remarked, "Oh, Mrs. Strawberry, I am surpise [sic] that you say this. They tell me that this word sun-on-the-beach is very bad word!" Later Angeli married a California woman and settled happily in Weston, Connecticut (due to his connection with De Lamar), creating wallpaper designs and painting in his studio. After becoming an American citizen and experiencing a successful marriage of some twenty-two years, in 1953 he and his wife, Claire,

traveled to Italy to celebrate their anniversary. Sadly, during the trip he fell to his death in La Spezia while trying to board a moving train.[7]

In 1923 Mizner traveled to Venice to meet with the controversial yet fashionable artist José Maria Sert y Badia (1874-1945) and approve his sketches for the Cosden ballroom at Playa Riente. Mizner thought the artist's drawings were "lovely beyond any dream" and Sert began to work in oils on the murals.[8]

Soon after he was hired by Mizner, Sert completed the spectacular Orientalist panels depicting the voyages of Sinbad from the *Arabian Nights,* and after a brief exhibition in 1924 at New York's Wildenstein Galleries, they were put in place (see fig. 47). The murals thoroughly enhanced Playa

Fig. 46. Dressing room (or hallway) at Playa Riente. (Courtesy HSPBC)

Fig. 47. Sert murals at Playa Riente; *Sinbad Recounting His Adventures at the Feast* is above the fireplace. (Courtesy HSPBC, photograph by Frank E. Geisler)

Riente's cavernous ballroom; *Vogue* deemed it a privilege just to view them. Light from the windows and Sert-designed tubular lanterns enhanced the paintings, a base of gold leaf contrasted by dramatic black delineation detailing each scene. Trompe l'oeil (fool the eye) red velvet curtains throwing off a faux sheen framed each panel as if the viewer were watching a grand theatrical production. While decidedly unique, one can't help but note the influence from late Baroque palace murals to early Rococo works by artists such as Giovanni Battista Tiepolo.[9]

One of the panels portrayed Sinbad's Seventh Voyage (see fig. 48). In the story, a pirate sells Sinbad as a slave to a hunter who commands Sinbad to shoot several elephants with a bow and arrow. Surviving members of the herd capture Sinbad by wrapping their trunks around his leg and carry him to the elephant graveyard, knowing that its cache of ivory will save them from future hunts. Notice how Sert cleverly formed the compositional off-centered jumble of elephants. Although these and other wild beasts purportedly frightened Playa Riente's staff so much that they refused to serve in the ballroom, many grand events nonetheless took place.[10]

The Cosdens sold Playa Riente to Horace Dodge's widow, Anna Thomson Dodge, in 1925. Dodge's fine art dealer, Joseph Duveen, visited Palm Beach the following year to oversee the redecorating of the manse, but the Sert murals remained in place until 1957, when their auction would engender a large amount of excitement, gossip, and speculation.[11]

Meanwhile, in November 1923 New York's Milch Galleries displayed Caroline Van Hook Bean's series of paintings depicting "Palm Beach Doorways and Gardens" (see fig. 49). The exhibition received favorable attention from both the *New York Times* and *Art News,* which further boosted the connection between Palm Beach and the New York art world.[12]

By 1927, the Palm Beach County Art Club's then president, Frank Landon Humphreys, had changed the club's name to

Fig. 48. José Maria Sert y Badia, *Elephants Capturing Sinbad,* Detroit Institute of Arts, USA City of Detroit, gift of Anna Thomson Dodge. (Bridgeman Images)

Fig. 49. Caroline Van Hook Bean, *Palm Beach Doorway,* ca. 1923. (Courtesy Robert Livingstone and James D. Julia Auctions, Fairfield, Maine, USA, www.jamesdjulia.com)

the Palm Beach Art League. The Art League's goals, like many other art associations in the South, included stimulation of art appreciation, the discovery of talent in schools, and, as Daisy Erb had written, the determination to establish a permanent exhibition space—a fine art museum—where they could educate other artists and raise the public's taste level for art. Humphreys, a sculptor, concurred with that premise. He loved art and strived to preserve Palm Beach's artistic beauty. In fact, Humphreys spoke civically on that subject and extended his aesthetic sensibilities to his sons, Malcolm and David, who became fine artists, Malcolm especially catching New York's attention.[13]

Further championing the cause of art in Palm Beach, in 1924 art booster, critic, and connoisseur Velma Glenn Hodges opened a gallery on Palm Beach Avenue (now County Road), near Royal Palm Way, and began organizing exhibitions of European tapestries and prominent American painters' and sculptors' works. Participating sculptors were among the finest in the nation, including Gertrude Vanderbilt Whitney, Paul Manship, Edith Barretto Parsons, Jo Davidson (who frequently visited Hodges), Harriette Gowen (Mrs. Henry Payne) Bingham, and Harriet Whitney Frishmuth. All had exhibited together in New York and had a connection to Hodges; in fact, no one brought the spirit of innovative American sculpture to Palm Beach quite like she did. Hodges had assistance from Whitney, who acted as patron to the gallery's 1924 "American Sculptors' Show." Whitney could entice her New York colleagues with declarations of not only Palm Beach's beauty and amenities but also its marketing possibilities. Furthermore, the sculptors grasped the opportunity of exhibiting in such an inviting, warm atmosphere in the middle of winter. Hodges also hired local artists, such as C. Percival Dietsch, Frank L. Humphreys, and his son Malcolm.[14]

Accenting the tropical sculpture garden of Hodges' gallery was Edith Barretto Parsons's appealing *Frog Baby* (fig. 50), portraying a little girl holding onto two frogs and grinning with delight. In the right-hand background, standing between two palm trees to the left of the gallery's sign, was Janet Scudder's (1869-1940) *La Douche,* in which a toddler stares fascinatingly at a frog.

Scudder's exposure in Palm Beach, acquaintance with Hodges, and knowledge of a proposed third Episcopal Church of Bethesda-by-the-Sea likely led her to invite James Sheldon, National Cathedral Association treasurer, to visit her studio in Paris in hopes of winning a commission for the church's sculpture. Sheldon and his prospective patrons approved of Scudder's studies and hired her for the marble statue of the angel above the Bethesda pool at the church (see fig. 51).[15] The pool commemorates a miracle in the Gospel of John in which an angel stirs the water of a pool that then cures ailments. The memorial, erected with funds from Cornelius Vanderbilt Barton and Jessie Cluett Barton in 1926, was dedicated to their forbearers.

In 1924 sculptor Jo Davidson modeled a portrait bust of

Fig. 50. Detail, sculpture garden at Mrs. Glenn Hodges' Gallery, County Road, ca. 1925. (Courtesy HSPBC, photograph by Joseph Dickoff)

Fig. 51. Janet Scudder, *Angel,* Episcopal Church of Bethesda-by-the-Sea. (Courtesy HSPBC)

PALM BEACH VISUAL ARTS

Addison Mizner (see fig. 52), who patiently posed at the Glenn Hodges Gallery. (Mizner's bust cast in bronze can be seen in the Gioconda and Joseph King Library at The Society of the Four Arts.) Hodges knew Mizner well and had no problem organizing this event; after all, the noted architect had built her house at 306 Worth Avenue.

The same year Addison Mizner posed for Jo Davidson, British illustrator Charles William "Bryan" de Grineau (1883-1957) visited Palm Beach and drew numerous sketches while observing the lively activities on the island. The illustrator remarked that "Palm Beach is quite a thing by itself" and found the island far more delightful than the French Riviera. He especially enjoyed the Lake Trail and boasted that his depiction of the resort would capture its spirit more than the work of any other artist in history.[16] In an uncanny way, it did. Several sketches (see fig. 53) denoted the event-filled day of a young female visitor. From the upper left, to begin her "strenuous day" she would take a morning stroll through the long corridors of the Hotel Royal Poinciana, ride a bicycle around the island, and then play eighteen holes of golf at the Everglades Club. Next she would take a "wheelchair ride to the beach" and participate in the boardwalk parade of the fashionable. Then she would toss a ball on the beach and bathe in the ocean, have lunch at the Poinciana Grill, partake in "gentle afternoon exercise" on roller skates, pursue her athletic ability during "the tennis hour," and shop at The Breakers. After this, she and her friends would view the "progress of the new Spanish palaces" and return to the hotel to dress for the evening and make the most important decision of the day—"Shall I wear pearls or emeralds or both?" The central panel portrayed "Dine and Dance Deluxe at the Everglades Club" as the

Fig. 52. Jo Davidson modeling the bust of Addison Mizner at Mrs. Glenn Hodges' gallery, 1924. (Courtesy HSPBC, photograph by Joseph Dickoff)

Fig. 53. Bryan de Grineau, *Palm Beach,* 1924, lithograph, 421/500, from the private collection of Cindy and Ted Mandes. The original pen-and-ink drawing is in another private collection.

highlight of the evening, followed by a midnight boat ride on Lake Worth (the last sketch at mid-left).

Art continued to flourish during the 1925 season. The Society of Arts, headquartered at Whitehall, primarily offered musical concerts; but in 1924-1925, Ethel (Mrs. Charles V. G.) Clark, followed by Velma Hodges, directed several successful art exhibitions. In keeping with Palm Beach's Spanish heritage, Addison Mizner and Paris Singer invited leading Hispanic painters Ignacio Zuloaga and Federico Beltrán-Massés to the island in 1925. Mizner had an ulterior motive for inviting Beltrán-Massés to Palm Beach: he wanted the artist to paint his portrait, which was achieved successfully. Both artists created a sensation when the Society of Arts organized their exhibitions at Whitehall. Exhibited in January, the Beltrán-Massés paintings were a triumph, and in March Zuloaga wowed his audience and enjoyed Irving Berlin serenading him. Zuloaga's paintings hung along with portraits by William Van Dresser, who painted the likenesses of notables from Billie Burke to Clara Bow.[17]

One of the highlights of the Beltrán-Massés exhibition was *La Maja Marquesa* (fig. 54), which depicted three sensual young women, the central figure having just removed her clothing. The inherent sexuality is balanced by a delicacy and variation in color and texture of prismatic skin tone and fabrics. Two of the women peer curiously at the viewer, as if they are about to invite him or her into their group and are not at all startled that after a formal fête their private moment has been interrupted. In 1915 the painting sparked much controversy in Spain; the jury of the *Comité del Exposición Nacional de Bellas Artes* rejected it, considering it immoral in its allusion to a real-life, prominent, rebellious marquesa who had divorced her husband and taken part in lesbian relationships. The committee also resented the presence of the mantilla, a Spanish headdress worn on formal occasions. (One could liken it to a recognized Palm Beach society doyenne wearing nothing but a tiara.) The dismissed painting was moved to the Sala de Arte Moderna

and received more publicity than Beltrán-Massés could have imagined, with countless postcards reproducing the work and hoards of curious visitors clamoring to see what some perceived as an effrontery to decency.[18]

The general public in Spain lined up to view the painting not for its superb color, compositional balance, or exquisite technique, but for its notoriety. Not so in Palm Beach. Despite the fact that the Palm Beach exposure of the painting was ten years later, the reaction from the press was commensurate with the sophistication of the island. The critics raved about the artistry of Beltrán-Massés and

Fig. 54. Federico Beltrán-Massés. *La Maja Marquesa,* 1915, private collection. (Courtesy Maria Antonia Salom de Tord, administrator of the Federico Beltrán-Massés estate, www. beltranmasses.com, and Stair Sainty Gallery)

the beauty of the women without a hint of moral outrage: "The paintings hung in the two rooms of the society were mutely eloquent of the absolute genius of the master. The ladies that the eminent painter portrays are all of the high, aristocratic type. His nude and semi-nudes show a very delicate sense of form and perfect delineation of figure." This was great *art* they were describing, with critical opinions free from prudish bias and rising above convention or prejudice towards sexual proclivity. However, if the nude woman had been an identifiable Palm Beach socialite the press might have not been so enthusiastic.[19]

Also in 1925, Paris Singer commissioned British portraitist of royalty, Oswald Birley (1880-1952), to paint his portrait and had Mizner build an apartment and studio for the artist on the upper floor of a building adjacent to the Everglades Club. While Singer was tall and distinguished looking (Alice De Lamar thought he resembled Renaissance royalty), Birley found him a difficult sitter, as he would not remain still for any length of time unless the artist played music Singer enjoyed. Birley finally completed Singer's likeness, which was placed in the entranceway of the Everglades Club. The artist thoroughly relished Palm Beach and enthused, "Nowhere in the world have I seen so luminous quality of light as there is in Palm Beach. The sea and all of the foliage has a quality of color that I have never observed anywhere else in the world." He painted the portrait of Edward T. Stotesbury, and Birley's works also graced a Society of Arts exhibition at Whitehall.[20]

In 1927 the Oasis Club—designed by artist/architect Joseph Urban, founded in part by Anthony Drexel Biddle Jr., and opened by Col. Edward R. Bradley—featured bas-relief sculpture of camels carved by Urban's employee, Vienna secessionist sculptor Franz Barwig (1868-1931). According to Alice De Lamar, the camels not only evoked the Middle East; they also referred to prohibition.[21] Urban, also from Vienna, had created fantastical illustrations for children's books and over-the-top theatrical scenery before designing

his unique Palm Beach buildings. He hired Barwig and the sculptor's son to carve the decorative Dorian stone imported from Genoa at Marjorie Merriweather Post's mansion, Mar-a-Lago, opened in January 1927.

The secessionist style, lasting between 1900 and 1918, remained in the Barwigs' Mar-a-Lago carvings, especially in the depiction of the fluid yet exaggerated snake-like necks of wild swans (see fig. 55). A secessionist (and art deco) geometric formation is found in the swans' feathers and in the cluster of cackling parrots (see fig. 56). The Barwigs' sculpture also reveals intricate ornamentation, no doubt the influence of fellow Vienna secessionist Gustav Klimt, also a member of the Wiener Werkstätte (Vienna Workshop), popular in Europe from 1903-1932.[22]

In the meantime, Palm Beach artist Charles Bosseron Chambers (1883-1964) kept a studio in West Palm Beach until 1916, when he moved to New York and

Fig 55. Franz Barwig I and II, *Swans*, Mar-a-Lago, ca. 1926. (Historic Map Works, historicmapworks.com)

maintained his atelier at Carnegie Hall. In his New York studio he created numerous stunning examples of beautiful women wearing exotic clothing, as well as the most reproduced painting of its time, *Light of the World,* depicting the Christ Child.[23]

Chambers continued to winter in Palm Beach for many years. During the season the artist exhibited his religious and Orientalist paintings, such as *Scheherazade* (fig. 57), at venues including Michaelyan Galleries, owned by Harutunc Michaelyan, who was born in Constantinople in 1875 and arrived in Palm Beach in the early 1920s.[24]

Chambers explained that he had his model don an elaborate headdress to transform herself into *Scheherazade.* The artist quipped, "I could take any quiet little homebody,

Fig. 56. Frans Barwig I and II, *Parrots,* Mar-a-Lago, ca. 1926 (detail). (Historic Map Works, historicmapworks.com)

Fig. 57. Charles Bosseron Chambers, *Scheherazade,* ca. 1921. (Courtesy Papillon Gallery)

give her a headdress like that and a gilded robe to match and she would unconsciously imbibe some of the spirit of the country that costume represents."[25]

In December 1926 Alice De Lamar brought her close friend Mary Duggett Benson (see fig. 58) to Palm Beach due to Benson's bout with bronchitis. Benson, later known as Palm Beach's "first lady of art," would initiate Worth Avenue's first major commercial gallery and forever change Palm Beach's artistic profile.

Mary Duggett was born on March 30, 1890, to a devout Catholic family in New York and was educated at Mount St. Mary's, a convent in Burlington, Vermont, where her piano teacher instilled in her a love of art. In December 1917 the tall, fashionably slender twenty-seven-year-old tyro actress with flawless skin and thick, lustrous red hair met the stage star Eva Le Gallienne while Duggett was performing as an extra in a New York theatrical production. Duggett (whom Le Gallienne called Mimsey) and Le Gallienne were immediately attracted to each other, moved in together, and became loving companions. Le Gallienne wrote in her diary that she was completely happy after spending the night "in Mimsey's arms" and often expressed her deep love for Duggett. Le Gallienne's mother and father also thought Duggett was "a darling" and thoroughly approved of the relationship due to her sweet nature. Some nine years older than Le Gallienne, she nurtured and cared for the actress, especially in times of ill health and crisis. "There is always a sense of comfort where Mimsey is," Le Gallienne wrote in her autobiography. "Somehow one has the feeling that everything will be all right."[26]

The two young women lived together for over three years, during which time several men courted Mary Duggett, making Le Gallienne furiously jealous. However, she remained devoted to the soft-spoken Duggett, obtaining theatrical parts for her, emotionally supporting her at the hospital when her younger sister, Frances Mathews, underwent major surgery, and while on a theatrical tour

Fig. 58. Mary Duggett (Benson) at seventeen (left) with her sister Frances, 1907. (Courtesy Susan Mathews Sperandeo)

accompanying Duggett on a visit to Frances and Edward Nash Mathews' home in Cleveland, Ohio.[27]

In August 1920, when Mary Duggett returned to New York after traveling to England, Spain, Italy, France, and Belgium to pore over the arts, Eva Le Gallienne asked her to join the actress on a national tour. Duggett declined and instead remained in New York to study music and voice. While Le Gallienne was out of town, Duggett, bowing to pressure from her family and society to adopt a more accepted relationship, married the stockbroker, art editor, and sculptor Stuart Benson on February 8, 1921. This devastated Le Gallienne, but in time she and the new Mrs. Benson reconciled. After Le Gallienne had moved on to other relationships, Benson deeply regretted leaving her and marrying Stuart, sobbing over her decision on Le Gallienne's staircase. They remained intimate friends, and during the off season Le Gallienne would visit the Bensons at their home, Folding Key Farm, in Weston, Connecticut.[28]

In 1926, Mary Duggett Benson became Eva Le Gallienne's personal secretary and the business manager of Le Gallienne's Civic Repertory Theater, where Benson's winning personality helped considerably in fundraising for the organization. This position gave her the opportunity to socialize with the theater's most loyal backers, including the wealthy and cultured Alice De Lamar and art collector Otto Kahn, both of whom nurtured her love for the visual arts. Furthering Benson's cultural education, Alice De Lamar hosted Benson and Le Gallienne during their tour of Europe in 1927.[29]

As mentioned, Mary Benson's hopes for a happy marriage were not enough to sustain it, despite the fact that she and her husband took active leadership roles in Weston society for around five years. They spent less and less time together and in 1926, the same year she visited Palm Beach with Alice De Lamar, Stuart gave Mary the option to move to the South of France with him or remain in the United States. She declined to move to the French Riviera and the couple separated. Four years later Benson divorced her husband on the apocryphal grounds of constant cruelty, charges necessary to obtain a divorce in New York State. In the courtroom, as lawyers read aloud the claims of Stuart's alleged abuse and abandonment, Mary couldn't bear hearing them and jumped repeatedly out of her seat exclaiming, "That's not true!" Despite her declarations to Benson's innocence, the judge handed her the divorce. Sadly, many years later Stuart Benson died while traveling alone by apparently falling overboard during a tempestuous night at sea.[30]

In the interim, Alice De Lamar's godfather, William Nelson Cromwell, who had been more like a real father, asked Mary Benson to befriend his goddaughter and move in with her. De Lamar lived almost as a hermit and Cromwell felt that Benson, with her gregarious nature, could draw Alice out of her excruciatingly shy, reclusive behavior. Benson agreed and the two women became close friends and, later, domestic partners.[31]

Mary Benson's appreciation of art grew with the influence of Alfred La Liberté, an esteemed Canadian pianist and composer who regularly took her on New York gallery excursions. Benson's friendships with famed mega-art collectors Bernard Berenson and Alfred Erickson and renowned art dealers Carroll Carstairs and Joseph Duveen also cultivated her interest in art. Duveen and Benson remained great friends for many years. One day he asked Benson to choose any painting she wanted from his London gallery. Gleefully anticipating a strong reaction from the dealer, she picked an impressive Augustus John portrait, the most expensive painting in the entire place. A shocked Duveen raised his arms and exclaimed in horror, "Oh, my dear child!" before realizing it was a joke. After her friend became Lord Duveen, Benson continually referred to him as such, although he simply called her Mary.[32]

While Mary Benson was gleaning art appreciation from the influence of her notable friends and associates, one of them, Otto Kahn, began to winter in Palm Beach due to a heart condition. Kahn brought a lasting reputation as an arts supporter. In Palm Beach he hosted guests such as Bernard Baruch and sculptor Jo Davidson.[33]

Another important art collector and admirer of Benson, Jules Bache, joined Kahn as a winter resident in Palm Beach by 1929. Bache had been vacationing on the island as early as the 1910s. His fine-art dealer, Joseph Duveen, would visit Bache in Palm Beach yet shun seeing any other of his other prominent collectors in town. According to Duveen's biographer, the art dealer once stated, "It bores me to death to have to visit so many people I may know there."[34]

Duveen, who had sold Eva and Edward Stotesbury much of the art for their Pennsylvania homes, had not assisted them in decorating their Palm Beach mansion, El Mirasol. Eva instead had chosen a rather subdued collection of various tapestries, old-master school paintings, and British

portraits, including several by George Romney. Tapestries, paintings by or after Murillo and Velasquez, and other old-master paintings—some religious or depicting Italian ruins—decorated several of the other Palm Beach homes designed by Mizner, Marion Sims Wyeth, and Maurice Fatio. Mizner, interestingly enough, mixed old-master paintings and tapestries with modern art in his home.

Frances Bingham Bolton and Chester Bolton decorated their Palm Beach estate, Casa Apava, with a sparse mix of decorative landscape murals, Spanish school paintings, and Italianate capriccios. What they lacked in fine art, they made up for in Portuguese tiles (see fig. 59), later donated to the Preservation Foundation of Palm Beach by Mr. and Mrs. Irwin Kramer and now displayed at Pan's Garden in Palm Beach.

In 1927 Eva Stotesbury (see fig. 60) announced a meeting of the most powerful society and cultural leaders at El Mirasol to form the visual arts support group the Friends of the Arts and Crafts. Spurred on by the ongoing taste for aestheticism and the Arts and Crafts movement born in the nineteenth century, they planned to advance the cause of artistic achievement in Palm Beach by sponsoring exhibitions with the work of painters,

Fig. 60. Douglas Chandor, *Portrait of Eva Stotesbury* wearing her famous Cartier emeralds, 1926. (Courtesy Russell W. Kuteman, with permission from the estate of Ina Kuteman Chandor, all rights reserved)

Fig. 59. Detail, Wall from Casa Apava, Pan's Garden, Preservation Foundation of Palm Beach. (Photograph by author)

sculptors, printmakers, and craftspeople. During the previous winter season the Society of Arts no longer held art exhibitions, and those culture boosters present at El Mirasol, including architect Marion Sims Wyeth, felt that the Friends of the Arts and Crafts should concentrate more on the visual arts rather than primarily music. After the new organization's formation was approved, the group elected officers, including socialite Edith Rea as president and Frank Gair Macomber, honorary curator of art at the Museum of Fine Arts, Boston, as vice president. Amy Phipps Guest, Mary (Mrs. Joseph) Urban, and Mrs. E. F. Hutton (Marjorie Merriweather Post) were among the executive committee members.[35]

While the Society of Arts had exhibited only European artists, the Friends encouraged and supported local artists and artisans. A flyer asking for regular membership at twenty-five dollars per year stated that "many of us feel that we lose touch with what is going on in the world of Art by being absent from the north during the winter months when the most notable exhibitions and artistic events take place. Although [the Friends of the Arts and Crafts] bring to Palm Beach the best that is to be had in the world of Art today, their success and growth depend entirely upon the appreciation and encouragement accorded them by the community. It is hoped that Palm Beach will wish to prove itself the leader in developing both arts and crafts."[36]

The group cultivated further growth of the island's tropical artistic civilization; however, one of their first exhibitions displayed not the work of local artists but that of a European, Sir John Lavery, whose portraits were exhibited at Whitehall in 1927. Lavery stayed at The Breakers and painted glorious impressionist scenes of its tennis court and salon. He also rendered *The Peoples' Pool, Palm Beach* (fig. 61).[37]

Concurrently, in 1927 many of the same members from the Friends of the Arts and Crafts formed the Palm Beach Association for Artists. The association hoped to promote the best of nationally known American artists' works for annual Palm Beach exhibitions.[38]

While Alice De Lamar was not listed as one of the founding members of the Friends of the Arts and Crafts or the Palm Beach Association for Artists, she no doubt anonymously supported both groups. She also helped Addison Mizner and simultaneously provided creative work for local photographer Frank E. Geisler (1867-1935). De Lamar hired and drove Geisler throughout Palm Beach and Boca Raton to create a large folio volume (which she financially yet anonymously backed) of Mizner-built properties in order to protect his architectural legacy. Geisler (born Franz E. Geisler in Hoboken, New Jersey) had previously worked in Manhattan photographing Broadway stars and illustrating magazines. Florenz Ziegfeld, one of Geisler's patrons,

Fig. 61. John Lavery, *The Peoples' Pool, Palm Beach,* 1927, private collection. (Photograph © Christie's Images/Bridgeman Images)

introduced the photographer to wintering in Palm Beach, where he exhibited his work with the Palm Beach County Art Club and maintained a winter studio at The Breakers. He achieved success with patrons such as the Binghams, who hired him to photograph their property, but his greatest achievement was the 1928 book that De Lamar created, *The Florida Architecture of Addison Mizner* (see example in fig. 47). In gratitude for such a tribute, Mizner aptly denoted Alice De Lamar as a Medici figure when he inscribed the following sentiment beneath his photographic portrait by Geisler: "To Allice [*sic*]—My Lorenzo the Magnificent. Addison."[39]

Mizner himself broadened visual arts culture when he sponsored an exhibition inviting three hundred guests to his Worth Avenue showroom to see the works of celebrities by portraitist Byron Higgins. The artist's subjects included Charles Lindbergh and Tallulah Bankhead.[40]

In the meantime, an American sculptor of Italian heritage, Leo Lentelli (October 29, 1879-December 31, 1961), designed his most famous Palm Beach work, *The Breakers Florentine Fountain* (fig. 62), in 1926. Lentelli graduated from schools in Bologna, including the Scuola Professionale per le Arti Decorative and the R. Istituto de Belle Arti. He emigrated from Italy when he was twenty-four and less than a decade later became an American citizen. At the Panama-Pacific Exhibition in 1915, his sculpture impressed spectators and his other prominent work graced many buildings throughout the nation.[41]

The *Fontana del Carciofo* (Fountain of Artichokes, Francesco Susini, installed in 1641) on the terrace above the Grotto of Moses at Palazzo Pitti adjacent to Boboli Gardens in Florence, Italy, (see fig. 63) inspired Lentelli's Breakers fountain. However, Lentelli's version is not an exact replica. One difference is in the religious symbolism inherent in *Fontana del Carciofo* but absent from The

Fig. 62. Leo Lentelli, *The Breakers Florentine Fountain* (restored), Palm Beach, 1926. (Photograph by author)

Fig. 63. Francesco Susini, *Fontana del Carciofo* (Fountain of Artichokes), Florence, Italy. (Courtesy Wikimedia Commons, photograph by Rufus46)

Breakers fountain, which is secular in iconography. Lentelli also incorporated his penchant and skill in depicting the fit female figure, and based on Greco/Roman mythology, The Breakers fountain features four beautiful naiads (water nymphs) riding dolphins and supporting the middle basin, whereas the *Fontana del Carciofo*'s basin is supported by muscular male angels.

The four water nymphs in The Breakers fountain may perhaps be directional symbols or may represent the four seasons in which Florida bears fruit and flowers throughout the year. Indeed, fruit and flowers decorate The Breakers fountain's upper basin, as opposed to the *Fontana del Carciofo*'s top portion, which is adorned primarily with two clothed figures. While putti accent the edge of both fountains, the *Fontana del Carciofo*'s putti ride turtles, dolphins, and play with bows. The Breakers fountain putti wrestle playfully with herons and alligators—symbolic of Florida.[42]

Over the decades since its installation, Lentelli's fountain had unfortunately deteriorated and was in such disrepair that in 2015 conservators replicated it. Lentelli wrote a prophetic phrase that relates to giving new life to his fountain: ". . . for art does renew and is alive again, to never die out—the spirit and mind of humanity."[43]

The devastating 1928 hurricane did not hinder Palm Beach in its quest for a tropical artistic civilization. During the season the Friends of the Arts and Crafts, already affiliated with the National Federation of Arts, held exhibitions at various venues. Addison Mizner chaired the hanging committee at one of the exhibits that featured old-master paintings. Other shows displayed tapestries (some loaned by Joseph Duveen) and stained glass. Participating craftspeople included those from Mizner Industries' Las Manos Pottery, with potters showing off their wares in the famous color "Mizner blue" (see fig. 64). Mizner himself joined in the exhibition with his wrought iron designs, and other artisans showed sterling implements as well as jewelry and furniture.[44]

At one of the 1928 Friends' exhibitions, Oswald Birley's sister-in-law, professionally known as Olive Snell, painted the portrait of movie star Gloria Swanson, and Mary McKinnon (de Vries Johnson) (aka MacKinnon DeVries) painted Gertrude Lawrence's portrait. McKinnon, who grew up in Greenwich Village and studied at the Art Students League, illustrated *Harper's Bazaar* and showed her work at New York's Ferargil

Fig. 64. Mizner Industries jardinière with lion-head decoration, "Mizner blue" glaze. (From the collection of the Boca Raton Historical Society & Museum)

Galleries. She first came to Palm Beach in 1925 and spent summers in Southampton, Easthampton, and Newport, where she depicted members of society. McKinnon, who would become fundamental to Palm Beach's visual arts development, also exhibited at the Glenn Hodges Gallery.[45]

Another member of the summer Southampton colony was George Inness's granddaughter and daughter of noted sculptor Jonathan Scott Hartley, Rachel Hartley (1884-1955). The talented painter spent time painting in South Carolina and Florida and displayed her art in a January 1929 Palm Beach exhibition.[46]

In the interim, Amy Phipps Guest admired Caroline Van Hook Bean so much that she commissioned a portrait of Amelia Earhart in 1928, which Caroline painted in her Worth Avenue studio in Via Kaufer (now Via Demario). Guest financed Earhart's historic flight as the first woman trans-Atlantic passenger that year, and Bean executed the portrait shortly after Earhart made the flight.[47]

Several women involved in the Friends of the Arts and Crafts also became members of the Garden Club of Palm Beach in 1928; and far more than merely planting posies, they advised town officials on the beautification of Palm Beach. Alice De Lamar offered the club five hundred dollars if they would clear a large section of dead cabbage palms in the north end that had been decapitated during the hurricane. They accepted her offer, removed the dead stalks, and turned an eyesore into valuable real estate.[48]

It wasn't long before the town of Palm Beach began to form a municipal art league, just as northern cities had done in the late nineteenth century and southern cities had emulated in the early twentieth. In 1928 Palm Beach mayor Major Barclay H. Warburton proposed the organization known as the Palm Beach Art Jury to pass judgment on "plans for all bridges, walls, and other forms of construction." The town council thoroughly approved the committee (the concept of today's Architectural Commission); however, oddly and unlike other urban centers where artists were

Fig. 65. Harriet Whitney Frishmuth, *Call of the Sea,* 1924, bronze, Rovensky Building, The Society of the Four Arts, purchase, April 1, 1992, from the estate of Margaret M. Miller. (Photograph by author, courtesy The Society of the Four Arts, Palm Beach)

called upon as members, the mayor and Palm Beach town council invited only architects and landscape designers for its first art jury.[49]

The same year, Amy Phipps Guest, Eva Stotesbury, Mary (Mrs. Joseph) Urban, and other prominent women acted as continuing patrons of the Palm Beach Association for Artists by holding several exhibitions at 334 Australian Avenue. Members of "The Philadelphia Ten," a group of fine women painters and sculptors, including Harriet Whitney Frishmuth (1880-1980), participated. The Association for Artists also held a solo exhibition devoted to Frishmuth, who after studying with Auguste Rodin forged new pathways in American sculpture with her bronzes of lithe female figures. At her Palm Beach exhibition, *Crest of the Wave, Desha,* and *Joy of the Waters* immediately found buyers. (The purchaser of *Desha* owned the Vineta Hotel—now the Chesterfield.)[50]

Frishmuth, whose work has been collected by many major museums, often utilized dancers for models, moving to music emanating from a Victrola. One of the models, the young ballerina Madeleine Parker, introduced to Frishmuth by her favorite model Desha Delteil, posed for the garden fountain bronzes *Playdays* and *Call of the Sea* (fig. 65), the latter currently located in Palm Beach's The Society of the Four Arts' Rovensky Building. Parker, who died tragically of leukemia at age twenty-five, was around twelve when she modeled for Frishmuth in 1924. The sculptor deftly captured adolescence as the young girl rides a dolphin as if it were a bronco. Indeed, the exuberant joy of unbridled, youthful freedom comes alive in the work.[51]

At the end of the decade, Oscar G. Davies (publisher of the *Palm Beach Daily News*) and Addison Mizner decided

Fig. 66. Addison Mizner and August Godio, Mizner Memorial Fountain, Palm Beach. (Photograph by author)

Fig. 67. Fountain, Villa Borghese (Charles Latham, *The Gardens of Italy,* New York: Scribner's, 1919, 73. This book was once owned by Addison Mizner; Mizner special collection, Gioconda and Joseph King Library, The Society of the Four Arts.)

to beautify the town with a tribute to the pioneers who helped establish it (most notably Henry Morrison Flagler and Elisha Newton Dimick). The fountain for which Mizner donated his services portrays hippocamps rising from the sea (see fig. 66). Mizner, who kept copious large folio tomes and scrapbooks with innumerable illustrations of European design, was inspired by the *Fontana dei Cavalli Marini* in the Borghese Gardens in Rome, Italy (see fig. 67).[52]

With its accompanying planted median and pool, the Mizner Memorial Fountain gained immediate approval and encouragement by Mayor Barclay Warburton, who had campaigned for more parks in the town. Numerous wealthy gentlemen of Palm Beach funded the project, and sculptor August Godio (1862-1933) carved the fountain out of quarried keystone. Godio, who was born in Paris of Italian descent, studied art in Europe before immigrating to the United States in 1880. Eight years later he became a naturalized citizen. Relocating to the Palm Beaches in 1919 from New Jersey, Godio became most well-known for the memorial fountain but also created a trophy base for Palm Beach's Sailfish Club. His beautiful work on the fountain, completed just before Christmas 1929 and presented by the town in 1930, was restored in 2015.[53]

The Mizner Memorial Fountain marked the end of an art-filled decade. However, Palm Beach had only begun to build on its foundation created by visual arts pioneers and those they inspired. These cultural boosters took up the challenge of bringing additional fine art, crafts, and photography to the tropical resort and looked forward to a promising future.

Chapter Five

1930-1940: Further Artistic Growth and the Birth of Two Art Centers

In the midst of the Great Depression, Palm Beach and West Palm Beach continued to thrive in the visual arts. The New Deal established art centers throughout Florida and built the art deco armory in West Palm Beach that would later become the Armory Art Center. During the 1930s, ornate Palm Beach mansions continued to please art collectors, including mega-patron Joseph E. Widener, whose Philadelphia art holdings were later placed in the National Gallery of Art. Widener, however, did not include a substantial fine art collection in his Palm Beach palace, Il Palmetto, designed by Maurice Fatio and completed in 1930.

While the county's artistic growth was steady, glamour flourished in Palm Beach. However, something was different about the island; it seemed to relax its formal atmosphere and there was, according to *Vogue* magazine, a "wholesale reversion to a more casual and simple life. No one is trying to live up to a delusion of grandeur and pomposity."[1]

Artist Constantin Alajalov, who illustrated countless covers of *The New Yorker* and many for *The Saturday Evening Post*, came to Palm Beach in the 1930s and thoroughly enjoyed its new, casual approach to life. He attended private parties until 4:00 a.m. and gambling jaunts at E. R. Bradley's Beach Club. He also admired socialites such as Adele Astaire Cavendish and Kentucky-born Margaret Edmona "Mona" Travis Strader Schlesinger Bush Williams, who resided in a Maurice Fatio-designed house. Alajalov socialized with Alice De Lamar and her intimate friend, aviatrix pioneer Lucia Davidova, as well.[2]

Alajalov recorded his thoughts about Palm Beach for *Vogue*: "The pattern of life is well organized, comfortable, polished, *bien soignée*. Every one gathers . . . around the private pools splashed with bright coloured cushions and mattresses, men taking sun-baths, women almost never. People drop in for tennis, a cocktail or two, and stay to lunch outdoors. Every one looks better . . . with no trace of tenseness. I liked the casual feeling of life, fresh, lazy, and easy-going."[3]

Painter, designer, and photographer Cecil Beaton, whom *Vogue* hired when he was destitute, enjoyed Palm Beach and sold his sketches at the Everglades Club after raising their former New York prices. Beaton first came to Palm Beach in the 1920s with his associate, writer Anita Loos (*Gentlemen Prefer Blondes*), who often wintered on the island (see fig. 68). With help from Loos, he quickly became part of the popular Addison Mizner crowd but later wrote, "Although more than anything I wanted to be accepted by these vital people, I could not bring myself to believe that they really accepted me as one of them."[4]

In 1931 Beaton depicted leading actress Gertrude Lawrence, who posed for him on a patio during a stay in Palm Beach (see fig. 69). Beaton commented that Lawrence looked "divine" in fashion designer Edward "Molyneux's polka-dotted pajamas or white satin sheaths but then Miss Lawrence was always a wonderful exponent for everybody connected with the making of all sorts of clothes. . . ."[5]

Fig. 68. Cecil Beaton and Anita Loos in Palm Beach, January 16, 1930. (Corbis collection, photographer unknown)

Fig. 69. Cecil Beaton, *Gertrude Lawrence in Palm Beach,* from *Vogue,* April 15, 1931, 79. (Cecil Beaton/Vogue, © Condé Nast)

Beaton not only painted and photographed Palm Beach personas; he also wrote commentary about the resort for *Vogue:*

Oh, those Spanish patios! A strange place this that has grown as if by magic from the waste clearing! Gigolos, Argentines with pet white mice on their shoulders, and beazles with hennaed hair and clumsy jewellery [*sic*] all are caught at the Ambassador Hotel, at The Breakers, or Cocoanut Grove. . . . The sun pours down, shoulders blister and peel, and away goes all determination. It is impossible to leave on the day you had originally planned; it is a wonder that you ever leave this place. The shops here in Palm Beach are magnificent but there is no Northern hustle about them—not on account of the slump depressions, but because of the laziness in this tropical climate. It is almost impossible to imagine that the slump has occurred.[6]

Beaton frequently stayed at the home of his close friend the aforementioned Mona Williams. A group of Parisian designers including Cristóbal Balenciaga and Coco Chanel elected Williams (later the countess of Bismarck) the best-dressed woman in the world more than once. A woman of exquisite taste, she enjoyed an annual wardrobe budget of $50,000 as her third husband—Harrison Williams, more than two decades older than she—was worth almost $700 million. Aside from Beaton and Constantin Alajalov, Mona Williams was a patron and friend of many involved in the visual arts—for instance the outstanding surrealist Salvador Dali, who portrayed Mona as dressed in rags. She was also a major art collector with holdings in her gleaming New York residence by artists such as Goya and Boucher.[7]

Cecil Beaton flat out adored Williams and admitted this in correspondence effervescing in affection and illustrated by hearts, butterflies, and flowers. He photographed her numerous times in ultra-glamorous poses wearing the finest of haute couture and also captured her on film informally with her favorite pet, a mixed-breed dog named Micky (fig. 70).

Fig. 70. Cecil Beaton, *Mona Williams and Micky.* (Filson Historical Society, Louisville, Kentucky)

Constantin Alajalov wrote at least one letter to the pet, illustrating a glamorous "Greta Garbo of lizards" and promising to give it to Micky. In fact, Micky was so famous among Mona's friends that his death prompted almost the same number of condolence cards as her husband's death.[8]

Beaton's photograph of Williams brings to the forefront her humanness and affectionate nature, as well as her polished glamour. He wrote that her beautiful "aquamarine eyes, her short silver curling hair and very pink cheeks" epitomized the "American quality of freshness" and later described her as "the perfect example of all that taste and luxury could nurture."[9]

Beaton also chose to depict Williams and her husband with their pets casually sitting in their colorful Palm Beach living room designed by Syrie Maugham (formerly Mrs. William Somerset Maugham) and highlighted by eighteenth century Chinoiserie wallpaper. This painting (see fig. 71), featured in *Vogue* in 1937, was part of a series Beaton painted on American fashion icons exhibited in New York's Carroll Carstairs Gallery.

Like Cecil Beaton and Salvador Dali, French artist Bernard Boutet de Monvel (1884-1949) depicted the popular Mona Williams. Boutet de Monvel also worked for *Vogue* and other magazines as well, and he knew what he was doing when he joined Beaton and Constantin Alajalov in Palm Beach. Maurice Fatio built the artist's beautiful house, *La Folie Monvel* (Monvel's Folly), on Hi-Mount Road in 1936, where he painted in his octagonal studio.[10]

The artist, whose work is in several museums, including the Metropolitan Museum of Art, portrayed Palm Beach socialites with an art deco yet dark, ultra-realist style. In contrast, the illustrated paintings (see figs. 72 and 73) with a linear, sleek design reflect a lighthearted, stylish atmosphere. Around 1930 frequent Palm Beach visitor Helen Brady Cutting (widow of James Cox Brady) commissioned Boutet de Monvel to create these tennis and tropical foliage-inspired paintings for her New Jersey home.

Fig. 71. Cecil Beaton, *A Palm Beach Conversation Piece: Mr. and Mrs. Harrison Williams at home with their dogs, against a Chinese wallpaper that's as vivid as the tropical vegetation outside,* from *Vogue,* February 15, 1937, 46. (Cecil Beaton/Vogue; © Condé Nast)

Fig. 72. Bernard Boutet de Monvel, *1900,* ca. 1930. (Courtesy Barridoff Galleries)

Fig. 73. Bernard Boutet de Monvel, *1930,* ca. 1930. (Courtesy Barridoff Galleries)

In the summer of 1932 Mary Duggett Benson spent extra time in Europe, trying to recover from health complications resulting from six years of strenuous fundraising for Eva Le Gallienne's Civic Repertory Theater. Benson had found something at which she excelled and continued to raise funds for actors, artists, and musicians. By then she had led both Alice De Lamar (see fig. 74) and Le Gallienne to buy properties in Weston and had become more intensely interested in finc art while De Lamar began to collect surrealist paintings.[11]

In Weston, De Lamar would keep many fine and performing artists afloat, including jazz legend Dave Brubeck, fine artists Isamu Noguchi and Pavel Tchelitchew, and choreographer George Balanchine, allowing them to live in one of her houses when they were struggling. Tchelitchew would later exhibit at Mary Benson's Palm Beach gallery.[12]

While Benson and Alice De Lamar had become closer friends, the two women maintained intimate relationships with other female companions and also remained part of Eva Le Gallienne's extended family. Benson continued her nurturing of Le Gallienne and also took care of her own family. When her sister's daughter, Mary Frances ("Didi"), became rebellious against her parents, Benson stepped in and brought up her niece for years. Benson's beneficent nature later helped cultivate countless Palm Beach artists whom she would discover.[13]

Meanwhile, photographer Robert Yarnall Richie, known for artistry in his photographs, was in Palm Beach. He convinced *Town and Country* magazine to hire him to capture many aerial views of Palm Beach mansions, including Mar-a-Lago and the residences of Alice De Lamar, Otto Kahn, and Joseph Kennedy.[14] Other artists with a camera included Frank Turgeon, a former World War I aerial photographer. Born in 1898, Turgeon became successful at shooting scenes at several charity balls, expertly creating formal portraits of notables such as Jules Bache (see fig. 83) and later working for the Duke and Duchess of Windsor (see fig. 108) and Pres. John F. Kennedy.

Fig. 74. Alice De Lamar (left) and Mary Duggett Benson in Weston, Connecticut, 1933. (Photograph by Arnold Genthe, Library of Congress Prints and Photographs Division)

In the early 1930s, Palm Beach Art League member Mabel Jane Hess provided sculpture in town from a studio at the First American Bank building and later at The Breakers and on Worth Avenue. Around that time, New York rug and antiques dealer Ohan S. Berberyan built a home to accentuate his lovely gardens on Peruvian Avenue. First arriving in Palm Beach for the 1915 season, Berberyan had during the 1920s partnered with Mizner in providing fine Persian and Spanish carpets and art objects to Mizner's clients as well as other Palm Beach estate owners. In 1935 Berberyan held an exhibition of paintings by the famed British artist Alfred J. Munnings on loan from New York's Howard Young Galleries, along with decorative objects lent by socialite decorator Elsie De Wolfe.[15]

On February 26, 1933, sculptor Hugo Gari Wagner modeled banker Edward T. Stotesbury's likeness for his eighty-fifth birthday party at El Mirasol, captured by

Fig. 75. Hugo Gari Wagner modeling the bust of Edward Stotesbury at his eighty-fifth birthday celebration at El Mirasol in 1933. (Courtesy HSPBC, photograph by Ray Dame)

photographer Ray Dame (see fig. 75). After photographing European battles during World War I, Dame worked for the Mizner Development Corporation and provided images for Mizner Industries' catalogues. Like several other Palm Beach photographers, Dame also created filmed glimpses of the Duke and Duchess of Windsor.[16]

Hugo Wagner, whose father was also a sculptor, was born in Detroit and studied with the noted American sculptor Karl Bitter. Maintaining a studio in Syracuse, New York, Wagner arrived in Palm Beach around 1920 and worked with Addison Mizner in creating stone sculpture for several of the architect's houses, including the Stotesburys' El Mirasol. Other architects who reaped the talent of Wagner included Marion Sims Wyeth for E. F. Hutton's house, Hogarcito, and Maurice Fatio for Otto Kahn's mansion, Oheka, Mona and Harrison Williams' house, Blythedunes, and Joseph Widener's manse, Il Palmetto. In 1929 the sculptor formed his own company in West Palm Beach, Wagner Stone Products. He also created a bronze plaque of *Florida Pioneers* for the Seminole Chapter of the Daughters of the American Revolution.[17]

Painter Frank T. Hutchens was also in town, painting in gardens and rendering other local landscapes, which he exhibited with the Palm Beach Art League. At least two other Palm Beach artists—society portraitists Cavalier Frederick Roscher and Frank C. Von Hausen—kept busy by portraying Addison Mizner. Roscher, who studied at the Royal Academy of Munich, rendered likenesses of regal clients, heads of state, celebrities, and papal subjects. He became Mizner's good friend and chess partner after the artist depicted Eva Stotesbury, who introduced the two men. Roscher's painting of Mizner portrays him as robust, relaxed, and wearing a smoking jacket (see fig. 76).[18]

Frank C. Von Hausen, an aristocratic German American who studied at the Royal Academy in Vienna, first drove his Lincoln phaeton convertible from Maine to Palm Beach in the 1920s, set up a studio on Worth Avenue, and flourished

Fig. 76. Frederick Roscher, *Addison Mizner,* HSPBC. (Courtesy Mignon Roscher Gardner, © Mignon Roscher Gardener)

there in the 1930s and beyond. He became-well known for his posthumous portrait of Henry Flagler (Henry Morrison Flagler Museum), as well as portraits of Albert Einstein, Edward T. Stotesbury (while the multi-millionaire relaxed in the courtyard of El Mirasol), and, like Roscher, Eva Stotesbury. Von Hausen recollected Eva as "charming and beautiful" and recalled that Edward Stotesbury declared as he watched Von Hausen paint, "I don't see how you do it."[19]

Von Hausen's 1932 portrait of Addison Mizner depicts the jacketless architect appraising the viewer while holding a lit cigarette in one hand, the other resting on a chair (see fig. 77). The artist later recalled, "Mizner was the hardest one to paint. You could almost feel the building schemes coursing in the brain of that huge body. He wouldn't sit still. I had to limit myself to two sittings. His pet monkey, Johnny [*sic*] Brown, scampered about." Von Hausen thought that after all the problems he had in executing the picture, Mizner would be disappointed in it, but the architect surprised Von Hausen after the painting's completion when he "stood before his portrait and exclaimed, 'Why it's great.'"[20]

Von Hausen remained active for over fifty years in Palm Beach and in his seventies maintained a home studio on Indian Road on the north end of the island. In the interim, he exhibited with other artists at the Palm Beach Art Center established by Ogunquit/St. Augustine artist Nunzio Vayana (1878-1960) in 1933. The center, first on Royal Palm Way until it was relocated by 1935 to the former Bradley Oasis Club on East Main Street (north of The Breakers) (see fig. 79), made a significant impact on Palm Beach. It spread visual-arts encouragement to members of the Palm Beach Art League and, by inviting nationally and internationally-acclaimed artists to exhibit, enticed art lovers from other regions to the island. The center also hosted operatic concerts and maintained the Palm Beach Art School, which included outdoor sketching classes in its curriculum, extending Laura Woodward's legacy of painting en plein air.[21]

PALM BEACH VISUAL ARTS

Fig. 77. Frank C. Von Hausen, *Addison Mizner*, 1932, HSPBC, on loan to the Boca Raton Historical Society and Museum. (Boca Raton Historical Society and Museum)

Henry Strater (1896-1987), who assisted director Vayana in organizing the exhibitions, also summered in Ogunquit, Maine. A painter of landscapes (see fig. 78), figures (primarily nudes), and an ardent lover of many women, Strater ("Mike" to his friends) lived a fascinating life before wintering in Palm Beach. He roomed with F. Scott Fitzgerald at Princeton and ignited the inspiration for the author's character of Burne Holiday in *This Side of Paradise*. "I taught Scott not to be afraid of the devil or the dark," Strater later recalled. He took his place as a central figure of the "Lost Generation," the motley yet brilliant group of American expatriate writers in Paris in the 1920s. There he became dining companions with James Joyce (who, according to Strater, was henpecked by his wife), and illustrated Ezra Pound's controversial work *The Cantos*. John Dos Passos also considered Strater a friend during the time when Strater was toying with the idea of becoming a writer. However, Strater later said that after he took a month's instruction at the Académie Julian, "I decided I would rather spend my life sitting before

Fig. 78. Henry Strater, *Pier: Inlet at Palm Beach*. (Courtesy Nicholas Strater)

a beautiful girl than a typewriter." Consequently he also studied with artists Édouard Vuillard, Ignacio Zuloaga, and Arthur B. Carles. Through Ezra Pound, Strater met Ernest Hemingway and became his close friend and fishing buddy after earning the writer's respect by brawling with him on a Paris street corner. The long-lasting friendship survived a major difference in political ideologies; Strater's conservative political views were in direct opposition to the socialist leanings of Hemingway.[22]

Strater taught Hemingway how to catch large fish like marlin, and they bonded further when they were stranded together in a storm during a fishing trip in the Dry Tortugas. In 1936 Strater became furious at Hemingway when Strater caught a nine hundred-pound marlin but Hemingway took credit for the catch and posed with it. Contrary to published accounts, their friendship didn't end because of the marlin; on the contrary, Hemingway continued to visit Strater and his wife after the incident. However, when one of Strater's sons began to resemble Hemingway to such a remarkable extent that it provoked commentary and controversy, the two men parted company for life.[23]

Strater, who had three wives throughout his life, once remarked, "I just love to have love. Women inspire me and I need lots of inspiration." He certainly had plenty of inspiration in Palm Beach. At least one server at Testa's restaurant and a female lifeguard at the Sailfish Club became his muses, and several other women posed for him as well.[24]

In the spring of 1934, the Civic Arts Association was established, led by Maud Howe Elliott, artist Mary McKinnon (Mrs. Frederick Johnson), and Mary (Mrs. Lorenzo E.) Woodhouse. Some in the group, such as Eva Stotesbury, Amy Phipps Guest, and Frank G. Macomber, had been members of the Friends of the Arts and Crafts and acted as patrons of Nunzio Vayana's Palm Beach Art Center, vowing to support and continue its efforts.[25]

Being a painter and illustrator, Mary McKinnon had ample reason to support visual arts in Palm Beach, and Maud Howe Elliott not only had studied fine art and was a recognized art advocate, her husband was an artist. A love of culture had also been instilled in Mrs. Elliott by her mother, Julia Ward Howe, suffragist and lyricist of the *Battle Hymn of the Republic.*

Elliott believed strongly in American art and praised it in her writings and lectures. She also knew Oscar Wilde, a major proponent of aestheticism. She and her husband had been members of the previously mentioned American Renaissance Movement, comprising the finest sculptors and painters in the Northeast who summered with the Elliotts at the Cornish Art Colony in New Hampshire. The Elliotts carried forth the movement's purpose, to promote the beauty of classicism in all forms of the visual arts, by

Fig. 79. Palm Beach Art Center, ca. 1936, formerly the Oasis Club. (Courtesy HSPBC)

PALM BEACH VISUAL ARTS

helping form the Art Association of Newport before Mrs. Elliott extended the cause for culture in Palm Beach.[26]

Mr. and Mrs. Lorenzo Woodhouse were also fervent art patrons and cultural supporters. In 1916 the couple founded a library and in 1930 established a museum on Long Island. Mary Woodhouse also inaugurated the Marjorie Leidy Prize (in memory of her artist daughter who had tragically drowned in an automobile accident), given to outstanding participants exhibiting at the Palm Beach Art Center.[27]

With firm support from steadfast doyennes, the Palm Beach Art Center continued to thrive. In 1936 artists from throughout Florida exhibited at the center, including Miami's Denman Fink and Henry Salem Hubbell, and Fort Pierce's Albert E. Backus (1906-1990), who won an award at the show and was described by a critic as showing "unusual promise." Northern artists joined the Florida painters, such as Nicola D'Ascenzo, who exhibited studies of stained glass for the Baptistry at the Episcopal Church of Bethesda-by-the-Sea. Graphics and sculptures were also on view, including the work of Anna Hyatt Huntington. Participating artists had one aspect in common—none of them embraced modernism, a disdain shared in many southern regional art centers in the 1930s. Nunzio Vayana, who abhorred the movement, gave a lecture in 1936 on the very subject: "The Moderns—Their Honesty or their Insanity."[28]

The year 1936 marked the tenth anniversary of Laura Woodward's death. Daisy Erb and other members of the Palm Beach Art League, with the support of the Woman's Club, acknowledged Woodward's importance as their pioneer by planning a memorial exhibition of her work. Artist and teacher Erich John Geske (1873-1934), who had designed the Art League exhibition catalogue logo just before he died, was also memorialized in 1936 by an exhibition of his etchings. In another section of the show, Jane Peterson exhibited a "brilliant" still life of *Zinnias* and Albert and Adele Herter displayed their floral works as well. After the exhibition closed, Peterson donated her *Zinnias*

and Mary Woodhouse gave her *Asters* by Albert Herter to Palm Beach's brand new arts center.[29]

The center's draft procedure was first set in place in 1935 when the Civic Arts Association, which included painter/sculptor C. Percival Dietsch, met at Mary McKinnon Johnson's home and planned an organization devoted to art, drama, music, and literature. They reconvened on January 14, 1936, in a vacant store on the ground floor of the Spanish Provincial Apartments on Royal Palm Way, thanks to the generosity of Col. Edward Bradley, who donated the space. There they adopted their new name, The Society of the Four Arts, and held their first exhibition in that store (see fig. 80).[30]

The Four Arts would become Palm Beach's most significant and longest-lasting cultural institution. Alice De Lamar, not listed among the founding committee, supported the cause wholeheartedly but remained in the background.[31]

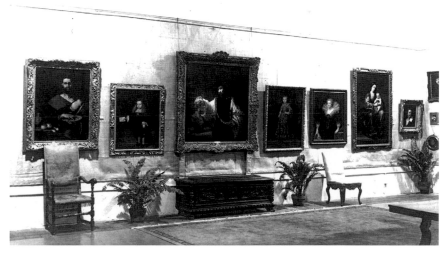

Fig. 80. First exhibition at The Society of the Four Arts, 1936, reproduced in the *Palm Beach Daily News,* January 1969, in a special supplement commemorating the paper's seventy-fifth anniversary. (Courtesy HSPBC and The Society of the Four Arts, Palm Beach)

Hugh Dillman (a former actor and previous art director of the Society of Arts who had married Anna Dodge in 1926) became the Four Arts' president. Architect Marion Sims Wyeth and Amy Phipps Guest (both former members of the Friends of the Arts and Crafts) sat on the board of directors, as did Elizabeth Norton. She and her husband Ralph had become prominent collectors ever since Ralph had given up golf for his health, as he put it. Frank G. Macomber served as consulting director, and Mary McKinnon Johnson and artist/doctor Donald J. McCarthy helped round up paintings for the first show.[32]

New York/London/Paris art dealer Joseph Duveen, who no doubt saw the opportunity of a possible Palm Beach sale, loaned the first show's most important painting, Rembrandt's *Aristotle Contemplating the Bust of Homer* (fig. 80, center of the wall), now in the Metropolitan Museum of Art. Frank Macomber, who owned several old master paintings, loaned his vivid *Macaroni Eater* by Jusepe de Ribera (fig. 80, far left), depicting a rough-hewn, semi-bare-chested peasant eating pasta with his hands, which had previously hung at the Museum of Fine Arts, Boston. Jules Bache loaned paintings by Giovanni Bellini and Francois Clouet, and an astounding amount of fine art poured from other local private caches. Nettie Reynolds presented a tender *Madonna and Child* attributed to Murillo (see fig. 80, largest painting on the right), which she later donated to the Episcopal Church of Bethesda-by-the-Sea. (It was reportedly stolen in 1979.) The groundbreaking exhibition received rave reviews.[33]

The next show that season consisted of modern paintings (see fig. 81). Palm Beach winter resident Audrey Chadwick, a passionate art collector and good friend of art dealer Velma Glenn Hodges, became the chairman of the membership committee for the show. She arranged a loan exhibition with the cooperation of the Museum of Modern Art and also provided art from her own collection, including an exquisite Marie Laurencin (see fig. 82), a Leger, and a Brancusi.

Other important artworks, such as Picasso's *Harlequin* and *Seated Woman* (see fig. 81) and Matisse's *Odalisque,* were selected from prominent New York sources. The show created a sensation.[34]

Marie Laurencin's *La Danse* lives up to the artist's quip about subject matter: "Why should I paint dead fish, onions and beer glasses? Girls are so much prettier." The pretty girls in this painting entice the viewer to enjoy their sultry dance. One of them, dressed androgynously, indicates that a lesbian relationship might be occurring in the couple at the right. The series of triangular shapes, apparent in the v-necks, bow, and drapery, shows cubism's influence on the artist—albeit a softened, feminine version of the movement.

Fig. 81. Modern art exhibition held in the first gallery of The Society of the Four Arts, 1936. Picasso's *Seated Woman* is at the far right. (© 2015 Estate of Pablo Picasso / Artists Rights Society [ARS], New York, The Society of the Four Arts Scrapbooks, courtesy The Society of Four Arts, Palm Beach)

The same year of the Four Arts premiere shows, architect Maurice Fatio continued to provide employment for talented artists by utilizing their services to decorate homes. In 1936 Fatio brought Robert Bushnell (1896-1960) to Palm Beach to adorn one of the architect's own houses. A successful business relationship between Fatio and Bushnell endured as Fatio called upon the artist to decorate several other resort homes. Two decades later Bushnell would create a mural for a very special Palm Beach building that hosted some of the greatest stars in the world.[35]

In the meantime, Mary Benson added the title of curator to the list of her professional achievements. The Civic Repertory Theater had closed years before due to the Depression, and Benson was eager to conquer new territories. In 1937 she readily accepted a curatorial position when her close friend Joseph Duveen (who eventually sold Rembrandt's *Aristotle* to Benson's friend, collector Alfred Erickson) recommended that she oversee the prestigious Jules Bache collection, housed in Bache's posh mansion at 814 Fifth Avenue in New York City. While Bache continued to winter in Palm Beach during the season (see fig. 83), his impressive New York holdings contained highly important paintings by Rembrandt, Goya, Vermeer, Holbein, Gainsborough, and other masters.[36]

By that time Mary Benson lived in a Manhattan apartment on East 60th Street that she shared with two other women. Although occupied frenetically with her new career as art curator, she took the time to bring Eva Le Gallienne to see the Bache collection before it opened to the public. The collection (now at the Metropolitan Museum of Art) was so popular that in the first five months of its public showing it attracted more than twenty thousand visitors. Mary recommended that the artwork be catalogued, which prompted national news coverage.[37]

Fig. 82 (left). Marie Laurencin, *La Danse,* exhibited at the first modern show at The Society of the Four Arts, loaned by Audrey Chadwick (Berdeau). (© Foundation Foujita / Artists Rights Society [ARS], New York / ADAGP, Paris 2015)

Fig. 83. Jules Bache in Palm Beach. (Courtesy HSPBC, photograph by Frank Turgeon)

Meanwhile, the New Deal continued to provide funds for art nationwide, including in Palm Beach. In fact, the Treasury Department's Section of Fine Arts funded New Hope, Pennsylvania, impressionist Charles Rosen's murals in the Palm Beach Post Office. Rosen (1878-1950) and his wife traveled to Palm Beach in 1938 just for this particular project. He spent many days with Seminoles and carefully observed, photographed, and sketched them to produce a lovely, historical result.[38]

The murals consisted of a horizontal central panel portraying Seminole life flanked by vertical panels of a landscape of coconut palms along Lake Worth and a palm-lined ocean view. The Seminole-inspired panel (see fig. 84) depicts a man fishing in the Everglades by his dugout canoe opposite other men who pluck a wild turkey they have hunted. The center portion portrays the three ages of women: a young woman grinds corn in front of a *chickee* (Seminole hut) using a mortar and pestle made from cypress, an older woman crafts dolls to sell to visitors at local festivals, and a young girl watches as she learns this tradition from her elder.[39]

While the New Deal financed Palm Beach art, The Society of the Four Arts began a summer school by 1937. Palm

Fig. 84. Seminole Indians by Charles Rosen, oil on canvas. © 2016 United States Postal Service. Photograph by Christopher Ziemnowicz.

PALM BEACH VISUAL ARTS

Beach Art League member Frank Edward Lloyd (1895-1945) directed its courses in art, commercial sketching, and life class for several years. Lloyd, born in Northampton, England, became a naturalized American citizen at an early age. He studied at the Pennsylvania Academy of the Fine Arts and at the Albright Art School in Buffalo.[40]

Also in 1937, Bernard Boutet de Monvel enjoyed a one-man show at The Society of the Four Arts. The same year, the Four Arts announced that their new building on Ceiba Avenue (designed by Maurice Fatio) would be opening in 1938. It housed an art gallery on the ground floor with an addition of a library on the second floor. (The building now contains the Gioconda and Joseph King Library.) As soon as the new gallery opened its doors on January 2, 1938, word hit New York art circles. The *Museum News* published an article entitled "Public Art Gallery for Palm Beach" lauding the new facility. Other publications praised it as well; for example the *Christian Science Monitor* declared the Four Arts responsible for the arts flourishing in Florida.[41]

Four Arts exhibitions in 1938 included *Origins of the Modern Movement in Art,* organized by Mary McKinnon and replete with art loaned by the Museum of Fine Arts, Boston, New York galleries, and collectors such as Audrey Chadwick. Other shows consisted of fantastical murals by Nicholas De Molas (sponsored by architect Maurice Fatio) and the art holdings of Ralph and Elizabeth Norton. Paintings shown from this notable collection included Childe Hassam's *Off Marblehead* and Ernest Lawson's *Railroad Track* (fig. 85), exemplifying the artist's metamorphosis from delicate American impressionism towards the broader brushwork of a more expressionist technique. By then, the Palm Beach Art League had become a member of the Florida Federation of Art and planned to work with The Society of the Four Arts to promote art and artists as well as to find their own exhibition and teaching facility.[42]

In 1938 Amy Phipps Guest donated to the town a stone fountain (see fig. 86) that was once at her home, Villa Artemis. Possibly carved by C. Percival Dietsch or Hugo Wagner, both of whom worked with several Palm Beach architects, the fountain has remained in Bradley Park for decades.[43]

During the 1938 season, the Four Arts held their annual flower show at which Auguste Rodin's *The Age of Bronze* (fig. 87), loaned by the Phipps family was a highlight. The Four Arts later acquired the sculpture and it is presently located in the Esther B. O'Keeffe Gallery Building, their exhibition and auditorium space.[44]

Originally modeled in 1876 and called *The Vanquished One, The Age of Bronze* reveals Rodin's genius in portraying the naturalistic human figure—so much so that the sculptor

Fig. 85. Ernest Lawson, *Railroad Track*. (Courtesy Norton Museum of Art, West Palm Beach, Florida, bequest of R. H. Norton, 53.106)

Fig. 86. Stone fountain, Bradley Park. (Photograph by author)

Fig. 87. Auguste Rodin, *The Age of Bronze,* 1876, bronze, Esther B. O'Keeffe Gallery Building, The Society of the Four Arts, acquired in 1939, gift of Right Honorable Mrs. Frederic E. Guest. (Photograph courtesy The Society of the Four Arts, Palm Beach)

was accused of casting a live human model to produce the work. Rodin also ignored the suggestion of an art critic to add two spears for the figure to carry in his left hand. This decision on Rodin's part downplayed an actual historical or biblical subject matter and focused the viewer's entire attention on the man himself. The figure, once perceived as a defeated warrior in anguish, became the more optimistic vision of a man awakening to the dawn of a new civilization. While officials at the Paris Salon disdained this sculpture for its lack of an obvious subject matter and departure from previous, more academic works, it is one of the first bronzes that cast Rodin into immortality.[45]

In 1939 The Society of the Four Arts generated a huge amount of publicity when it featured Frank Macomber's idea of "The Festival of the Sea" with works by such artists as Winslow Homer (see fig. 88) and nautical artifacts.

Children attended in droves and a yacht parade was held in conjunction with the popular exhibition. The same season, the Four Arts again showed a varied exhibition schedule, setting an annual standard for the center with displays reflective of the traditional, the modern, and the contemporary. It became the perfect formula to continually attract public interest. The esteemed Alfred H. Baur, director of the Museum of Modern Art, and Lloyd Goodrich, director of the Whitney Museum of American Art, judged subsequent exhibitions consisting of living artists' works.[46]

Also in 1939 Mary Woodhouse donated a lasting cultural gift—she commissioned the renowned artist Albert Herter

Fig. 88. Winslow Homer, *The Gale,* 1883-93, exhibited at The Society of the Four Arts "Festival of the Sea," 1939. Worcester Art Museum, Worcester, Massachusetts, museum purchase 1916.48. (Courtesy Wikimedia Commons)

Fig. 89. Albert Herter holding sketches. (Charles de Kay, "Albert Herter," *Art and Progress,* February 1914, 131)

LEFT HAND CENTRAL PANEL

Fig. 90. Albert Herter, study for "Art," left hand central panel, Gioconda and Joseph King Library, The Society of the Four Arts. (Photograph by author, courtesy The Society of the Four Arts, Palm Beach)

Fig. 91. Mary Woodhouse (in white) at the unveiling of the Herter murals, 1939, from The Society of the Four Arts Scrapbooks. (Courtesy The Society of the Four Arts, Palm Beach)

(1871-1950) (see fig. 89) to paint the façade of The Society of the Four Arts building on Ceiba Avenue (now Four Arts Plaza). Herter had painted Mary Woodhouse's portrait and knew her well as they both summered in Easthampton, Long Island. But Herter had another connection with Four Arts supporters: his father, Christian, partner of the Herter Brothers who designed aesthetic furniture and provided other kinds of decoration, employed Maud Howe Elliott's husband as a painter.[47]

Herter, who admired Maud Howe Elliott for her talent in persuasion, studied at the Art Students League in New York and in Paris and won numerous medals at exhibitions. He was also a successful manufacturer of tapestries known

Fig. 92. Albert Herter, *Art*, mural, exterior of the Gioconda and Joseph King Library, The Society of the Four Arts. (Photograph by author, courtesy The Society of the Four Arts, Palm Beach)

Fig. 93. Albert Herter, *Music*, mural, 1939, exterior of the Gioconda and Joseph King Library, The Society of the Four Arts. (Photograph by author, courtesy The Society of the Four Arts, Palm Beach)

as the Herter Looms, which depicted galleons, maidens, knights, and troubadours of the fourteenth and fifteenth centuries; Herter utilized the same courtly motif in his murals for the Four Arts' exterior. After carefully plotting out the murals on large boards (see fig. 90), Herter went to work outdoors, executing scenes representing art, music, drama, and literature (see figs. 92 and 93). He was assisted by landscape artist Leonard Lester, whose wife, Marian, posed for some of the figures. In March 1939 Mary Woodhouse, dressed entirely in white (see fig. 91), officiated the unveiling of the Herter murals.[48]

Mary Woodhouse also commissioned Albert Herter's wife, Adele McGinnis Herter (1869-1946), a noted portrait and still life painter who had studied at the Académie Julian, to paint the portrait of Maud Howe Elliott (see fig. 94), currently in the Gioconda and Joseph King Library at The Society of the Four Arts. Mrs. Elliott, who along with Mary Woodhouse became an honorary president of the Four Arts, is shown wearing a Chinese robe, an accessory of aestheticism. She holds a scroll; often an artistic symbol of law, in this instance it likely refers to one of her numerous citations, such as her honorary doctor of letters degree, World War I citation from the US government, or illuminated scroll from the Art Association of Newport, which she helped found. She also wears her and her husband's medals of which they won many.[49] Elliott did not display these awards to boast; on the contrary, she wore them as a memorial to her husband and his humanitarian achievements, a lasting reminder of her legacy of cultural attainments, and perhaps to uplift and inspire the viewer to accomplish the same. And although she is elderly, her thoughtful gaze tells us that her mind is still as brilliant as it was when she won the Pulitzer Prize for cowriting the biography of her mother, Julia Ward Howe.

Mary Woodhouse continued to enhance The Society of the Four Arts by giving it a remarkable Chinese garden: a peaceful heaven on earth with a lotus lily pond, symbolic exotic plants, and Chinese statuary. Woodhouse called the

Fig. 94. Adele Herter, *Maud Howe Elliott*, 1939, Gioconda and Joseph King Library, The Society of the Four Arts, gift of Mrs. Lorenzo Woodhouse. (Courtesy The Society of the Four Arts, Palm Beach)

garden "Happiness and Harmony" and dedicated it to her deceased artist-daughter, Marjorie. The Kuan Yin (see fig. 95), or goddess of mercy and compassion, is a focus of the tranquil outdoor space and is seen wearing her usual draped robes and a rosary around her neck.[50]

By the 1930s, painter and sculptor Charles Knight (1874-1953) had delighted in yearly visits to friends and patrons in Palm Beach and had studied its lush palm trees to create large paintings of the prehistoric. Also modeling dramatic sculpture of cavemen (see fig. 96), mammoths, and dinosaurs, Knight soon spent entire winters in Palm Beach, exhibiting at The Society of the Four Arts, and in 1942 lecturing there on "Animal Life in Prehistoric Florida." He is most renowned for the backgrounds of dioramas at New York City's Museum of Natural History—inspired in part, Knight said, by the jungles of Palm Beach.[51]

In 1939 the New Deal's Treasury Relief Arts Project (TRAP) commissioned Stevan Dohanos (1907-1994) to paint six murals portraying *The Legend of James Edward Hamilton, Mail Carrier,* for placement in a West Palm Beach post office (fig. 97). Hamilton, known as a "Barefoot Mailman," trekked along the shore from Miami to Jupiter while delivering mail along his perilous way. Dohanos earned $2,400 for the project, and in March 1939 officials approved the space at Olive and Evernia Streets.[52]

Dohanos rigorously studied the legend and had help from pioneer Charles Pierce, himself a barefoot mailman and postmaster of Boynton Beach, who sent the artist a photo of James Hamilton wearing similar clothes to what he wore when he tragically perished in the Hillsboro Inlet. As a result, Dohanos used explicit realism in his depiction of Hamilton walking or boating amid a distinct Florida atmosphere and also conveyed sheer determination in the mail carrier's face.[53]

At the end of the 1930s, The Society of the Four Arts held optimistic hopes for the future. They envisioned a school of applied art focusing on tropical décor, they strove to "abolish

Fig. 95. Kuan Yin, Goddess of Mercy, in the style of the Tang Dynasty, possibly sixteenth century, Chinese garden, The Society of the Four Arts. (Photograph by author, courtesy The Society of the Four Arts, Palm Beach)

Fig. 98. Paul Gauguin, *Christ in the Garden of Olives,* 1889, Norton Museum of Art, West Palm Beach, Florida, gift of Elizabeth C. Norton, 46.5. (Courtesy Norton Museum of Art)

Fig. 99. Norton Gallery and School of Art, West Palm Beach, original east entrance, ca. 1942. (Courtesy HSPBC, photograph by Samuel R. Quincey)

Garden of Olives, a depiction of Christ (as a self portrait of Paul Gauguin) awaiting his fate (fig. 98). Gauguin, who knew well the sadness of isolation, felt that this was his greatest painting to date. He would later abandon Paris for the island of Tahiti.[4]

Mary E. Aleshire, a former director of The Society of the Four Arts, became director of the Norton Art Gallery; noted Palm Beach painter and sculptor J. (Joy) Clinton Shepherd was appointed director of the school and an instructor in life classes; J. Eliot O'Hara was named watercolor instructor; and Joseph J. Hollenbeck, who had been painting Palm Beach blossoms for some thirty years, began teaching classes in flower and still life painting.[5]

In the meantime, when art supporter/architect Marion Sims Wyeth (who built the Norton Gallery and School of Art) saw Paul Manship's plaster figure of *Diana* at the 1939 New York World's Fair, Wyeth suggested that the sculptor have his *Diana* and *Actaeon* cast for the niches at the Norton Gallery. Manship (1885-1966) had already modeled versions of *Diana* and *Actaeon* in 1925, but Wyeth felt they would complement the Norton Gallery's art deco style of architecture. Wyeth proposed a change in the *Actaeon* statue, however, to have his arm curved so that it would fit better into the niche, rather than outstretched as in the first bronze cast in the 1920s. Manship complied with the alteration and the niches were filled (see figs. 100 and 101).[6]

The art of the ages had inspired Manship during his European studies, and the sculptures of *Diana* and *Actaeon,* as in Manship's other work, combine ancient themes with a modern, sleek, art deco technique. They portray a version of the Greco-Roman myth in which Actaeon spies on the nude goddess Diana (the Roman equivalent of Artemis) while she is bathing. She becomes so angry at him she aims her bow and shoots him, transforming him into a stag. His own hunting dogs then proceed to tear him apart, and only then does Diana's anger dissipate.[7]

Adept in chiseling stone due to his studies with Solon

PALM BEACH VISUAL ARTS

Fig. 100. Paul Manship, *Diana*, Norton Museum of Art, West Palm Beach, Florida, purchase, the Palm Beach Art League Construction Account, 41.14.1. (Courtesy Norton Museum of Art)

Fig. 101. Paul Manship, *Actaeon*, Norton Museum of Art, West Palm Beach, Florida, purchase, the Palm Beach Art League Construction Account, 41.14.2. (Courtesy Norton Museum of Art)

Borglum, Manship also carved stone panels in bas- and mid-relief set into the niches atop the original entrance of the museum (see fig. 102) and above *Diana* and *Actaeon*.

Wyeth explained to Ralph Norton that *Diana* should be placed in the southern niche and *Actaeon* in the northern one to accurately portray the myth, but by 1942 Norton felt rather irritated that the sculptures were not architecturally correct as a pair, with angles facing each other. Thus, he had *Diana* placed in the northern niche with her drawn bow aimed away from *Actaeon,* which did not correspond to the myth (see fig. 99). It was not until the twenty-first century when museum officials finally switched the statues back to their original positions to accurately portray the ancient tale.[8]

Sculptor Wheeler Williams (1897-1972) added to the Norton Gallery's cache of treasures when he extended the legacy of the famous Ponce de León myth utilized by Palm Beach and West Palm Beach artists in the past. Williams' impressive limestone work *The Fountain of Youth* (1941),

Fig. 102. Paul Manship, *Inspiration,* atop the original central entrance of the Norton Gallery and School of Art, photograph stamped "from Art Keil Publicity Director, City of West Palm Beach, Florida," companion photo stamped "Walter J. Russell." (Courtesy HSPBC)

Fig. 103. Sculptor Wheeler Williams and Ralph Hubbard Norton in front of the *Fountain of Youth* by Wheeler Williams, Norton Gallery and School of Art, courtyard, ca. 1942. (Courtesy HSPBC, photograph by Herb Davies)

PALM BEACH VISUAL ARTS

placed in the Norton's courtyard and dedicated in 1942, portrays a rejuvenated woman holding her former elderly face as if it were a mask (see fig. 103).

Williams also enhanced Palm Beach by his outdoor limestone statue of *Maya* (1928). Additionally, winter resident Andrew Jergens (as in the lotion) and Byron D. Miller presented to The Society of the Four Arts a pair of male and female bronze panthers (see fig. 104) that Williams had created in 1933. Like other sculpture in Palm Beach, a version of Williams's panthers also prowl Brookgreen Gardens in South Carolina.[9]

Williams, who studied at the Art Institute of Chicago,

Fig. 105. Members of the Palm Beach Art League in the courtyard of the Norton Gallery and School of Art, winter 1942, surrounding *The Fountain of Youth* by Wheeler Williams. According to Jean Wagner Troemel, known artists are Jean Wagner (Troemel), standing at far left; Mrs. William McKim next to her; Lucille Stonier seated in front; Ann Weaver (later Norton) seated to her right, hatless, and wearing a plaid jacket; J. Clinton Shepherd, seated in front to the left of the statue; J. Eliot O'Hara, is seated in the center front; Jane Peterson, wearing dark cable-knit sweater, is standing to the right of the statue and looking to her left; next to her is Theodora (Theda) Tilton; seated in the front row are (with hat and sunglasses) Mrs. Woolley-Hart and Mrs. Bemis; and flanking them are Alice Swain and Dorothy Henderson. Daisy Erb is seated in the second row at the far right and in front of her is Richard Albany. (Courtesy Jean Wagner Troemel from her scrapbook, photographer unknown)

Fig. 104. Wheeler Williams, Pair of life-sized bronze panthers (1933) in front of the Gioconda and Joseph King Library, The Society of the Four Arts, gift of Andrew Jergens and Byron D. Miller. (Photograph by author, courtesy The Society of the Four Arts, Palm Beach)

Copley Society, and École des Beaux-Arts, won numerous prizes. A member of the National Academy of Design and Municipal Art Society in New York, he also helped lead the Architectural League and the National Sculpture Society. He advised young sculptors, "Don't strive to be modern, just strive to excel. Automatically you will reflect your times either realistically or aspirationally. You will find sculpture a hard way of life in this commercial age, but in a true sense a most rewarding one."[10]

The Palm Beach Art League delighted in their new home and school of art (see fig. 105), and Elizabeth Norton could not have chosen a more consummate director of the school than J. Clinton Shepherd. Born in Iowa in 1888, Shepherd was an accomplished painter and sculptor who maintained a Palm Beach home and studio for over thirty-five years until he died in 1975. After studying at the Art Institute of Chicago and the Beaux-Arts Institute of Design in New York Shepherd moved to Miami, where he directed art at Barry College. He came to Palm Beach when Mrs. Norton requested him to head the school.[11]

Shepherd was renowned for his paintings and sculptures of the American West as well as a World War I commemorative statue of a doughboy. He also provided breathtaking murals of the Everglades for Florida's Clewiston Inn and handsome sporting scenes for the Pebble Hill plantation in Georgia. In the meantime, his works became housed in several museums. Aside from his instructorship at the Norton Gallery and School of Art, he established an art school in Palm Beach.[12]

The same year the Norton Gallery and School of Art opened to rave reviews, The Society of the Four Arts held their annual contemporary exhibit, praised by none other than art collector Jules Bache. "Modern art is out of my sphere," he told Lee Rogers of the *Palm Beach Daily News.* "However . . . I do think that the present show is exceptional. I didn't see a single picture I couldn't live with."[13] Like the Norton Gallery, the Four Arts gave ample opportunity to young artists to achieve success when it annually showed current works by members of the Palm Beach Art League. The Four Arts also mounted a show in 1941 comprising realistic works from the Florida Watercolor Society, which was praised by both the general public and Maud Howe Elliott. She wrote it was "like an oasis in the desert of this war torn world." She felt that Florida artists and subject matter gave "an added interest to the collection" and went on to frankly state, "The first impression I received was of peace and sanity, elements rarely found in exhibitions of modern art today." (One would hardly expect a proponent of the American Renaissance and aesthetic movements to appreciate abstract art.) Mrs. Elliott remained outspoken for the cause of fine art until her death in 1948.[14]

In the meantime, photographers, including the talented and ubiquitous Morgan brothers, capitalized on Palm Beach's seasonal allure for celebrities and socialites. One of the brothers captured a haughtily serene Barbara Hutton (Countess Haugwitz-Reventlow) (see fig. 106) while she watched a tennis match at the Everglades Club. *Palm Beach Daily News* columnist Emilie Keyes reported that Hutton and her friend golfer Robert "Bob" Sweeny "tried to hide behind the crotons . . . courtside but the bloodhound news reporters tracked them down."

In the photograph Hutton epitomizes the cool, wealthy, and stylish sophisticate from her ultra-chic upsweep to the tips of her perfectly-manicured fingernails. During that season she attended an exhibition at The Society of the Four Arts where she bought a painting by American regionalist Clarence Carter, and then whistled and tapped her foot while waiting for Sweeny to escort her to the Colony Hotel.[15]

The Morgan brothers (see fig. 107) also photographed Marjorie Merriweather Post, Mary Sanford, Eva Stotesbury, the Duke and Duchess of Windsor, and numerous other socialites and celebrities. Bert Morgan was reportedly the only one who could get away with calling the Duke of Windsor "Eddie." In fact, anytime a distinguished person was in Palm

Fig. 106. Barbara Hutton watching tennis at the Everglades Club. (Courtesy HSPBC, photograph by the Morgan brothers)

Fig. 107. The Morgan brothers, 1941, standing from left to right, Bert and Fred, seated from left to right, Ralph and Leonard. (Courtesy HSPBC)

Beach, either walking on Worth Avenue or at charitable events, the Morgan brothers succeeded in photographing them. Bert's son Richard later joined him and continued the artistic legacy of fine society photography.[16]

Along with the Morgan family, Palm Beach photographer Frank Turgeon remained busy in the 1940s. In 1941, during one of the Duke and Duchess of Windsor's many Palm Beach visits, Turgeon offered to photograph them and was commissioned by the duke to do so. Later, armed with 250 pounds of camera equipment and accompanied by his wife and another assistant, Turgeon flew from Palm Beach to Nassau for the job. The result was some of the most attractive images of the couple ever taken (see fig. 108). The duchess framed and treasured Turgeon's photographs and some were later sold in her estate sale.[17]

Other respectful photographers, such as Herb Davies, captured the Kennedy family—and not always formally—while they enjoyed their winter home in Palm Beach (see fig. 109). By revealing their subjects' varied personalities as Ernest Histed did before them, Davies, Turgeon, and the Morgans illustrated precisely why fine photography is another form of the visual arts. Another photographer,

Samuel R. Quincey, who worked for the *Palm Beach Post* and other periodicals, was also a ubiquitous figure in the Palm Beaches, capturing civic events, educational activities, notables, and hurricanes.

While fine photographers, the Norton Gallery, and the Four Arts continued to progress steadily, Alice De Lamar and Mary Duggett Benson did more than their share to encourage and support the artistic in Palm Beach. So important were these two cultured women to the history of the island's visual arts that without them, Palm Beach would never have the varied and rich artistic heritage it has

Fig. 109. Kennedy children in Palm Beach, ca. 1940, from left to right, Eunice Kennedy (Shriver), Robert F. Kennedy, Edward "Teddy," Kennedy, and Jean Kennedy (Smith). (Courtesy HSPBC, photograph by Herb Davies)

Fig. 108. Frank Turgeon, *Duke and Duchess of Windsor,* 1941. (Courtesy HSPBC)

PALM BEACH VISUAL ARTS

enjoyed. The domestic partners spent many summers abroad and part of the spring and autumn months either in Weston, Connecticut or in New York until returning to Palm Beach for a long winter season.

On December 7, 1941, Alice De Lamar was in New York in the midst of a housewarming party for her new apartment. When guests heard the shocking news on the radio of the bombing of Pearl Harbor, one of them exclaimed "My God, this is it," and they all wondered how their lives would change. The Second World War decidedly altered Palm Beach. The Biltmore Hotel morphed into a training ground and The Breakers became a hospital, as did Amy Phipps Guest's palatial oceanfront home, Villa Artemis. The Four Arts supported the US military by holding a GI artists' exhibition in 1942. The show was so successful that they repeated it in 1943, prompting brisk sales and attention from New York art publications, including the *Art Digest,* which headlined their article, "Soldier Art Sells at Palm Beach." The Four Arts also gave soldiers the opportunity of displaying their artistic skill relating to the military at the Museum of Modern Art in New York and the National Gallery of Art in Washington, DC.[18]

During the war years, Benson and De Lamar lived at De Lamar's house on 247 Brazilian Avenue, as her oceanfront mansion was in a blackout zone and had only one telephone after authorities removed the rest of them to use at military camps. Also, gasoline was difficult to obtain, and the in-town location of Brazilian Avenue was a convenient walking or biking distance to many shops.[19]

In 1942, amid the sound of countless bombers manufactured from all points of the nation flying overhead and German U-boats sinking American ships just off the Florida coast, the fifty-two-year-old Mary Benson established the first major commercial gallery on Worth Avenue. In doing so, she forever changed the shape of Palm Beach art and how the art world looked upon Palm Beach galleries. Influential art critic Lawrence Dame later commented that words could

not express the amount of good Mary Benson provided, both "culturally and otherwise." And as critic Elizabeth Vaughan later put it, "Palm Beach had to wait for the arrival of Mrs. Duggett Benson to really get down to business."[20]

While some have reported, assumed, and/or claimed that Alice De Lamar secretly owned the Worth Avenue Gallery, legal documents filed with the State of Florida, sworn affidavits signed by Mary Benson, and intimate letters written by Alice De Lamar prove otherwise. Prominent art critics of the day and nearly all the artists exhibiting at the gallery were also fully aware that it was Benson's. But in order to understand the gallery's accurate history, one must realize its connection to family. As mentioned, Benson retained a close relationship with her sister, Frances, after Frances married Edward Nash ("Ned") Mathews in 1914. After Ned and Frances moved to Miami Beach in 1926, Ned and his brother James purchased an enormous warehouse facility on Washington Avenue—the Washington Storage Company. Mathews and his brother became successful from the need for seasonal residents to store their items in a safe place while out of town. (The building was so sturdy that in the 1980s Mitchell Wolfson Jr. purchased it to house his important collection of culture material; it is now known as the Wolfsonian-FIU.) A respected art dealer and art restorer, Mathews also maintained a gallery on the first floor of the storage building and named it the Washington Art Gallery and Studio, with connoisseur Eric Carlberg employed to direct it.[21]

After Mary Benson and Ned Mathews (see fig. 110) opened the Palm Beach annex of his gallery at 310 ½ Worth Avenue (between Saks Fifth Avenue and Bonwit Teller), the partners named it the Washington Art Studio. Benson ran the operation and she and Mathews hired Eric Carlberg to direct it until Benson became more involved with its day-to-day dealings, after which Carlberg returned to directing the Miami Beach gallery. The two galleries occasionally shared painting and sculpture exhibitions and displayed crafts as well, such as handmade jewelry.[22]

Fig. 110. Mary Benson and Ned Mathews at Alice De Lamar's house, Palm Beach, 1945. (Courtesy Pamela Nash Mathews)

Fig. 111. Mary McKinnon Johnson, photograph by Richard A. Little, 1948, clipping from *Palm Beach Life,* March 9, 1948. (Courtesy HSPBC)

Mary soon changed the Washington Art Studio's name to the Worth Avenue Gallery. She advertised in a flyer, "Tired of that stuffed marlin? Create wider horizons for the walls of your home."[23]

One of the Worth Avenue Gallery's first one-man shows displayed the work of a woman—the often-cited Mary McKinnon (Johnson) (see fig. 111). This accomplished portraitist, who helped establish The Society of the Four Arts, maintained her studio for a time at Major Alley at the corner of Peruvian Avenue and Coconut Row. McKinnon and important modern art collectors Mr. and Mrs. William McKim were among those cultural leaders who supported Mary Benson in her efforts; and, of course, Alice De Lamar offered unyielding support anytime Benson or one of her discovered artists needed it. The gallery was also a space where De Lamar's artist-friends could frequently exhibit. It was a perfect arrangement between the two women, but again De Lamar did not own the gallery—Benson did.[24]

In West Palm Beach, progress continued at the Norton Gallery and School of Art when Ann Weaver (see fig. 112) began to teach sculpture. Born in Selma, Alabama, Weaver, who studied with José de Creeft and at the Art Students League and National Academy of Design, also became Alexander Archipenko's assistant. She participated in several exhibitions, including at the Whitney Museum of American Art, Museum of Modern Art, The Society of the Four Arts, and the Norton Gallery.

Weaver was pleased that she could earn a living in South Florida and found it not the "cultural wasteland that she had feared." When she saw an exhibition at The Society of the Four Arts that the Museum of Modern Art organized, it helped assure Weaver that she had made the right move.[25]

After Elizabeth Norton died, in 1948 Ann Weaver married Ralph Norton. She influenced him in his collecting of modern art and established a studio on their property next to the Norton Gallery. Exhibiting with the Palm Beach Art League, Weaver won prizes at the Lowe Art Gallery in Coral Gables

Fig. 112. Norton Gallery and School of Art sculpture class, Ann Weaver, left of model. (Courtesy HSPBC, photograph by Herb Davies)

(now the Lowe Art Museum) and other venues. She would later leave a tremendous legacy to West Palm Beach.[26]

Additionally of note, in 1942 the already famous Salvador Dali, after working on a Hollywood movie and enjoying a retrospective exhibition at the Museum of Modern Art in New York, came to Palm Beach at the age of thirty-eight. Columnist Emilie Keyes, who relied on her college French to communicate with the artist, interviewed Dali while he was on the island. He said he loved the United States, was planning to obtain American citizenship, and that while most people here did not understand his art, they still appreciated it.[27]

While in town, the flamboyant artist stayed with his

patron, George de Cuevas and his wife, Margaret Strong Rockefeller, on El Bravo Way, where they wintered. Dali had come to Palm Beach to paint a portrait of de Cuevas, a renowned Chilean-born ballet impresario.[28]

Palm Beachers gave Dali the warmest of receptions, and the artist thoroughly charmed reporters and all of his hosts. He was delighted with the island, especially when collector Audrey Chadwick Berdeau and her husband feted the artist with a luncheon in the dining room of their home, Villa Today, where a Dali painting was displayed. The artist was thrilled to have come upon this particular work, as he thought it had been lost.[29]

Dali's portrait of de Cuevas standing in a surreal landscape was exhibited in 1943 at Knoedler in New York, but it eventually went missing. In the 1990s an affable artist/vintage furniture dealer, who lived in a New Jersey trailer park, discovered the rolled-up canvas marked $40 in a New York City thrift shop. The shopkeeper informed the artist that the painting was a fake, but the artist, believing it to be an authentic Dali, purchased it. He brought it to Sotheby's, whose experts agreed; consequently the auction house sold it for $184,000. In 2013 the Dali was exhibited at the Norton Museum of Art as an acclaimed masterpiece.[30]

Other artists thrived in Palm Beach during the war years. In 1944 Constantin Alajalov, who lived above a Worth Avenue decorator's shop, chronicled the island's World War II atmosphere for *Vogue* in his depictions of the Coast Guard Women's Reserve, or the SPARS—standing for "Semper Paratus, Always Ready." His lively scenes portrayed them marching to the beach accompanied by a band and exercising in their daily drills at The Breakers golf course (see fig. 113). The SPARS schooled women in fire fighting and first aid at the Biltmore Hotel, and according to *Vogue*, these women numbered around one thousand, led by female officers addressed as "Sir." When not contributing his time and talent to the war effort, Alajalov served on the jury of The Society of the Four Arts.[31]

Fig. 113. Constantin Alajalov, *Palm Beach, 8 AM, the Spars do Setting Ups,* from *Vogue,* March 1944, 82. (Courtesy HSPBC; Constantin Alajalov / Vogue, © Condé Nast)

In the meantime, Mary Benson launched another cause for Palm Beach art. After hearing a suggestion by Philadelphia/Palm Beach artist Marguerite Idell, Benson initiated the annual Palm Beach clothesline show with over one hundred art students and professionals participating, first held in the patio of her 310 ½ Worth Avenue Gallery around 1943. Benson's Worth Avenue clothesline exhibits became very successful, and after she moved the gallery to 347 Worth Avenue, she held them in the courtyard of the adjacent Via Parigi (named for Paris Singer). In ensuing years Benson's ongoing clothesline shows influenced artists and art patrons to participate in the same kind of exhibitions at several other Palm Beach locations, including The Breakers.[32]

After the end of World War II in 1945, Palm Beach returned to a sense of normalcy. By then Mary Benson had found a codirector in Emily Rayner, whom she met through Alice De Lamar. Mrs. Rayner, who began wintering in Palm Beach

Fig. 114. Sisters in paradise; from left to right, Emily Rayner, Betty Parsons, and Suzanne Pierson McCarter in Palm Beach. (Courtesy HSPBC and William Rayner)

around 1937-38 with her husband, Archibald ("Archie"), had not ventured into any kind of employment until she became involved in World War II efforts by driving an ambulance and working in a canteen. But when the war ended, Mrs. Rayner tired of playing golf and bridge and determined that a gallery position would be much more interesting. She possessed a strong artistic sensitivity instilled in her by her older sister, prominent New York artist and art dealer Betty Parsons, who pioneered the marketing of abstract expressionism. Betty and Emily (see fig. 114) were very close with no sibling rivalry between them, and Betty not only exhibited at the Worth Avenue Gallery and The Society of the Four Arts, she also helped Emily in obtaining works from other New York artists for the Worth Avenue Gallery.[33]

There was no particular school that Mary Benson and Emily Rayner selected—it just depended on a certain something possessed by an artist: "A painting must have an intangible part that you intuitively recognize as art," Mary explained. "It is an indefinable, inspirational quality. And when you find it, the reward is a wonderful, exciting experience."[34]

Benson continued to "set standards" for later art galleries. Critic Lawrence Dame remarked that "Mary had heart, knowledge, and rare intuition" and that she considered the cause of art "sacred." She believed that "the artist is the all important factor, not the gallery. The gallery is there simply to serve the artist and of course, the public." And serve she did. Her attitude as an art dealer was much like Edith Halpert, who owned New York's Downtown Gallery. They both offered the public the privilege of owning a great work of art by an artist they believed in. As one artist put it, "Mary Benson doesn't sell paintings, she allows people to buy them." She was devoted to her artists unequivocally and gave Palm Beach debuts to portraitist Channing Weir Hare, famed painter Bernard Buffet, Piero Aversa, Franz Bueb, and many other talented artists who achieved world renown. She also provided a well attended space to show off the work of longtime Palm Beach artists of the past, such as C. Percival Dietsch.[35]

Zoe Shippen, Channing Hare, and Mary McKinnon (Johnson) made up the gallery's roster of portraitists along with Mary Benson's ex-husband, Stuart, who provided portrait sculpture before he died in 1949.

Channing Hare (1899-1976) (see fig. 115) stood by Mary in all her decisions. Originally from Park Hill Avenue in Yonkers, New York, Hare became a leader of the mid-twentieth century Palm Beach art world. He had studied with the best of American painters including Ashcan School members George Bellows and Robert Henri at the Art Students League.[36]

Hare stated, "Palm Beach is a game one has to learn how to play," and he certainly played it well. A member of high society primarily through his marriage to an heiress but also due to his impeccable social manners, he mingled with royalty and celebrities he depicted. Aside from stunning portraiture, Hare painted haunting "magic realist" works in which the real and imagined were combined, inspired by his friendship with artist Paul Cadmus. Hare also became acclaimed for his poignant scenes of African American subjects, one of which earned him a prize in 1943 at The Society of the Four Arts. Several museums would collect his art, including the Museum of Fine Arts, Boston and the Pennsylvania Academy of the Fine Arts.[37]

In Palm Beach Hare lived in Consuelo Vanderbilt's former palatial house on El Vedado Road with a view of Lake Worth, sharing it with his partner, Ogunquit postimpressionist landscapist H. Mountfort Coolidge. By 1948 the two gentlemen were joined by Stephen Hopkins Hensel (1921-1979), professionally known as Hopkins Hensel and "Stevie" by his friends. Hare was a longtime friend of Hensel's family (they all summered together in Ogunquit, Maine) and Hare knew Hensel from the time Stevie was a toddler. (As a youth Hensel called Hare "Uncle Bunny" and later referred to him as just "Bunny.")[38]

Fig. 115. Channing Hare in his Worth Avenue penthouse, 1964, reproduced on the cover of the *Social Pictorial*, March 23, 1964. His *Fourth of July* is hanging behind him and his portrait of Beatrice Lillie is against the lower portion of the easel. (Courtesy HSPBC, photograph by Bert and Richard Morgan)

Coolidge died in 1955 and by 1960 Hare and Hensel resided in Hare's grand penthouse on Worth Avenue. In the early 1970s, when Hare was in his seventies and Hensel in his fifties, Hare adopted Hensel and made him his heir, and thereafter Hensel became known as Stephen Hopkins Hensel Hare. The two gentlemen also lived together in Hare's ninety-seven-room castle in Majorca, complete with sixteen servants, until Hare died at the age of seventy-seven in 1976.[39]

In the meantime, Channing Hare's dealer, Mary Benson, formally registered her name with the State of Florida on April 29, 1946, as "doing business as" the Worth Avenue Gallery. While Benson made the major decisions about the business with input from Emily Rayner and suggestions by Alice De Lamar, Benson's brother-in-law, Ned, still retained a part-ownership. The two maintained this business relationship for over a decade.[40]

By this time the Worth Avenue Gallery had become one of the most distinguished galleries in the United States and along with The Society of the Four Arts and Norton Gallery and School of Art, enhanced recognition of the Palm Beaches as an important, if not small, art center. Mary Benson annually borrowed and exhibited major paintings from the then prestigious Knoedler in New York (the association between the two galleries continued for several years) and shared her artists with Knoedler and Carroll Carstairs Gallery. Along with great European masters such as Pierre-Auguste Renoir, Toulouse Lautrec, and Pablo Picasso and American luminaries such as Childe Hassam (see fig.116), many young and obscure artists' works graced the Worth Avenue Gallery's walls. These painters and sculptors relied on Benson's gallery to sell their art to discriminating Palm Beach collectors and an international clientele. Often sales occurred during Benson's famous Worth Avenue Gallery openings, which she pioneered, where throngs of art enthusiasts would mingle every week, reaching a crescendo some two decades later.[41]

Fig. 116. Childe Hassam, *At the Grand Prix,* exhibited at the Worth Avenue Gallery annual show of important paintings. (Courtesy Skinner, Inc., www.skinnerinc.com)

Fig. 117. Kyril Vassilev, *Helen Rich,* 1940. (Courtesy Aspire Auctions, www. aspireauctions.com)

Palm Beach attracted many more artists who thrived in the 1940s; some of them European, such as portrait painter Kyril Vassilev (1908-1987), born in Russia of Bulgarian descent. Vassilev, whose mother was a gypsy, painted the portrait of Archbishop Angelo Roncalli, who became Pope John XXIII. The artist's portraits also included Amy Phipps Guest, Mona Williams, the Samuel Paleys, and Jack Dempsey.[42]

In 1940 Vassilev attended a soiree where he met Palm Beach socialite, fashion expert, and *Miami News* society writer and editor Helen Rich, whose Palm Beach parties were so lavish, they compelled "Cholly Knickerbocker" to call her the "Elsa Maxwell of the South." The artist was so taken by Rich's presence that he asked to paint her portrait (see fig. 117). She considered the work "perfect," although she was aware of a slightly exaggerated figure length to achieve a more elegant result, similar to the method of Jan Van Eyck and other fifteenth century Netherlandish masters. Her likeness shows Vassilev's adeptness in precisely depicting his graceful subject down to the sheen of her satin dress, and why Vassilev was such a sought-after Palm Beach portraitist. His wife, Rosa Tusa, was a food editor of the *Palm Beach Post.*[43]

By 1945 Leo Lentelli (who by 1943 had become a member of the National Academy of Design) regularly wintered in Palm Beach. He loved the island, maintained a studio at The Breakers, and formed many friendships. His wife, Mimi, owned an art gallery on Brazilian Avenue and County Road, where she exhibited works by numerous artists.[44]

His free-standing works displayed in Palm Beach in the mid 1940s graced the patio at 310 ½ and 312 Worth Avenue, where the Worth Avenue Gallery was first located (see fig. 118). Painted blue to match the pool tiles beneath it, Lentelli's *Fountain of Diana* with her faithful hunting dog at her feet greeted viewers at the entrance. In the mid-ground, *Leda and the Swan* stood on a pedestal and *The Bather (La Baigneuse)* could be seen in the back, sensuously bending over to wash one of her limbs. Unfortunately, these statues are no longer in this public courtyard.[45]

PALM BEACH VISUAL ARTS

Lentelli's superlative's Breakers fountain design (see fig. 62) and expert stone carving at the Cathedral of St. John Divine in New York earned him a commission in 1945 for the western portal of the Episcopal Church of Bethesda-by-the-Sea. With financing provided by Mrs. Neville Fahs-Smith in memory of her husband, Lentelli carved the tympanum above the portal portraying Christ blessing and protecting the church flanked by angels offering prayer and

Fig. 118. Leo Lentelli, sculptures, *Fountain of Diana* (foreground), *Leda and the Swan* (mid-ground), and *The Bather* (back), formerly at the patio of 310 ½ and 312 Worth Avenue. (Courtesy HSPBC)

Fig. 119. Leo Lentelli working on the Episcopal Church of Bethesda-by-the-Sea in Palm Beach, Florida, March 1946, Edward Buehler Delk, photographer. (Leo Lentelli Papers, Archives of American Art, Smithsonian Institution)

sacrament (see fig. 119). On either side of the portal, Lentelli carved the figures of Saints Matthew, Mark, Luke, and John with their attributes (see fig. 120), some mentioned in Ezekiel 1:5, 10.

Artistic growth in Palm Beach continued in many forms,

Fig. 120. Leo Lentelli, sculptural work on the west portal of the Episcopal Church of Bethesda-by-the-Sea, including tympanum and saints. (Used by permission, Church of Bethesda-by-the-Sea, photograph by author)

Fig. 121. Audrey Chadwick Berdeau and LeRay Berdeau, ca. 1940s. (Courtesy HSPBC)

PALM BEACH VISUAL ARTS

unimpeded by the 1947 hurricane. That year The Society of the Four Arts acquired the former Embassy Club, once a swank restaurant and nightclub built by Addison Mizner and operated by Col. Edward R. Bradley, and during the war a canteen for soldiers. In 1948, after architects such as John Volk completed renovations, it opened as the primary location for exhibition space (now the Esther B. O'Keeffe Gallery Building). Their building on Ceiba Avenue became devoted solely to a library (now the Gioconda and Joseph King Library) and remains one of Palm Beach's interactive treasures.

To initiate their new home, the Four Arts held an important loan exhibition of contemporary paintings, garnering nationwide attention. The exhibition could not have taken place without collectors such as Mr. and Mrs. William Lee McKim and Col. LeRay Berdeau and Audrey Chadwick Berdeau (see fig. 121), who retained connections with major New York galleries and museums.

The Berdeaus' holdings included two original models for the art deco panels on the SS *Normandie* by Jean Dunand (French, 1877-1942), displayed in the foyer of their home, Villa Today (see fig. 122). They also owned a 1910 painting by Franz Marc entitled *Liegender Hund im Schnee (Dog Lying in the Snow)* (fig. 123). The painting was previously in the collection of the Städel Museum, who purchased it from Marc's widow in 1919. Unbeknownst to the Berdeaus, the Nazis had stolen the painting from the museum and auctioned it at the infamous 1939 sale at Galerie Fischer in Lucerne. Subsequently, an art dealer sold *Liegender Hund im Schnee* to the Berdeaus, who held it until Col. LeRay parted with it in 1960. A gallery owned the pilfered war loot by 1961, but later the painting (worth several million dollars) returned to the Städel Museum, where it is housed today.[46]

William Lee McKim, whose wife, Charlotte, was an artist, was a trustee of The Society of the Four Arts and served as an influential leader of substantial Palm Beach art lovers. McKim, whose holdings included works by modernists Marsden Hartley and Jean Dubuffet, pioneered the collecting

of post-war contemporary art when he purchased a painting by Robert Motherwell entitled *In the Sun* (1946) (fig. 124). *In the Sun* was a gem of the McKims' collection and relates in palette and concept to other works of that period by the artist. The composition fills the canvas and packs a stunning juxtaposition of the sun on the left and more somber forms that would soon become typical of Motherwell's motif.[47]

Fig. 122. Jean Dunand (French, 1877–1942), *La Chasse (The Hunt)*, panels once flanking the main entranceway of Villa Today, 1935, lacquer, gold leaf, paint, plaster, 49 ⅛ x 98 ⅜ x 1 ½ in. (124.8 x 249.9 x 3.8 cm), the Wolfsonian–FIU, gift of the Frederick and Patricia Supper Foundation, Palm Beach, Florida, 2004.3.1–2. (Courtesy Wikimedia Commons, photograph by Wmpearl)

In 1947 artist Philip Brinkman, well-known for his World War II patriotically-decorated airplanes called "nose art," painted a mural behind the reception desk of the Colony Hotel depicting the history of Palm Beach. In the some four years in which he lived in the area he provided murals for the Palm Beach County Courthouse (see fig. 125) in West Palm Beach, a Worth Avenue toy shop, and other locations.[48]

Concurrently, Eric Lundgren taught at the Norton Gallery and School of Art. Lundgren, born in Sweden, received his primary art tutelage in China, instilling in him a deep respect for nature, which he studied prodigiously (see fig. 126).[49]

In 1948 a public work of art became controversial when Palm Beach's mayor, James M. Owens succeeded in having Burt Johnson's statue of Elisha Newton "Cap" Dimick (see fig. 37) moved from the front of the Health Department building in West Palm Beach across the lake to Royal Palm Way, one of Palm Beach's most prominent boulevards. Owens was justified in his wish for the statue's relocation; after all, Dimick had been one of Palm Beach's most significant pioneers and had lived on Royal Palm Way. However, by 1948 modernism had largely taken hold of the national artistic zeitgeist. Surrealist and cubist sculptures were en vogue and realistic commemorative statues were no longer au courant. Emilie Keyes disclosed that some Palm Beachers "whispered" that Royal Palm Way, across from The Society of the Four Arts, "should not be the spot for the statue as it was not in keeping with the highest art standards of today." They suggested relocating it to Royal Poinciana Way, a boulevard more connected with Palm Beach's historical background. Alice De Lamar wrote a letter protesting the Royal Palm Way location as well and proposed that the statue's life size (rather than a monumental, or over-life size) would be more suitable for the interior of a building. Yet while some of her stylish friends criticized the statue, she felt it a matter of opinion as to the quality of the piece. Despite the naysayers, the statue remained, and today "Cap" Dimick still stands on Royal Palm Way, surveying one of his many accomplishments—the Royal Park Bridge—and welcoming in a friendly, humble manner all those who enter Palm Beach.[50]

The same year Johnson's statue of Dimick arrived in Palm

Fig. 123. Franz Marc, *Liegender Hund im Schnee,* Inv. No. 2085, formerly in the Berdeau collection. Property of the Städelscher Museums-Verein e.V, Frankfurt, Germany. (Courtesy Wikimedia Commons)

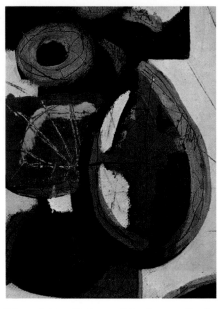

Fig. 124. Robert Motherwell, *In the Sun*, 1946, private collection, London, formerly in the collection of William Lee McKim. (Art © Dedalus Foundation, Inc. / Licensed by VAGA, New York, NY)

Fig. 125. Philip Brinkman painting a mural for the Palm Beach County Courthouse. (Courtesy Phylis Brinkman Craig)

Fig. 126. Eric Lundgren, *Sketch, Old Croker Home, Ocean Drive, Palm Beach,* inscribed "Copy from Orville Bulman, 1947, E. L.," mixed media. (Courtesy HSPBC, photograph by author)

Beach, Mary Benson exhibited surrealist trompe l'oeil capriccios executed in gouache by Ricardo Magni (1903-1956) (see fig. 127) along with paintings and drawings by important New York neo-romantic/surrealist Eugene Berman. Alice De Lamar, who admired surrealism, collected both artists' works.

On August 12, 1949, Theodora Alice Ruggles Kitson's *The Hiker* (fig. 128), was dedicated in West Palm Beach's Howard Park. The posthumous cast was among some fifty-two statues of the bronze that commemorated veterans of the Spanish-American War, the Philippine Insurrection, and the Chinese Relief Expedition. Kitson (1871-1932), born in Brookline, Massachusetts, studied at the Museum of Fine Arts, Boston and joined the multitude of Americans who received instruction in Paris in the late nineteenth century. After she married one of her teachers, sculptor

Fig. 127. Ricardo Magni, painting Lilly (Mrs. Herbert) Pulitzer's portrait, 1955. (Courtesy HSPBC, photograph by Paul Ilyinsky, a Romanov descendant and a later mayor of Palm Beach)

Henry Hudson Kitson, she became one of the first women accepted into the National Sculpture Society. She designed the original *Hiker* (also known as the *Spanish American War Veteran*) in 1904, utilizing an Allentown, Pennsylvania, Spanish-American war veteran named Leonard Sefing, Jr. as the model. Theo sold her rights to Gorham, which cast the original bronze, and they subsequently replicated the statue in many cities throughout the nation.[51]

The hiker's expression is one of determination and intelligence, signifying the legions of college students who volunteered for the Spanish-American War. Monumental and heroic, the 8 ½-foot high, handsome bronze utilizes the classical style of realism; yet *The Hiker* transcends any

Fig. 128. Theodora Alice Ruggles Kitson, *The Hiker*, 1904, Howard Park, West Palm Beach. (Photograph by author)

semblance of formality. The shirt sleeves of the rugged soldier's wrinkled uniform are rolled up. He holds his gun in a rather unconventional manner, not upright, like other portrayals of gallant soldiers (such as Daniel Chester French's 1875 *Minuteman*), but across his body, influenced by Kitson's husband's *Minuteman* in Lexington, Massachusetts, modeled in 1900.

The end of the 1940s exemplified a continued variety at The Society of the Four Arts, with three diverse shows.

The Norton Gallery boasted important new acquisitions by Paul Klee and Juan Gris. Mary Benson closed out the 1949 season by celebrating springtime with paintings by American masters such as John Marin, old masters, and nineteenth and twentieth century French masters, along with moderately priced works by emerging artists. The next year would mark the beginning of Palm Beach's golden age of galleries with Benson at the center of it all.[52]

Chapter Seven

1950-1960: The Fabulous Fifties

The year 1950 marked the start of the "golden years of Palm Beach galleries." By then Caroline Van Hook Bean, still actively painting in town, exhibited with the Artists' Guild of the Palm Beach Art League at Worth Avenue's Alex 14 Gallery. Mary Benson, who turned sixty in 1950, still owned the Worth Avenue Gallery with her brother-in-law, Ned Mathews. However, Alice De Lamar continued wielding her influence in getting her artist-friends to exhibit there. One of them was the previously mentioned Pavel Tchelitchew, who exhibited a one-man show at the Worth Avenue Gallery in 1952. An internationally acclaimed artist with works in numerous museums, Tchelitchew loved Alice and was quite fond of Mary Benson as well, calling her "a beautiful magnificent woman."[1]

Benson also gave a Palm Beach debut to the talented artist Ouida George (1916-2014) (see fig. 129), who began exhibiting her one-woman shows at the Worth Avenue Gallery in 1950. George studied at the Art Institute of Chicago, the Escuela Nacional de Pintura, Escultura y Grabado in Mexico City, and sculpture with José de Creeft and Ann Weaver (Norton) before turning to painting. George met her husband, Harold, in art school and moved to the Palm Beach area by 1949. Encouraged by Pavel Tchelitchew, Betty Parsons, and Alice De Lamar, George felt confident enough to display her works at Benson's gallery. It would be the first of many solo exhibitions, and George would remain a dynamic Palm Beach artist for decades. Her lyrical artwork ranged from colorful Bonnard-inspired French

Fig. 129. Ouida George with her paintings and English spaniel puppies, photograph by Bert and Richard Morgan, cover, *Social Pictorial,* February 21, 1972. (Courtesy HSPBC)

postimpressionist landscapes and figural pieces inspired by worldwide visits to charming, whimsical studies of her friends posing outside, in bed, or in claw-foot bathtubs. Some of her many collectors included the Duke and Duchess of Windsor, Ethel Kennedy, prominent art lover Algur Meadows, the Walter Gubelmanns, the Museum of Phoenix, and, of course, Alice De Lamar, who championed her. George had wanted to be an artist from the time she was a little girl. Smart, insightful, and not afraid to express an opinion, she declared, "My art is my life." She not only painted portraits of the rich and famous but also illustrated at least one children's book.[2]

John Franklin "Jack" Hawkins, who had been associated with the Worth Avenue Gallery since 1947, was also a frequent exhibitor there. A friend of Betty Parsons and Emily Rayner, he had previously shown his works at Parson's gallery and Knoedler in New York. Living at Alice De Lamar's house for many years, Hawkins swam three miles per day in the ocean. He specialized in surrealism, portraying a strange realm above the sea or dense coral life below (see fig. 130). In 1950 his undersea work garnered a prize at The Society of the Four Arts.[3]

Other artists made their mark in Palm Beach during the 1950s, such as Vincenzo Maria Zito (1900-1966), who first came to town in 1953. Born into a wealthy family, Zito studied painting and sculpture at the Accademia di belle arti in Palermo and Rome He was primarily a caricaturist and traveled to Palm Beach to render large panels of caricatures after Toulouse Lautrec for a nightclub named Nino's Moulin Rouge. Like so many other visual artists, Zito became enraptured with the town and its natural beauty and wintered in his home and studio on Cocoanut Row. Zito thrived as an artist and drew caricatures of practically everyone of note in Palm Beach.[4]

Artist J. Clinton Shepherd also flourished in town; along with teaching, painting, and sculpting, he owned an art gallery on Royal Poinciana Way, where he provided exhibition

Fig. 130. John Franklin Hawkins, *Full Fathom Five,* exhibited at the Worth Avenue Gallery. (Courtesy HSPBC)

PALM BEACH VISUAL ARTS

space for several local artists. In 1950 he gave Grand Rapids businessman/artist Orville Bulman (1904-1978) (see fig. 131), who wintered in Palm Beach each season, his debut. Bulman's work at that time portrayed Midwestern regional or social realist scenes and African American southern shanty towns. Unsure of himself as an artist as he had not pursued it as a career until his forties and had taken only a few lessons from Eric Lundgren, Bulman exclaimed, "I can't

believe I am actually to have a show; I'm almost embarrassed." After the first of the paintings sold at Shepherd's opening night party, the astonished Bulman took a bottle of scotch from the gallery's bar and ran down the street to give it to the buyer in gratitude. The show quickly sold out and Bulman began his magical rise to phenomenal success.[5]

During this time, Mary Benson continued to choose her artists assertively and nurture their talent. When she noticed Orville Bulman's 1950 sold-out show at the Shepherd gallery, she asked the artist to exhibit at her gallery in 1952. Knowing what a fine reputation the Worth Avenue Gallery had, the modest, self-effacing Bulman declared, "Gosh, I was overwhelmed that they'd think of asking me." By this time Bulman's work had become

Fig. 131. Orville Bulman with his painting *Delilah and the Preacher*, exhibited at the Worth Avenue Gallery in 1952. (Bulman family papers, photograph by Ramon)

Fig. 132. Orville Bulman, *New Orleans Jazz Club*, 1954, exhibited at the Worth Avenue Gallery, ca. 1955. (Courtesy Edward and Deborah Pollack Fine Art, Palm Beach, © Estate of Orville Bulman)

influenced by the Caribbean culture, but he also continued to paint scenes of Florida African Americans, jazz club renderings inspired by New Orleans (see fig. 132), and Midwest regionalism.[6]

Bulman's first Worth Avenue Gallery opening was a tremendous success, attracting the largest crowds in the gallery's history. All of the paintings sold out (twenty-seven selling on the first day), and critics from Florida to Michigan reviewed the show favorably. The following year Bulman repeated a successful sold-out show at the Worth Avenue Gallery, but the already-wealthy businessman/artist refused to accept any profit from it. Bulman in fact gave all the money earned by his exhibitions to other artists, museums, or back to galleries. He would often purchase another artist's work and then donate the work to a museum. Indeed, Mary Benson wrote that Bulman's motive was to "reveal . . . the rich personal rewards of an art interest—and so to promote a wider recognition of our artists and our art centers."[7]

Orville Bulman became Palm Beach's most successful artist in history. His patrons ranged from Palm Beach's mayor to J. Patrick Lannan, the important collector of modern and contemporary art who established a fine art foundation in 1960. The Duchess of Windsor waited patiently in line for Bulman's preview parties, and Marjorie Merriweather Post (see fig. 133) collected more than thirty of his paintings. In fact, anyone who was anyone in Palm Beach simply had to own a Bulman. When Bulman flew to Paris in 1959 for his opening at the Andre Weil Gallery, Mary Benson traveled there to support him. That exhibition was a sell-out, as were Bulman's shows in New York and Raymond Burr's gallery in Los Angeles, where Hollywood stars clamored for Bulman's work. By then the artist had created a fantasy world called "Bulman's Island," inspired by the Caribbean and fueled by his imagination. In the future, his whimsical style would evolve considerably.[8]

At one of Mary Benson's ongoing clothesline exhibitions,

Fig. 133. Marjorie Merriweather Post square dancing as her daughter, actress Dina Merrill, looks on; Orville Bulman painting in the background, ca. 1960s. (Bulman family photographs, photograph by Bert Morgan)

she discovered the art of handsome teenager Keith Ingermann (1929-2012), who sold his works for $5 each. The art student, who studied with J. Eliot O'Hara at the Norton School of Art and Mexican artist Xavier Gonzalez, could not have found a more apt showcase than Benson's gallery, sharing a two-man exhibition with Jack Hawkins in 1951. Ingermann's subsequent one-man shows launched a highly successful career, resulting in Hammer Galleries selling a group of his works in the early 1960s for over $50,000. He continued to return to Palm Beach from his worldwide sojourns to exhibit in the gallery that gave him his start.[9]

Art collectors found Ingermann's paintings charming, with outlined figures reduced to their simpler form yet remaining fluid, rounded, and poetic. This style extended from his studies in Japan while enlisted in the Air Force and the influence of Italian modernist painters, such as Giorgio Morandi. In Ingermann's painting *Zebras* (fig. 134) he implemented the simplified style, which fit right in with other dreamy Palm Beach art of the 1950s, '60s and '70s. He also created hammered frames that complemented his work. Jack Hawkins wrote about Ingermann's work: "These are comforting paintings in a time not without its anxieties, and they bring a feeling of reassurance by their forthrightness and awareness of the lasting beauty of humble things." The same sentiment applies today.[10]

Alice De Lamar collected Ingermann's paintings, became his close friend, and emotionally and financially backed him. She also did not cease supporting many of the other Worth Avenue Gallery painters and sculptors. In fact, De Lamar continued assuming the role of Medici-like patronage of many artists and artisans. Aside from her continued arts boosting, De Lamar was an animal rights activist and environmentalist; but in all her philanthropic endeavors, she remained largely anonymous.

Several other artists became favorites at the Worth Avenue Gallery. In 1956 artist John (Johnny) Baggs joined Jack Hawkins as a gallery associate. "Stevie" Hopkins Hensel's first

Fig. 134. Keith Ingermann, *Zebras,* 1968. (Courtesy Edward and Deborah Pollack Fine Art, Palm Beach)

one-man Palm Beach show also occurred at Worth Avenue Gallery. Born in New York City in 1921, Hensel had won a prize at The Society of the Four Arts in 1945 for his painting *Acrobats,* a.k.a. *Performers* (fig. 135). Among other Palm Beachers, Mary Benson and Alice De Lamar owned paintings by this artist, whose style could be described as post-surrealism with a linear motif portraying translucent, well-defined figures combined with geometric forms. In 1958 he would earn another award at The Society of the Four Arts for a self-portrait. The Museum of Fine Arts, Boston, Toledo Museum of Art, and others would collect his art. Hensel once commented, "I'll paint anything, in any medium—the sun, the moon, classical heads, mystical diagrams. You see, it all amounts to the greatest pleasure I can possibly find anywhere." He died in 1979 at the young age of fifty-seven in Majorca, Spain.[11]

Fig. 135. Hopkins Hensel, *Performers,* prize-winner at The Society of the Four Arts, 1945. (Courtesy HSPBC, photographer unknown)

Local art centers continued to grow in the 1950s thanks to their supporters. With the death of Ralph Norton in 1953, the Norton Gallery acquired important American paintings as part of his bequest, including Ernest Lawson's *Railroad Track* (fig. 85) and works by Edward Hopper and Charles Sheeler. The Society of the Four Arts held stunning exhibitions; in 1955 they were the first art organization in the South to hold a major Vincent Van Gogh retrospective (see fig. 136). The following year a Paul Gauguin exhibition took place, the Four Arts hosting the show before it traveled to Miami, Havana, Cuba, and Birmingham, Alabama. The Four Arts also carried on the nineteenth- and early twentieth-century traditions of tableaux vivants.[12]

Fig 136. Vincent Van Gogh, *The Langlois Bridge at Arles with Road alongside the Canal,* 1888, Van Gogh Museum, Amsterdam, Netherlands, exhibited at The Society of the Four Arts in 1955.

In 1955, Kyril Vassilev painted a full-length portrait of longtime art supporter Amy Phipps (Mrs. Frederick) Guest at her home, Villa Artemis, wearing a gardenia pinned to her dress symbolizing her passion for gardening. The same year at the identical location, photographer Slim Aarons photographed Mrs. Guest's daughter-in-law, socialite C. Z. Guest, with C. Z.'s son and their pets against an azure sky and aqua ocean (see fig. 137). Aarons photographed the privileged in glamorous settings and expressed in full color

Fig. 137. Slim Aarons, *Nice Pool* (C. Z. Guest and son, Palm Beach). (Photography by Slim Aarons/Getty Images © Getty Images)

the term "beautiful people." In this photograph, Guest represents an American goddess juxtaposed with the bronze Greek goddess behind her.

In 1956 French expressionist Bernard Buffet (1928-1999) had his Palm Beach debut at Mary Benson's Worth Avenue Gallery. Buffet, whose work is recognizable by its linear, flat, and angular compositions of figural content, had enjoyed much success in New York and Paris. But Buffett's canvases, priced reasonably at Benson's show—under $500—failed to find a buyer. Benson felt the fault was not with the artist but that her taste was too far advanced for the art-buying public at that time. In the future, Buffet would fare far more successfully in Palm Beach and prices for his art would skyrocket.[13]

Mary Benson and Alice De Lamar continued to live together at De Lamar's oceanfront house with Benson ensconced in her own apartment within the mansion. De Lamar's guest rooms were almost always filled, although she preferred only having two to three occupied bedrooms at one time so social activities didn't hinder her solitary hours of reading and rest. Haute couture designers Philippe Venet and Hubert de Givenchy became regular guests at her home, and she entertained Hollywood celebrities such as Charlton Heston (see fig. 138), who appeared in Palm Beach theatrical productions during the early 1950s. Eva Le Gallienne reunited with De Lamar and Benson in 1956 when the actress stayed at De Lamar's house while performing in *The Corn is Green* at the Palm Beach Playhouse. Lucia Davidova, who remained one of De Lamar's longest lasting intimate friends, also visited De Lamar in the 1950s, as did artist/designer Eyre de Lanux. De Lamar also often invited her friend art collector Peggy Guggenheim to Palm Beach and offered her multilevel apartment in Paris to Pavel Tchelitchew, Channing Hare, Emily and Archibald Rayner, and many others. De Lamar maintained close friendships with other creative people, such as the surrealist artist Leonor Fini and Ludwig Bemelmans (1898-1962), famous for his *Madeline* illustrations and murals at New York's Carlyle Hotel. Alice avidly collected his work, as did countless other Palm Beachers.[14]

Not so famous but extremely important visitors included Benson's several grandnieces: Amanda, Pamela, Catherine, Susan, and Molly (De Lamar's goddaughter) (see figs. 139 and 140). Benson lovingly cared for her grandnieces. She devoted many hours to them and, to improve the children's

Fig. 138. Charlton Heston and Alice De Lamar at Alice De Lamar's Palm Beach home, ca. early 1950s. (Richard Adams Romney Papers, Beinecke Rare Book and Manuscript Library, Yale University, GEN MSS 462, photographer unknown)

Fig. 139. Pam and Amanda Mathews with Alice De Lamar, 1952. (Courtesy Pamela Nash Mathews)

PALM BEACH VISUAL ARTS

Fig. 140. Mary Benson with Amanda and Pamela Mathews at Alice De Lamar's Palm Beach house, 1950. (Courtesy Pamela Nash Mathews)

posture and grace, sent Catherine and Molly to ballet school. Benson also treated Pamela to an Elizabeth Arden haircut when it was time to lose her braids. Another important and frequent visitor was Emily Rayner's son William ("Billy"), whom De Lamar treated like a nephew. Spending a generous amount of time nurturing him, De Lamar presented him with books and art and took him with her on trips to her idyllic property on the Loxahatchee River. De Lamar also filled her commodious house with various animals, especially cats, which she adored (except while packing for a trip). Her domestic zoo included a monkey that had a taste for young children—at least Benson's grandnieces, who were warned repeatedly not to feed the naughty animal but insisted on doing so. Unfortunately, each time they offered the monkey food it would instead take a bite out of the girls' fingers. At least one time the rambunctious monkey also jumped on top of Catherine's head, causing her screams to awaken Benson from a nap, which annoyed her so much she told Catherine to walk to the hospital.[15]

Meanwhile, native Californian Grover Hendricks made his Palm Beach debut in a group show at the Worth Avenue Gallery. Mary Benson championed Hendricks. She purchased his art, such as a stunning work entitled *Galaxy,* and after taking the advice of an astrologer who predicted great success in Hendricks's future, Benson promptly had him move into Alice De Lamar's house, joining Jack Hawkins. De Lamar disagreed with Benson's valuation of Hendricks's talent; but as she wrote, it was, after all, Benson's gallery, and therefore De Lamar could and would not interfere with Benson's believing in his artwork (see fig. 141). Hendricks achieved some success with sculptures included in the collections of Steuben Glass and the Corning Museum of Glass, but today he remains unjustly obscure in the history of art.[16]

Hawkins and Hendricks provided their services as escorts or "walkers" for Benson and De Lamar, accompanying them to gallery openings and parties, and were also caretakers of the properties while the ladies were in Weston, Connecticut, or in Europe. In exchange for this, the women provided a home for them. Johnny Baggs, part of the Benson/De Lamar family who spent springs and autumns in Connecticut with the women, and Keith Ingermann also acted as their escorts.[17]

Benson's grandnieces thought of De Lamar and the artists as Benson's extended family. Their lifestyle seemed entirely natural, simply because it was how Benson lived—normal for her and therefore normal to the young girls. Consequently, they did not hold anti-gay prejudices so prevalent in the mid twentieth century. Like Benson's relatives, many Palm Beachers felt the same way.[18]

During the 1950s, photographer Ray Howard, a former actor who worked with Mary Pickford and Joan Crawford, captured many celebrities on Worth Avenue, including Prince Rainer who removed his sunglasses to give the photographer a better shot. Howard also covered the 1957 Four Arts contemporary American painting show (see fig. 142), with works by Sylvia Chilton, Paul Crosthwaite (1910-1981), John Sharp (1911-1966), Channing Hare, and Hopkins Hensel.[19]

Sharp and Crosthwaite met in New York City in the early 1930s at the Art Students League and became lifelong partners. Crosthwaite had studied with Raphael Soyer, John Sloan, and Yasuo Kuniyoshi; Sharp had been under the tutelage of regionalist giant Grant Wood at Stone City, Iowa. The year after the couple first wintered in Palm Beach in 1955, Mary Benson gave both artists their gallery debut at the Worth Avenue Gallery, which led to successful sales, prizes, and further exhibitions. Benson not only encouraged them, she also convinced collectors to purchase the artists' work. Sharp's paintings were soon found in the collections of the Pennsylvania Academy of the Fine Arts; the Museum of Fine Arts, Dallas; and the Philadelphia Museum of Art. Crosthwaite, whose work critic Lawrence Dame described as "poetic realism," found collectors such as James A. Michener.[20]

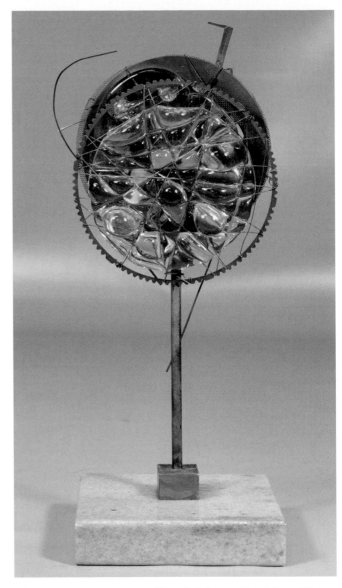

Fig. 141. Grover Hendricks, *Double Glass*. (Courtesy William Bunch Auctions, http://www.williambunchauctions.com, photograph by Laura Kiefer)

One of the most acclaimed artists to exhibit at the Worth Avenue Gallery was Gertrude Schweitzer (1911-1989) (see fig. 143). The New York-born artist had studied at the Pratt Institute and the National Academy of Design and began her career painting social realist works, but not the type associated with slums or the Great Depression. On the contrary, she mostly depicted children or lovely young women as ballerinas or debutantes (see fig. 144).

By the 1950s Schweitzer displayed her own modernist reduction of stylistic forms especially in her watercolors, perhaps somewhat inspired by John Marin. While she made detailed preparatory studies, she quickly executed the

Fig. 142. Paul Crosthwaite and John Sharp standing before a painting by Channing Hare at The Society of the Four Arts, 1957. At left, Paul Crosthwaite's painting of shacks, and at right, John Sharp's still life. (Courtesy HSPBC, photograph by Ray Howard)

Fig. 143. Gertrude Schweitzer in her studio, ca. 1940s. (Courtesy HSPBC, photographer unknown)

watercolors comprising translucent washes and ink highlighting the subject matter (see fig. 145). A National Academician, her unique form of feminine modernism did not go unnoticed by major art forces and she soon won numerous citations. She earned first prize for her work at the Norton Gallery and School of Art in 1947 and received awards at subsequent shows at the Four Arts. Curators at the finest museums, including the Norton Gallery, collected her work, and the great Marie Laurencin admired it as well.[21]

Aside from exhibiting, Gertrude and her husband, William, were instrumental to the development of the Palm Beaches' remarkable art world. William Schweitzer was a board member of the Norton Gallery and School of Art for years and Gertrude donated two important Picasso works to the institution. She advised, "Every artist finds the going rough at times, and wonders what it's all about. Why go on facing frustrations and failure? Then as you stay with a problem, and see it through, all of a sudden the sun bursts forth and you are rewarded with achievement."[22]

The Worth Avenue Gallery held a one-woman show of Schweitzer's work in 1955, and she and Mary Benson quickly became friends. Benson's gallery continued to thrive and on November 4, 1957, she registered it as a Florida domestic profit corporation with three principals—Mary as president, Ned Mathews as vice president, and Mary's sister, Frances, as secretary, treasurer, and director. By February 2, 1959, Ned was no longer a principal and Benson, at almost sixty-nine, signed a sworn oath notarized by Virginia Smith for the State of Florida that Mary maintained "100% ownership" of the Worth Avenue Gallery.

Fig. 144. Gertrude Schweitzer, *The Debutante,* ca. 1937. (© Estate of Gertrude Schweitzer)

Fig. 145. Gertrude Schweitzer, *Beaching the Boat, Number 2,* The Society of the Four Arts, donated in 1975 by the artist. (© Estate of Gertrude Schweitzer, courtesy The Society of the Four Arts, Palm Beach)

PALM BEACH VISUAL ARTS

While one could speculate that Alice De Lamar financially backed Benson's efforts after Mathews left the firm, Benson was still the only owner of the gallery and remained so. And according to Mary, the gallery was self-sufficient and never subsidized. However, there is no doubt that De Lamar, whose generosity extended to so many, financially supported Benson in various ways during her lifetime.[23]

Palm Beach also continued to host sumptuous private collections. Mr. and Mrs. Charles Wrightsman owned an impressive array of art in their Palm Beach mansion (the former home of Mona and Harrison Williams). Jayne Wrightsman had exquisite taste in all things beautiful. Cecil Beaton photographed her (see fig. 146) before the same eighteenth-century Chinoiserie wallpaper that formed the background of his painting of Mona and Harrison Williams. According to former Metropolitan Museum of Art director Thomas Hoving, Charles Wrightsman started scraping away the valuable wallpaper until Jayne stopped him before he could do further damage. Then, during a game of golf, Jayne outshone her husband so much that he hotly demanded she take up another hobby, such as art. As a result, she became a voracious art collector and learned much of her art history through study, her friendship with Bernard Berenson and art historian Kenneth Clark, and acquaintances with Hoving and his rival, National Gallery of Art director J. Carter Brown. Charles Wrightsman also believed that art was the perfect hedge against inflation, and he knew how to bargain with dealers. Consequently, the couple formed an impressive collection that included masterpieces housed in Palm Beach, such as Pierre-Auguste Renoir's *Girl and Cat* (fig. 147) and Johannes Vermeer's *Study of a Young Woman* (fig. 148), later donated to the Metropolitan Museum of Art. Jayne would, by the early 1960s, utilize her good taste when she served on Jacqueline Kennedy's Committee on the Arts.[24]

In 1957 Anna Thomson Dodge made the decision to raze Playa Riente and, in consequence, the nine José Maria Sert y Badia murals of Sinbad's adventures were offered at

Fig. 146. Cecil Beaton, Jayne Wrightsman in her Palm Beach home, 1956. (© The Cecil Beaton Studio Archive at Sotheby's)

auction on the premises. The sale received national attention and the press thought prospective bidder Huntington Hartford, art collector and heir to the A&P millions, would be the ultimate buyer of the dramatic panels. However, when Hartford arrived at Playa Riente, a coterie of women manning the front door mistook him for a delivery man and barred him from attending the sale. Hartford eventually gained entrance and left a sealed bid with the auctioneer but secretly planned to bid higher. Nevertheless, New York/Palm Beach antique and rug dealer Ohan S. Berberyan succeeded in buying the nine murals for $100,000. The dealer reportedly purchased the panels for an undisclosed collector who some whispered was none other than celebrity cosmetologist Elizabeth Arden; however, Berberyan relinquished his ownership in deference to Dodge's wishes of giving the murals to the Detroit Institute of Arts.[25]

Fig. 147. Pierre-Auguste Renoir, *Girl and Cat,* formerly in the Wrightsman collection, Palm Beach, private collection.

Fig. 148. Johannes Vermeer (Dutch, 1632–1675), *Study of a Young Woman,* ca. 1665–67, oil on canvas, formerly in the Wrightsman Collection, Palm Beach. (Metropolitan Museum of Art 1979.396.1)

Meanwhile, from 1952-57 the lively arts were held at the Palm Beach Playhouse, which occupied the Slat House on Cocoanut Row. Artist Franz Bueb painted murals in the lobby and designed some of its program covers. Bueb, who was Emily Rayner's favorite artist and described as "correct, German, very handsome, and very charming," lived part time in Austria as well as in Palm Beach after the close of World War II. Mary Benson gave the artist his Palm Beach gallery debut (as early as 1944), and Benson's patrons, including the Kennedys, avidly collected Bueb's art (see fig. 149). He painted portraits of both Jacqueline and Pres. John F. Kennedy as well. The artist remained grateful to his early Worth Avenue art dealer and would later comment that he "owed a great deal to Mary Benson." Museums, such

Fig. 150. Robert Bushnell, *Venetian Festival,* ceiling of the Celebrity Room (a.k.a. Poinciana Club), Royal Poinciana Playhouse. (Courtesy HSPBC, photographer unknown)

Fig. 149. Franz Bueb, *Portraits with Flowers.* (Courtesy Kaminski Auctions, Beverly, Massachusetts)

as the Los Angeles Museum of Art and the Grand Rapids Museum of Art, collected his work.[26]

After architect John Volk built a magnificent new playhouse—the Royal Poinciana Playhouse—New York artist Robert Bushnell earned the commission to paint the ceiling of its Celebrity Room, located across the hallway from the theater. Bushnell's trompe l'oeil mural entitled *Venetian Festival* (fig. 150) was inspired by Italian Baroque and Rococo masters such as Andrea Pozzo and Giovanni Battista Tiepolo, who painted dizzying architectural ceiling murals. Bushnell's work featured a constellation of Hollywood stars and prominent Palm Beachers peering down at patrons. The artist also decorated the Waldorf Astoria and other important buildings throughout the nation and painted murals for the Everglades Club's Bali Bar.[27]

Concurrently, J. Clinton Shepherd, aside from featuring local artists at his gallery, continued to provide murals; many decorated Palm Beach homes and venues such as the Everglades Club, the Palm Beach Towers, and the Palm Beach Athletic Club (one of three murals for the athletic club is illustrated in fig. 151). The club, which opened in 1956, unveiled Shepherd's murals for their "polo corner" on January 23, 1958, and received favorable publicity for the event.[28]

The end of the 1950s marked significant strides for both The Society of the Four Arts and the Norton Gallery and School of Art. In 1958 the Four Arts presented a show of Claude Monet's paintings, including the sun-splashed *Gladioli,* ca. 1876, loaned by the Detroit Institute of Arts and depicting Monet's wife, Camille, strolling through their colorful garden in Argenteuil (see fig. 152). The Four Arts would later acquire a masterpiece of American sculpture executed in the 1950s, *The Passing of the Torch* (fig. 153), better known as *The Torch Bearers,* by Anna Hyatt Huntington (1876-1973), one of the most significant American women sculptors of her generation. Huntington, who had exhibited at the Palm Beach Art Center in the 1930s, conceived the piece as early as 1949 and completed the clay model in 1953.[29]

Fig. 151. J. Clinton Shepherd, *Horse Race,* formerly in the Palm Beach Athletic Club, private collection. (© Estate of J. Clinton Shepherd)

The sculpture portrays two men, one fallen who passes a torch to the other astride a horse. There are several symbolic meanings: passing the torch of victory, youth, or—the consensus of critical opinion—civilization and culture. Inspired by her love of animals and her husband, Archer Milton Huntington, who established the Hispanic Society of New York, the sculptor wrote that she had in mind "the heroism of the Spanish people who have held for centuries to their ideals." Huntington also shows us that cultural enlightenment cannot live unless older generations pass it forward to the young, and that culture builders as well as those who maintain it are equally important to a civilized

Fig. 152. Claude Monet, *Gladioli,* ca. 1876, exhibited at The Society of the Four Arts in 1958. (Detroit Institute of Arts, USA City of Detroit, Purchase / Bridgeman Images)

society a crcdo most apparent at The Society of the Four Arts.[30]

A splendid loan exhibition of works by John Singer Sargent and Mary Cassatt closed out the decade at The Society of the Four Arts. At the same time, the Norton Gallery and School of Art, directed by Willis F. Woods, hosted numerous shows by members of the Palm Beach Art League and mounted exhibitions from important caches. In 1958, world-renowned actor and art collector Vincent Price attended the Norton's opening of the Walter P. Chrysler Jr. collection of old masters, which included *The Temptation of St. Anthony* by the studio of Hieronymus Bosch, 1450-1516 (see fig. 154). The Norton also continued showing off its collection, which included a wealth of old masters, a priceless cache of jade, and works by Constantin Brancusi,

Fig. 153. Anna Hyatt Huntington, *The Passing of the Torch,* 1953, aluminum, the Philip Hulitar Sculpture Garden, The Society of the Four Arts, 70.27, gift of Ogden Phipps. (Photograph by author, courtesy The Society of the Four Arts, Palm Beach)

Georges Braque, Claude Monet, and George Bellows (1882-1925). Bellows studied with Robert Henri in New York, and as an Ashcan School member he achieved success with striking works exemplifying bold brushstrokes and dramatic light and shadow interplay. The illustrated *Winter Afternoon* depicts a scene on the Hudson River painted from Riverside Park (see fig. 155). The artist's use of rich tones of blue accented with a splash of red results in the antithesis of a monochromatic winter scene.[31]

In 1959 the Norton Gallery purchased an abstract expressionist work by Mark Tobey (see fig. 156), emphasizing their desire to keep current with major trends of post-war contemporary art. The painting, entitled *The Avenue*, was inspired by New York City's scurrying, disconnected masses, Chinese calligraphy, and the Baha'i religion Tobey adopted. It projects an inherent musicality and harmony of color while keeping with the non-objective style found within the abstract expressionist movement.[32]

Also in 1959, Keith Ingermann convinced poet/artist Henry Faulkner (1924-1981) (see fig. 157) to head from New York to Palm Beach in pursuit of a place on the walls of the Worth Avenue Gallery. Faulkner, knowing the gallery's fine reputation was far greater than any New York showcase

that would have him, leapt at the chance. The young poet/painter had studied art in Louisville, Kentucky, and in the mid-1940s flourished in New Orleans, the city inspiring his palette and bringing forth fresh, lyrical verses. He lived a tumultuous life that included spending time at a psychiatric facility in the early 1950s, where he met poet Ezra Pound, who influenced Faulkner's art. While exhibiting in Miami in 1958, Faulkner encountered Tennessee Williams, who purchased a painting and gave the artist confidence in his work. Faulkner instructed Williams in painting technique and the two became close friends who shared a kindred angst applicable to talented, gay souls living amid the prejudice of mid-twentieth century.[33]

Fig. 154. Actor and art collector Vincent Price chats with Norton Gallery director Willis F. Woods at a Norton Gallery and School of Art preview, February 2, 1958, in front of *The Temptation of St. Anthony,* studio of Hieronymus Bosch, 1450-1516, now in the Chrysler Museum. (Courtesy HSPBC, photograph by Samuel R. Quincey)

Fig. 155. George Bellows, *Winter Afternoon,* 1909, Norton Museum of Art, West Palm Beach, Florida, gift of R. H. Norton, 49.1. (Courtesy Norton Museum of Art)

PALM BEACH VISUAL ARTS

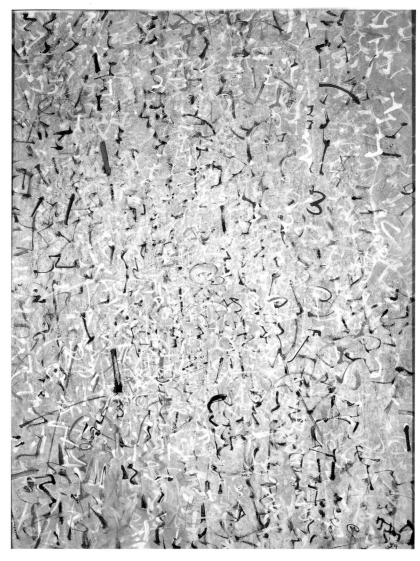

Fig. 156. Mark Tobey, *The Avenue,* 1954, Norton Museum of Art, West Palm Beach, Florida, purchased through the R. H. Norton Trust, 59.16. (Courtesy Norton Museum of Art, © 2015 Mark Tobey / Seattle Art Museum, Artists Rights Society [ARS], New York)

When Mary Benson arrived home after meeting Faulkner in 1959, she remarked to Alice De Lamar, "Quite a character turned up at the gallery today. He's from Kentucky and he says he's a hillbilly. He has a portfolio of pictures and they're quite nice." Benson invited Faulkner to participate in a group show that December along with Piero Aversa (see fig. 157) and other artists. Benson also had Faulkner's paintings properly framed, and under her influence he dropped all former shyness with the press and dove into the Palm Beach social publicity pool. He fascinated columnist Emilie Keyes,

Fig. 157. From left to right: Piero Aversa, Mary Benson, Henry Faulkner, Antoinette Johnson, and Alice De Lamar at De Lemar's Palm Beach home, ca. 1959. (Charles House, *The Outrageous Life of Henry Faulkner,* Sarasota: Pub This Press, 1988, 158, courtesy Charles and Nora House)

who called him an "engaging . . . puckish, slightly pixilated genius."[34]

Alice De Lamar became Faulkner's most generous patron. She paid $3,000 for a painting Faulkner priced at $300 and advised him to utilize the funds by studying in Italy and Sicily, offering to store his paintings in Weston, Connecticut, while he was in Europe. De Lamar did her share of nurturing Piero Aversa's work as well. As soon as he displayed his works at Mary Benson's gallery, De Lamar became his patron and in the future other notables purchased his art, including actors Marcello Mastroianni, Katherine Hepburn, and Agnes Moorehead.[35]

Following the 1958-59 season, Palm Beach art connoisseur George Vigouroux discovered artist Nicola Simbari's colorful oil paintings in Rome while on a European holiday. Vigouroux was a former artist, dancer, and actor and chaired the Everglades Club tennis committee before Mary Benson inspired him to realize that a gallery was in his future.[36]

Simbari (1927-2012), who was born in Calabria, Italy, had married a British actress named Elfrida, who remembered Vigouroux as having "a wonderful laugh and sense of humour." She recalled what happened in Rome: "We opened a flask of local wine and 'got down to business.' By the end of the evening, America was in our future. George bought the paintings he most loved and paid CASH, promising to be in touch with us soon, because he was to open a gallery, with friends, in a place called Palm Beach for 'the Season' whenever that was!"[37]

George Vigouroux was talking about Palm Beach Galleries, located at 336 Worth Avenue, incorporated on May 29, 1959, and set to formally open for the 1959-60 season.

Along with Benson's venerable Worth Avenue Gallery, the Palm Beach Galleries would usher in a decade filled with an abundance of lively openings, celebrated artists, and fantastical paintings and sculpture.[38]

Chapter Eight

1960-1970: An Abundance of
Galleries and Fantasy

The sixties opened with Nicola and Elfrida Simbari traveling from Rome to Palm Beach (via New York) for Simbari's one-man show at Palm Beach Galleries (see fig. 158). It would be Simbari's first major exhibition in America.[1] After George Vigouroux's limousine picked them up at the "tiny airport" in West Palm Beach and carried them across the bridge to the idyllic island, Elfrida and Nicola became overwhelmed at Palm Beach's beauty, calling it a "Garden of Eden." Elfrida was especially thrilled when Vigouroux hosted them at a party in his enormous oceanfront home to celebrate Simbari's first show. She later joked, "I'd leave Nicola some other time!"[2]

The Palm Beach Galleries had what George Vigouroux called a "billion-dollar board of directors" made up of prominent socialites. From the commencement these art enthusiasts included Mary Sanford, known as the "Queen of Palm Beach"; Texas oil heir Larry Sheerin; Joan Whitney Payson, daughter of Payne Whitney; Muriel Phipps, wife of Michael Phipps; and Barbara Vanderbilt Whitney Headley (Gertrude Vanderbilt Whitney's daughter, also an artist and married to artist George Headley). By the end of the decade the lovely Jane Volk, artist and wife of architect John Volk; Diana Guest Manning, an animal sculptor; and Lillian Phipps, wife of financier and horse-racing enthusiast Ogden Phipps, were on the gallery's committee.[3]

Elfrida fondly remembered how Vigouroux and his wife, Ethel, "created a 'fairy tale' in Nicola's rise to 'fame'" and credits them and his collectors for changing his career and

Fig. 158. George Vigouroux, Elfrida Simbari, and Nicola Simbari at Palm Beach Galleries, 1960. (Courtesy HSPBC, photograph by Bert and Richard Morgan)

encouraging Simbari to dedicate his life to art. She added that Palm Beach during that winter season "gave the impetus to Simbari's eventual success." She recalled the "wonderful gatherings of Nicola and his friends [including artists Franz Bueb and Piero Aversa] by the swimming-pool, on S. Ocean Blvd. . . . at the Vigourouxs' house . . . [where] there was always a great deal of laughter. Nicola created his 'Studio' by the pool house, with 'models' and several other artists living in the Palm Beaches."[4]

Elfrida especially enjoyed Worth Avenue and found it far more unique than Rome's Via Condotti in the 1960s, and far less commercial than today. "The sun and sea-air gave a timeless quality to each moment! No hurry. No stress. It was indeed a different world. Wealth of the sort that Palm Beach had . . . was 'accepted' as the norm; no need to 'show off!'"[5]

Simbari, who called himself a "neo-romantic realist" (as opposed to neo-romantic modernists, such as Pavel Tchelitchew), had already achieved some renown before his spectacular Palm Beach sell-out debut. Emily Rayner, who had joined Vigouroux by then as the associate director of Palm Beach Galleries, collected Simbari's paintings, as did entertainer Dinah Shore, connoisseur Henry P. McIlhenny, and director/producer Joseph Mankiewicz. These art appreciators were attracted to the beauty created by the love affair Simbari enjoyed with color, form, and light. Elfrida called him "an artist to his very soul," and Nicola Simbari himself declared, "I paint the way I make love."[6]

As compelling as a romance, Simbari's, thick, generous tints applied on canvas producing bursts of red, orange, yellow, and blue stir life itself. The viewer can feel the heat of a tropical, azure sky against a sun-washed beach at midday. In *On the Sea Wall* (fig. 159), the female figure sitting on the stone precipice turns her head away from the viewer, perhaps looking out to sea. It is the juxtaposition of her sun-kissed flesh and the wall's stone texture plunging into those rich, contrasting blues that transports the viewer to nirvana.

Fig. 159. Nicola Simbari, *On the Sea Wall.* (Courtesy Elfrida Simbari, © Nicola Simbari)

By 1960 Palm Beach had not only become a magnet for artists, galleries, and art collectors but also an important, internationally recognized art center, with works from local collectors and museums featured in significant art volumes. The Palm Beach Art League had become the Palm Beach Art Institute, which still owned and maintained the Norton Gallery and School of Art. The Norton Gallery began the new decade with a display of old master drawings and also works by modern masters Klee, Picasso, and famed Dadaist Marcel Duchamp from the Palm Beach collection of Isadore and Jeanne Levin, who hosted the artist. In town to lecture at the Norton Gallery, Duchamp spoke of Palm Beach's allure while reclining by the pool and admitted it was a pleasure to be among such wonderful art in such a desirable location. Prominent Palm Beach art collectors by then also included Peter and Faye Lavan and Chester Dale, one of the most significant art patrons in the nation.[7]

During the 1960 season, The Society of the Four Arts exhibited art of high stature, including works by French postimpressionist Camille Pissarro (1830-1903). The Worth Avenue Gallery's season began successfully with loyal patrons including Jacqueline Kennedy, who regularly purchased art at the gallery. Rose Kennedy was also a client, as were other family members. In fact, Mary Benson was close friends with Rose Kennedy.[8]

Other galleries by 1960 included the Thieme Gallery located in Via Demario or Via Parigi off of Worth Avenue, run by the widow of artist Anthony Thieme. It first opened in 1959 and featured not only Thieme's works but other artists associated with her gallery in Rockport.

Anthony Thieme, born in Rotterdam in 1888, studied painting in Europe and immigrated to Boston in 1917. He had already designed a New York theatrical production starring Anna Pavlova, and this gave him the confidence that he could succeed in the United States. Establishing a studio in Rockport, Massachusetts, in 1929, Thieme won numerous awards, including two Shaw prizes, and arrived in Florida in the beginning of 1948. In St. Augustine he became the most important member of the "Lost Colony" art group, which flourished from 1930-1950. Unfortunately, while on his way to Florida in 1954, Thieme ended his life in Greenwich, Connecticut.[9]

Upon viewing the illustrated work *Sailboats, Florida* (fig. 160), one can readily see why a Florida critic called Thieme "the master of light due to the deft way of capturing the transient play of sunlight on Florida waterways and foliage." It is also clear why the Metropolitan Museum of Art, Museum of Fine Arts, Boston, and many other distinguished museums collected his work.[10]

To add to Palm Beach's international recognition, in 1961

Fig. 160. Anthony Thieme, *Sailboats, Florida*, 1948, exhibited at the Thieme Gallery, Palm Beach. (Courtesy Edward and Deborah Pollack Fine Art, Palm Beach)

Walstein "Wally" Findlay opened a Worth Avenue branch of his galleries first established in Kansas City and then Chicago. Specializing in impressionist, postimpressionist, and modern art, Findlay's artists were international—European, Asian, and American. It was the grandest, most glamorous gallery in Palm Beach and reportedly the largest art house in Florida.

In 1961 Findlay displayed a wealth of Dali's jeweled art and Bernard Buffet paintings. So successful, another Buffet show took place the following year (see fig. 161). Wally Findlay would become Palm Beach's most ambitious art dealer and instrumental in bringing important and soon-to-be-important artists to the island, as long as their work was pleasing to the eye. Years later he would admit that if not for Palm Beach he wouldn't have expanded his galleries to New York and Paris.[11]

The Worth Avenue Gallery displayed an "ingenious" group show to start the 1961 season. Artist Patricia Massie Tavender Widener (see fig. 162)—who painted whimsical works of birds, shells, and flowers—enjoyed a one-woman show at the gallery in 1959 and 1961. Her impressive list of collectors included the Duke and Duchess of Windsor and

Fig. 162. Patricia Massie with one of her paintings at the Worth Avenue Gallery, ca. 1961. (Courtesy HSPBC, photograph by Bert and Richard Morgan)

Fig. 161. Wally Findlay, Annabel and Bernard Buffet, and Helen Findlay at the opening of a one-man Buffet show, ca. 1962 at Wally Findlay Galleries. (Courtesy HSPBC. Image of Bernard Buffet's painting © 2015 Artists Rights Society [ARS], New York / ADAGP, Paris)

J. Patrick Lannan. The beautiful artist, who married Peter Widener III in 1959, studied with Eric Lundgren at the Norton but also credited her colleagues Ricardo Magni and Orville Bulman for their influence and encouragement. Tragically, on February 4, 1963, at the young age of thirty-five, Massie was killed in a plane crash, stunning the island community.[12]

An artist who shared an exhibition with Patricia Massie was Zoe Shippen (Varnum). Specializing in children's portraiture, the engaging Shippen had taken instruction in Vienna and France in the 1920s and at the Detroit Institute of Arts, the School of the Museum of Fine Arts, Boston, and the Art Students League. Her depictions included Caroline Kennedy (see fig. 163), exhibited at the Worth Avenue Gallery in 1961; Joan Crawford's daughter, Christina; Walt Disney's children; as well as many other famous offspring.[13]

Joining the exhibiting artists at George Vigouroux's gallery was Charles Baskerville (1896-1994) with a 1961 show, followed by one in 1963 and 1965. A WWI and II hero and official artist of the US military, Baskerville, whose exotic paintings (see fig. 164 and 165) were extremely popular in Palm Beach and Hobe Sound, enjoyed a long list of collectors and an impressive résumé. The *Art Digest* called him "one of the leading portrait painters of the nation." With diverse subject matter from India, Nepal, Morocco, and Mexico, he came to Palm Beach in the 1930s and quickly became well-known from exhibitions at The Society of the Four Arts and his tropical murals painted in the finest homes. His mural *The Sultan of Morocco on his Stallion* prompted Marjorie Merriweather Post to build a ballroom around it. His patrons included royalty and celebrities, some of whom were close friends of the artist.[14]

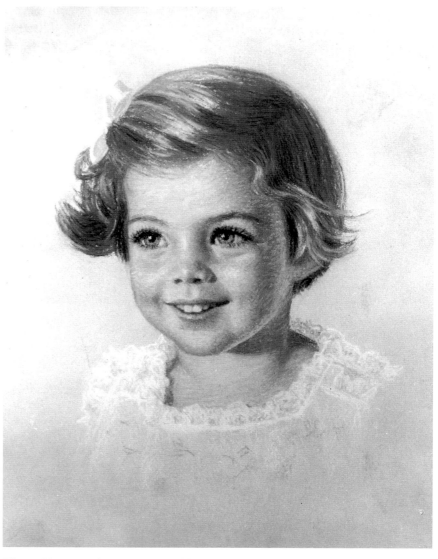

Fig. 163. Zoe Shippen, *Caroline Kennedy,* 1961. (Courtesy HSPBC, photograph by Gordon M. Potter)

In the meantime, photographer Mort Kaye was in town. He started his long-lasting career as a Waldorf Astoria banquet photographer earning two dollars per picture. A client first introduced him to Palm Beach in the 1940s and by the 1950s Kaye became an island resident.[15] While Kaye and his former associate, Bob Davidoff, as well as Bert and Richard Morgan, flourished, they were not paparazzi. On the contrary, for the most part society and celebrities thoroughly enjoyed getting their picture taken and welcomed these photographers. For instance, according to Mort Kaye's son, Corby, the rumor about Frank Sinatra swinging his fist at Mort Kaye is untrue.[16]

In 1962 Kaye photographed twenty Palm Beach working artists for *Palm Beach Life*'s March issue (see fig. 166). The artists inspired, influenced, and supported each other, and a joyous camaraderie among them would last for years.

The aforementioned Bob Davidoff, who had earned the Silver Star in World War II and had worked for Mort Kaye,

Fig. 164. Charles Baskerville, *Family of Monkeys in a Mango Tree, 1970.* (Courtesy Doyle, Auctioneers & Appraisers)

Fig. 165. Charles Baskerville, *Favourite Son of the Maharani,* private collection. (© Christie's Images / Bridgeman Images)

PALM BEACH VISUAL ARTS

Fig. 166. Palm Beach artists, 1962, photograph by Mort Kaye, reproduced in *Palm Beach Life,* March 1962, 55. From left to right, bottom row, Carl Brown (kneeling), Chaning Hare (standing), Franci Young (seated on step), Hopkins Hensel (seated next to Franci Young), Ron Hefler (seated cross-legged), Patrick Archer (with white jacket and glasses), Keith Ingermann (standing). Second row: Richard "Dick" Banks (standing next to Channing Hare), Ouida George (standing), Sheridan Crumlish (seated with white sweater), Dudley Huppler (seated with black jacket), Zoe Shippen Varnum (standing wearing brightly patterned dress). Top row: Orville Bulman, Paul Crosthwaite (wearing plaid jacket), Grover Hendricks, Piero Aversa (plaid pants), James de Vries (Mary McKinnon's son, kneeling), David Nemeroff (seated in front of de Vries), Henry Strater, and John Sharp (wearing plaid jacket in front of Strater). (Courtesy Corby Kaye, © Mort Kaye Studios)

Fig. 167. Kennedy Family, Easter Sunday, 1963. (Davidoff Studios, photograph by Bob Davidoff)

established his own studio on Bradley Place. Extremely successful, Davidoff became the official photographer of The Breakers and the Kennedy family, and would not miss an opening of the Royal Poinciana Playhouse. Davidoff's iconic 1963 image of the Kennedys in front of their private chapel on Easter Sunday remains internationally acclaimed (see fig. 167).[17]

During the early 1960s, Nicola Simbari continued to exhibit at Palm Beach Galleries. However, after a successful show of his works at Wally Findlay's Chicago gallery, Findlay and his sister Helen asked the artist to show at their gallery in Palm Beach. Simbari promptly came to George Vigouroux and asked for his advice; after all, Vigouroux had given Simbari his Palm Beach debut. Instead of selfishly insisting that Simbari exhibit at the Palm Beach Galleries exclusively, Vigouroux encouraged Simbari to grasp the opportunity to become part of the Wally Findlay group of artists. This, of course, was a great boon to Simbari's career, and he became even more internationally successful under Findlay's patronage.[18]

Although Piero Aversa had made his Palm Beach debut in a group show at the Worth Avenue Gallery in the 1959-1960 season, Wally Findlay gave the "happy, naughty" artist (as Elfrida Simbari called Aversa) his first Palm Beach one-man show in 1961. Aversa impressed Palm Beach with his Italian/East African heritage and could attend a gallery opening or the most formal parties barefoot and strewn with gold necklaces and anklets. After moving to Greece, he would stay at Lily Pulitzer Rousseau's house when visiting Palm Beach, and by the mid 1970s he lived in Key West, where he died in 1991.[19]

After visiting Europe, Henry Faulkner made a triumphant return to Palm Beach with successful shows at the Worth Avenue Gallery in 1961 and 1963. Faulkner taught art in Palm Beach, and the list of his collectors soon ballooned to include Bette Davis, Marlon Brando, Vincent Price, and the Corcoran and Phillips Museums in Washington, DC. Faulkner's *Leaning Tower of Pisa* (fig. 168), exhibited at the Worth Avenue Gallery in 1963, shows the influence of Italy and the vibrant coloration he implemented by traveling there—exactly what Alice De Lamar had hoped for him.[20]

In 1963 Orville Bulman reigned with another sold-out show at the Worth Avenue Gallery (see fig. 169), and his painting *Joyeux Noel* (fig. 170) graced the cover of December's *Palm Beach Life*. The magazine also reproduced Bulman's 1965 *C'est Ici* (*It's Here*) (fig. 171), which expressed the joyous beginning of the Palm Beach season; it also became the subject of numerous reproductions made by Lord and Taylor.

After Bulman moved to nearby Manalapan in the mid-1960s, he became inspired by its lush atmosphere (and Henri Rousseau) and introduced his popular jungle paintings (see fig. 172) to Palm Beach. Soon, other artists provided murals of jungles on walls of foyers and hallways.

George Vigouroux, in a spirit of friendly competition with Mary Benson, sold Cape Cod artist Ralph Cahoon's primitive, whimsical paintings of mermaids and sailors. Usually Cahoon's images depicted a New England theme, but he had painted a Palm Beach scene for Mrs. Walter Gubelmann, and Vigouroux was so impressed with it that he commissioned Cahoon for several paintings with a Palm Beach flavor (see fig. 173).[21]

By the early 1960s, Alejo Vidal-Quadras (1919-1994) was also in town and created a stir with his splendid portraiture. Born in Barcelona in 1919, he was influenced in determining a career by his artist-uncle as well as several popular painters, such as José Maria Sert y Badia. A commission brought Vidal-Quadras to Florida in 1959. In Palm Beach he enjoyed the patronage of the prominent Phipps family and exhibited at Wally Findlay Galleries. Like so many other artists, Palm Beach's beauty captivated Vidal-Quadras and he soon divided each year between his home in Paris and a winter residence on the island. "Palm Beach is about a long love story for me," he later said.[22]

One of Vidal-Quadras's subjects was Princess Grace of Monaco (see fig. 174), the former actress Grace Kelly, who

Fig. 168. Henry Faulkner, *Leaning Tower of Pisa,* exhibited at the Worth Avenue Gallery in 1963. (Courtesy John Stephen Hockensmith, Fine Art Editions)

Fig 169. Jean Bulman, Mary Benson, and Orville Bulman at the Worth Avenue Gallery, ca. 1963. (Courtesy HSPBC, photograph by Bert and Richard Morgan)

often visited Palm Beach. The artist recalled that after a number of sittings, he wondered how she could stare into space for so long without a blink and in such a natural manner. He finally asked her, thinking perhaps her theatrical training instilled that talent, but she confessed that it was due to the fact that she was terribly nearsighted and couldn't focus on anything in the distance.[23]

In mid-March 1965, Mary Benson became ill and Alice De Lamar made certain she was looked after at the South Ocean Boulevard house. At seventy-five years of age, Benson also began to have memory problems, and on March 28, 1965, she retired and closed her Worth Avenue Gallery, the most remarkable, groundbreaking art house in Palm Beach history. The closing marked the end of the island's "golden years of galleries."[24]

Benson felt worn out and planned on resting at home in Weston, Connecticut. George Vigouroux organized a Palm Beach farewell party (coinciding with Benson's birthday), which included many of her old friends and admirers. They gave the veteran art dealer a meaningful gold bracelet with charms including an artist's palette, and Benson also received a chest full of Kennedy half dollars, signifying her warm relationship with the renowned family. After the gathering, in which tears were mixed with laughter, columnist Emilie

Fig. 170. Orville Bulman, *Joyeux Noel,* 1963, private collection. (Courtesy Edward and Deborah Pollack Fine Art, Palm Beach, © Estate of Orville Bulman)

Fig. 171. Orville Bulman, *C'est Ici,* 1965. (Courtesy Edward and Deborah Pollack Fine Art, Palm Beach, © Estate of Orville Bulman)

Fig. 172. Orville Bulman, *La Princesse Arriveé.* (Courtesy Edward and Deborah Pollack Fine Art, Palm Beach, © Estate of Orville Bulman)

Fig. 173. Ralph Cahoon, *The Everglades Club.* (Courtesy Sotheby's, permission to reproduce work courtesy Cahoon Museum of American Art)

Keyes, who called Mary "gallant and lovely," wrote to Alice De Lamar, "Mary's party was sweet but sad—I hate to see the end of an era—but am glad to have been part of it."[25]

By the 1966 season at least fourteen commercial galleries, almost all following the honorable tradition set by Mary Benson, were in business. George Vigouroux made a point of extending his colleague's legacy and displayed the work of artists who previously showed at the Worth Avenue Gallery. Also by 1966, Lillian Phipps opened a fine gallery of her own, and Trosby Galleries (in town by 1950) auctioned the important Acosta collection, which included works by Modigliani, Picasso, and Lautrec. Exhibitions at the Four Arts were consistently outstanding. The Norton Gallery's reputation as a small but important fine art museum continued to skyrocket, boosting the economy of the Palm Beaches from tourism to real estate development. They expanded their collection and remembered local artists when they hosted Gertrude Schweitzer and Henry Strater exhibitions. It was clear that the Palm Beaches continued making an international statement in the field of art.[26]

Unfortunately, a thorn grew among the blossoming galleries on Worth Avenue when during the 1965-66 winter season Galerie Trianon opened, run by proprietor David Stein. For years on the French Riviera, Paris, and New York, the Frenchman had dealt in both originals and his own forged copies of works by artists such as Picasso, Marie Laurencin, Chagall, and even El Greco. Using the *Social Register* as an invitation list, Stein drew a large crowd of Palm Beach notables for Galerie Trianon's opening. According to Stein's wife, they intended to sell exclusively authentic paintings and had help from a rival Findlay family member who shipped legitimate paintings by major artists from New York to Palm Beach. But Stein still could not generate enough business to pay for the couple's lavish expenses, which included a chauffeur-driven Rolls Royce. As a consequence, the dealer decided to spice up the collection with his own forgeries. He did fairly well, selling a few fakes to collectors before returning to New York after the season ended. Fortunately, the Steins did not conduct business in Palm Beach the following season, for Stein's career ended abruptly in New York—courtesy the FBI and Marc Chagall, who assisted

authorities in their charges against the dealer. Ironically, years later Stein exhibited his own paintings legitimately, at a Worth Avenue gallery owned by Roslyn and Alex Sailor. Each painting was signed by Stein with the addition of the artist's name he copied.[27]

In the interim, George Vigouroux continued providing Palm Beach with artwork and opening-night parties. The gallery handled the dramatic marine paintings of Jack Lorimer Gray (1927-1981) after he had exhibited at Wally Findlay Galleries. In Gray's art (see fig. 175), the ocean, boat, and fishermen merge in a dynamic composition, uncompromisingly masculine in their power and unsentimentally beautiful in their grace. Gray also shows his skill at the interplay of light and shadow on waves, enhancing their movement, depth, and luminosity.

Gray was one of the most popular artists in Palm Beach. Born in Nova Scotia, he attended Nova Scotia College of Art for only a year before opting to obtain employment on fishing

Fig. 174. Alejo Vidal-Quadras painting a portrait of Princess Grace of Monaco. (Courtesy HSPBC and the Alejo Vidal-Quadras Foundation, photograph by Bert and Richard Morgan)

Fig. 175. Jack L. Gray, *Herring Ground*, 1962, oil on canvas 31 x 50 inches, exhibited at Palm Beach Galleries, private collection. (Courtesy Pierce Galleries, Nantucket, Massachusetts, © John S. Gray)

boats. Before arriving in the area, he enjoyed a successful career with his New York harbor scenes, becoming world famous and his art collected by Pres. John F. Kennedy. According to Gray's son, John, the artist was "an avid sailor and owned around eleven boats in his lifetime." He arrived in South Florida by 1960 and later "lived on various boats moored on Lake Worth." By 1968 Gray had sold a painting to the owner of the This Is It Pub in West Palm Beach, which the restaurant's owner displayed behind the bar for many years. Other Gray paintings and prints followed, admired by numerous diners. Gray's son thought his father "gave a special discount to the bar owner in consideration of many outstanding overdue tabs."[28]

Meanwhile, after Mary Benson's memory lapses became more severe, Alice De Lamar arranged for her to move into a Miami nursing home. Eva Le Gallienne became furious at this and considered it callous treatment, as she felt that Benson would miss her own home. But it was actually best for Benson, who could live nearby her Miami grandnieces in comfort with constant care. In the meantime, De Lamar had spent much of her time fighting for cultural preservation, stray animals, and the Florida environment, especially the Loxahatchee River.[29]

Fig. 176. Dorothy Thayer, Lettuce Ware, ca. 1970, created for Au Bon Gout, formerly on Worth Avenue. (Courtesy Cottone Auctions)

Fig. 177. Betty Kuhner, Lilly Pulitzer (Rousseau) and children, left to right, Minnie, Peter, and Liza, ca. 1967. (Courtesy HSPBC)

Fig. 178. James Hunt Barker in his gallery with his beloved Cavalier King Charles spaniels, invitation to a James Hunt Barker show. (Courtesy HSPBC, photograph by Bert and Richard Morgan)

Barker featured many artists whom Mary Benson had discovered, as well as others favored by Alice De Lamar. Ouida George, who had exhibited at Palm Beach Galleries in the 1960s after Benson closed her gallery, joined Barker and not only exhibited at his gallery but also worked as its art consultant. Her one-woman shows continued every two years until 1994. Barker also handled works by marine painter Jack L. Gray, who after exhibiting at Wally Findlay Galleries was thought to be exclusive with Palm Beach Galleries.[7]

Reorganization of Palm Beach Galleries ousted the dapper George Vigouroux by 1972. Several other galleries opened on Worth Avenue; one at no. 345, owned by Hilde Gerst, exhibited works by French impressionist and postimpressionist masters. In the 1930s, Gerst convinced her doctor husband to escape from the Nazis just before they overran her central European town; she arranged for her sister and brother-in-law to evade them as well. Settling in New York, she opened a gallery where her first client was Jacqueline Kennedy. When Manhattan crime rose considerably in the winter of 1971, Gerst hung a sign in her gallery's window: "Closed for the winter season. Gone to Palm Beach." Her fine taste was immediately recognized on the island, and her gallery's beautiful paintings engendered much success in the town that she loved. Her marketing technique was somewhat like Mary Benson's in that Gerst would not sell a customer a painting—she would instead allow them to buy it while educating them about the artist. Gerst went further than Benson, however, and after appraising a potential client would sometimes declare she didn't think they could afford the painting in question. Psychologically they would want the work even more.[8]

New York artist Albert Goldman opened his Gallery Gemini by 1970 to showcase his and other artists' works, some by contemporary masters. Grace Hokin's gallery, established ca. 1965, at first displayed primitive art and then added modern works and became Gertrude Schweitzer's representative in 1971. By 1972, New Jersey artist Ronni Pastorini kept a gallery in Via Mizner where she would paint on the spot. Other art dealers continued to succeed as they had in the past, including Galerie Jean Tiroche, originally established in Haifa, Israel; Tanya Brooks' Galerie Montmarte, which featured art by David Nemerov; Galerie Juarez; Lorraine Trester; the Upstairs Gallery, which featured Whitney Cushing's works; and Irving Gallery, akin to a small museum. There was also Flair Galleries, where Philip Standish Read (1927-2000), exhibited (see fig. 179). Read, who designed at least one program cover for the Palm Beach Heart Ball, trained at the Art Students League and the Académie Julian. His Venetian-inspired murals became quite popular and he was a well-known, well-liked artist whose work still enhances several Palm Beach collections. Read also exhibited at Tiffany's and Cartier's in New York, and Peggy Guggenheim, Max Ernst, and Jean Cocteau considered him a friend. Other artists working in town during the 1970s included marine painter Eldred Clark Johnson, magic realist Paul Riba, animal painter Guy Coheleach, and South Carolina artist Alfred Richardson Simson, who painted a series of Palm Beach historical paintings.[9]

Additional visual artists included Lucien Capehart, a former oceanography photographer who found that capturing social life above the water was far more fruitful than picturing underwater life; however, he did not relinquish artistic photography, which remains highly regarded. Other photographers, such as Bert and Richard Morgan and Bob Davidoff, also continued to depict celebrities and the stylish (see figs. 180-183).

In 1976 an important addition of sculpture entitled *Intetra* by world-renowned artist Isamu Noguchi (1904–1988) (see fig. 184) became an outdoor highlight at The Society of the Four Arts. The stainless steel *Intetra* has been widely described by art historians as a cosmic version of a pyramid, a spaceship, or a natural interstellar formation. It touched down at the Four Arts thanks to the generosity

Fig. 179. Philip Read and Ken Lloyd (director of Flair Galleries) in front of Read's paintings at a Flair Galleries reception for Philip Read. (Courtesy HSPBC, photograph by Bert and Richard Morgan)

Fig. 180. Gloria Vanderbilt Cooper with actor Emlyn Williams, April in Paris Ball, Palm Beach, 1970. (Courtesy HSPBC, photograph by Bert and Richard Morgan Studio)

Fig. 181. John and Julian Lennon at the Sun & Surf condominium, Palm Beach, December 1974. (Davidoff Studios, photograph by Bob Davidoff)

Fig. 182. Actor George Hamilton with his half brother, William "Bill" Potter, and their mother, Ann Spalding Hamilton, on Worth Avenue, ca. 1970s. (Courtesy HSPBC, photograph by Bert and Richard Morgan)

Fig. 183. Dame Margot Fonteyn and David Wall, after performing *Les Sylphides* and the *Sleeping Beauty* pas de deux at Mary Howes' annual Fine Arts Festival, 1972, Royal Poinciana Playhouse, Palm Beach. (Courtesy HSPBC, photograph by Bert and Richard Morgan)

of Ziuta and Joseph James Akston. A well-liked artist, diplomat, journalist, and collector, J. James Akston was an indefeasible champion for funding the arts and donated to the Norton Gallery, Flagler Museum, Four Arts, and major museums in New York.[10]

In celebration of the Bicentennial in 1976, metal sculptor Edward Ryneal Grove's gilded bronze *Eagle* (the iconic symbol of America), with a wing span of over seven feet, alit on a golden rock on Royal Poinciana Way (see fig. 185). The Bicentennial *Eagle* had arrived via funds raised by the town after a budget was approved, and the statue was unveiled on July 4, 1976. Grove (1912-2002), who with his sculptor

wife moved to West Palm Beach in the late 1960s, had already established a remarkable career before relocating south. He worked in Washington as an engraver and designed several monuments as well as a gold congressional medal presented by Pres. John F. Kennedy to actor Bob Hope. Grove's wife, Jean Donner Grove, provided artwork in Palm Beach County as well.[11]

By the 1970s the Norton Gallery acquired works by Louise Nevelson, Andy Warhol, Pierre Bonnard, and George Luks. Prominent Palm Beach art collector Dorothy Rautbord became president of the board of directors and gave the Norton significant artworks. In 1977 Ann Weaver Norton,

Fig. 184. Isamu Noguchi, *Intetra,* 1976, stainless steel, The Society of the Four Arts, 76.2, gift of Ziuta and Joseph James Akston. (© 2015 The Isamu Noguchi Foundation and Garden Museum, New York / Artists Rights Society [ARS], New York, photograph by author, courtesy The Society of the Four Arts, Palm Beach)

Fig. 185. Edward Ryneal Grove, *Eagle,* 1976, Royal Poinciana Way, Palm Beach. (Courtesy Eric Grove, photograph by author)

who had begun to create a sculpture garden in her backyard in the mid 1960s, endowed her house packed with her art and garden as a West Palm Beach legacy. The Ann Norton Sculpture Gardens filled with monumental shapes of gateways (see fig. 186), towers, and native figures made of stone or brick can be visited today. Her former home has been the venue of several exhibitions of works by other artists as well.[12]

In the interim, Edna Hibel Plotkin (who used the name "Edna Hibel" professionally) exhibited at her Worth Avenue gallery beginning in 1968, and the Edna Hibel Museum was established in 1977, formerly located in Royal Poinciana Plaza. Hibel was the recipient of multiple honors. Her highly decorative, sweet figures of children, with a colorful palette highlighted in gold, and her innovative implementation of stone lithography led to many prestigious international awards. Her collectors included Queen Elizabeth II and several museums throughout the world.[13]

In 1979 Palm Beach Galleries closed due to burgeoning rents and a "growing disinterest in its board of directors." Wally Findlay Galleries remained on Worth Avenue, exhibiting primarily works by the finest of impressionists, postimpressionists, and moderns and fanciful artists such as Chilean-born fantasy painter Gustavo Novoa. The gallery also exhibited American artists inspired by the French, such as Texas-born Huldah Cherry Jeffe (1901-2001).[14]

At the dawn of 1980 The Society of the Four Arts continued to grow. From 1979 to 1980, fashion designer/painter/sculptor Philip Hulitar designed a sculpture garden on land previously acquired by the Four Arts in the 1960s. Two of the many sculptures in the idyllic natural space are the endearing *Reaching* (fig. 187), by Philadelphia-born artist Edward Fenno Hoffman III (1916-1991) and the playful, lithesome *Giraffes* (fig. 188), by Henry Mitchell (1915-1980), incised in a modernistic way to indicate their spots. Mitchell studied at Temple University's Tyler School of Art. His lyrical animal sculpture was influenced by Marino Marini. Hoffman studied at the Pennsylvania Academy of the Fine Arts and was influenced by Paul Manship, whom he assisted. So important to Hoffman's oeuvre, *Reaching* highlighted the cover of a 1985 book devoted to the sculptor's work.[15]

By the 1980s art critic Gary Schwan had taken up the challenge of journalists before him and kept art lovers in the Palm Beaches aware of the latest cultural news as well as

Fig. 186. Ann Weaver Norton, *Gateway Number 3,* 1974. (Courtesy Ann Norton Sculpture Gardens, Inc.)

Fig. 187. Edward Fenno Hoffman III (1916-1991), *Reaching,* 1963, bronze, the Philip Hulitar Sculpture Garden, The Society of the Four Arts, 90.1, in memory of Margaret Richardson Trout, given by the family. (© Estate of Edward Fenno Hoffman III, photograph by author, courtesy The Society of the Four Arts, Palm Beach)

Fig. 188. Henry Mitchell (1915-1980), *Giraffes,* 1959, bronze, the Philip Hulitar Sculpture Garden, The Society of the Four Arts, 81.15, gift of Mrs. Eileen Zantzinger Holberg in memory of her husband Alfred Zantzinger (© Estate of Henry Mitchell, photograph by author, courtesy The Society of the Four Arts, Palm Beach)

local art history. In that decade the extraordinary amount of masterful art treasures held in private Palm Beach homes had multiplied. In fact, the legacy of all who encouraged the visual arts remained vibrant, with new members joining their ranks. Alice De Lamar lived until 1983, continuing to support the arts even beyond her death; for example, she bequeathed over a million dollars to her longtime friend, actress Eva Le Gallienne.[16]

In 1986 the Norton Gallery and School of Art discontinued its art school and changed its name to the Norton Museum of Art. To fill the need for artistic instruction, artists, teachers, and civic sponsors joined forces to form the Armory Art Center in 1987. Most prominent among the contributors were Robert and Mary Montgomery.[17]

Other art philanthropists in town included A. Alfred Taubman, owner of Sotheby's and collector of major artworks, such as those by Thomas Gainsborough and Amedeo Modigliani. Several masterpieces were displayed in his Palm Beach home, including Martin Johnson Heade's *The Great Florida Sunset,* which Heade sold to Henry Flagler in the 1880s and which later hung at Whitehall for years before Taubman purchased it at auction in 1988.

Artists in Palm Beach by the 1980s included Helmut Koller, born in Austria. He had photographed internationally-celebrated subjects such as Rudolph Nureyev and succeeded as a fine painter as well; his first art exhibition, entitled *Homage to Egon Schiele,* featured various media applied over photographs and engendered critical praise.

In the 1990s Koller became absorbed in depicting colorful portrayals of animal life, which has earned the artist a worldwide audience. His wife, Helga Wagner, has designed desirable pearl, shell, and coral jewelry.[18]

Portraitist Ralph Wolfe Cowan also made an impact on Palm Beach visual arts in the late twentieth century. When the young artist first came to town in the 1950s, he visited Channing Hare at his studio and asked for his advice. Hare curtly replied, "Get out of town." In reaction to such a rude response, Cowan left Palm Beach and didn't return to until 1979. By that time he had filled his résumé with the most famous names in history, including Elizabeth Taylor and Princess Grace. In 1989 Cowan painted Donald Trump's portrait, which hangs in his Mar-a-Lago Club in Palm Beach. A robust Trump is portrayed not in a traditional suit and tie but wearing a tennis sweater, reflecting the island's relaxed yet chic atmosphere.[19]

As for art organizations formed in the late twentieth century, one of the greatest artistic boons to the area is the Cultural Council of Palm Beach County, its establishment in 1978 led by generous and ubiquitous arts philanthropist Alexander W. Dreyfoos. Throughout the 1980s, '90s, and beyond, it has continued to flourish. Also, West Palm Beach formed the Art in Public Places program in 1987, integral to beautifying the city. These major forces led by art-boosting individuals served to secure a glowing future, endowing an assurance of support for artists, museums, and educational institutions.

Chapter Ten
1990-2015: An Enduring Legacy

With a solid, thriving visual arts foundation in place, the Palm Beaches' list of painters, sculptors, artisans, photographers, art supporters, collectors, and dealers has burgeoned since 1990. In that decade Alexander Dreyfoos greatly advanced an existing school of the arts in West Palm Beach, which since has been renamed the Alexander W. Dreyfoos School of the Arts and includes the visual arts in its curriculum. By 2013, younger children could attend the Center for Creative Education in West Palm Beach, which also enhances education through the arts.

During the 1990s, photographers Mort Kaye, Lucien Capehart, and Bob Davidoff remained busy photographing the rich and famous, such as Sylvester Stallone and Donald Trump (see fig. 189), as well as those who were unknown. No matter who posed before them, these artists with a camera made their subjects feel special, which led to a successful result.

The Norton Museum of Art more than doubled its size under the direction and fundraising capabilities of Christina Orr-Cahall. Reopening in 1997, one of its ceilings featured the work of glass sculptor Dale Chihuly. Under the leadership of Hope Alswang since 2010, the Norton has included many more photography exhibitions and has re-introduced its Old Master collection. Alswang has also continued the legacy of E. Robert Hunter and Richard Madigan by bringing major exhibitions of American art to the Palm Beaches. In addition, the Norton Museum of Art has been supported by numerous philanthropic organizations, including the Sydelle and Arthur I. Meyer Endowment Fund, Priscilla and

Fig. 189. *Sylvester Stallone and Donald Trump,* 1997. (Davidoff Studios, photograph by Bob Davidoff)

John Richman Endowment for American Art, Milton and Sheila Fine Endowment for Contemporary Art, Mr. and Mrs. Hamish Maxwell Exhibition Endowment, and Dr. Henry and Lois Foster Endowment for the Exhibition of Contemporary Art. Hopefully the flourishing organization, as in its history, will again honor regional artists from the past, a practice that has become highly effective in many other successful museums.

Whitehall, rescued from demolition in the 1950s, became the Henry Morrison Flagler Museum and has continued to inspire with resplendent exhibitions of Gilded-Age visual arts. Under the executive directorship of John Blades (who retired in February 2016) and chief curator Tracy Kamerer, Henry Flagler's artistic legacy remains essential to not only Palm Beachers but to the legions of international visitors who marvel at the museum's treasures. On December 11, 2010, a monumental statue of Flagler was unveiled on Royal Poinciana Way, donated by Flagler's great-grandson, G. F. Robert Hanke (see fig. 190). Like the monument to Elisha Newton Dimick, Flagler stands as if welcoming visitors and residents to Palm Beach. It replicated a Flagler monument in St. Augustine inscribed "Roma 1902 C.J.R." by the same artist whom Flagler's third wife, Mary Lily, commissioned to carve a marble bust of Flagler now at the museum.[1]

In 2008 the Richard and Pat Johnson Palm Beach County History Museum opened in West Palm Beach, featuring, among its many fascinating exhibits from the Historical Society of Palm Beach County's vast offerings, the visual arts. The Johnsons' generosity was similar to other philanthropists, such as Fitz Eugene Dixon and his wife, Edith, who helped engender the Campus on the Lake's Dixon Education Building at The Society of the Four Arts. Run by the indefatigable, innovative Molly Charland, it brims with diverse cultural programs including fine art and crafts classes, lectures, and demonstrations. The Four Arts's talented curator and executive vice president Nancy Mato, who has mounted numerous exhibitions since the late 1980s, has succeeded in carrying on the tradition of

Fig. 190. Henry Morrison Flagler Statue, Palm Beach. (Photograph © Flagler Museum, Palm Beach, Florida)

PALM BEACH VISUAL ARTS

Four Arts excellence. Its former director, Ervin Duggan, improved the arts center in several ways until he retired in 2014. Duggan's succeeding director, David W. Breneman, has extended the legacy of cultural leaders before him by continuing to make the Four Arts vital to the community.

In the twenty-first century, the Cultural Council of Palm Beach County has grown and assisted countless artists and artisans. The dynamic Rena Blades has led the organization towards the future, and it remains a primary force behind many arts organizations, extending the torch of culture first ignited in the nineteenth century. Many supporters of the Cultural Council include women, such as Irene J. Karp, Roe Green, and Jean Sharf, who seem to have the same resilient, aesthetic philosophy as feminine cultural leaders of the nineteenth century and early twentieth century.

West Palm Beach's Art in Public Places program has continued to enhance the city with several art objects, including the abstract *Arrival,* a 2009 twenty-five-foot stainless steel and glass sculpture by Ulrich Pakker, and *The Wave,* 2009, (fig. 191) by Arizona artist Barbara Grygutis. The monumental aluminum and computer-modulated, kinetic LED light sculpture, located at the Palm Beach Convention Center, is an integral part of West Palm Beach's main thoroughfare, Okeechobee Boulevard. As the sculptor has stated, *The Wave* "was designed to be completely integrated with the existing architecture, creating an elegant, dynamic canopy over the main ballroom balcony entry. Five semi-transparent forms evoke the roll of waves as they spring off the façade. . . . At night, gentle, undulating wave/tide patters of brilliant light emanate from the sculpture. During the day the sculpture displays ever shifting moiré patterns interactive with the viewer."[2]

Sculptor Marsha Montoya enhanced the artistic topography of the Palm Beaches and helped the city commemorate Henry Rolfs when she created his monument (see fig. 192), installed in 1996 on Okeechobee Boulevard in West Palm Beach. Rolfs had dreamed of a vibrant city,

Fig. 191. Barbara Grygutis, *The Wave,* West Palm Beach Convention Center. (Courtesy Barbara Grygutis, photograph by Dana Hoff)

Fig. 192. Marsha Montoya, Henry Rolfs Monument, installed 1996, Okeechobee Boulevard, West Palm Beach. (Courtesy Marsha Montoya)

and his extensive land purchases led to the modernization of the downtown area, so it is fitting that his likeness is represented with arms extended as if welcoming those who enter the urban hub. Montoya, who also designs unique jewelry, received a BFA from Pratt Institute and an MFA from the School of Fine Arts of San Fernando in Madrid, Spain. Her works have been collected internationally.[3]

There are so many other artists living and working in Palm Beach or West Palm Beach it is impossible to list them all. The lovely Sandra Thompson, one of the island's most popular painters, studied art in New York at the Cooper Union and was employed at *Redbook* as their art buyer. Her husband, David, came to the Palm Beaches as a four-year-old in 1925. He and Sandra purchased a home in Palm Beach County in the early 1980s and then rented a home in Palm Beach in the 1990s. Falling in love with its natural and designed beauty, Thompson began her "Palm Beach Collection" of exquisitely painted scenes of local buildings and nature with an impressionist palette and keen attention to light and shadow (see fig. 193). She has also written several books and contributed countless covers to the *Palm Beach Real Estate Guide*. In 2014 the BMO Bank gave Sandra a major retrospective attended by legions of her fans.[4]

Luis Montoya, born in 1950, received an MFA at the School of Fine Arts of San Fernando and exhibited at the Norton Museum of Art and numerous other venues. His prizes include the Ziuta and Joseph James Akston Foundation award among many other honors. His partner, Leslie Ortiz (born in 1957), took instruction at the School of the Museum of Fine Arts in Boston and also has earned awards. The team's work is in the collections of the Norton Museum of Art, The Society of The Four Arts, and several other art institutions, and they have continued to exhibit extensively on a local and international basis. They are most known for their beautiful, sleek, oversized bronze sculptures of vegetables and fruit.[5]

Part raconteur, humorist, curator, author, editor, and 100%

Fig. 193. Sandra Thompson, *Villa on Peruvian Avenue, Palm Beach*. (Courtesy Sandra Thompson, © Sandra Thompson)

genius, leading artist Bruce Helander has been an integral part of the area's art world for decades. His numerous, prestigious awards include being a White House Fellow of the National Endowment for the Arts and earning a fellowship from the South Florida Cultural Consortium. Born in Kansas in 1947, Helander received a master's degree at the Rhode Island School of Design, and since then over fifty museums have clamored for his work. He has been well-known for the art of collage and was inducted into the Florida Artists Hall of Fame in 2014.[6]

Helander at one time lived in a charming house brimming with antiques and collectibles located on Root Trail, the very street where Daisy Erb and the early 1900s Palm Beach art colony painted. Helander remarked that many other artists have had studios on Root Trail, "the nucleus" of the Palm Beach art community. The creative group would meet at sundown and stroll down the narrow lane to the ocean, no doubt for inspiration and relaxation. They included Barbara "Binny" Jolly, who won the National Still Life Award from The Society of the Four Arts, and painter and photographer Paul Aho. Aho graduated from Florida State University, received an MFA from the University of South Florida, and became a dean at the Armory Art Center. He has also received honors including the Ubertalli Award for Artistic Achievement from the Cultural Council of Palm Beach County.[7]

Helander also reminisced about artists who stayed at his house, such as "Larry Poons, Robert Zakanitch, Dan Rizzie, Dale Chihuly, Todd Oldham, Richard Merkin, and Kenneth Noland." Other visitors included "Robert Rauschenberg, James Rosenquist, John Chamberlain, Jules Olitzki, and Duane Hanson" (whose *Young Worker* is a popular feature of the Norton Museum of Art). Helander added that "Henry Geldzahler, [Andy] Warhol's great friend and former curator at the Met stayed with me for a month . . . while he was writing my book *Curious Collage*. He would get a call from David Hockney on our 'land line' nearly every day. It was fun and inspiring."[8]

Helander's 2015 *Stick Figures Walking* (fig. 194) is an

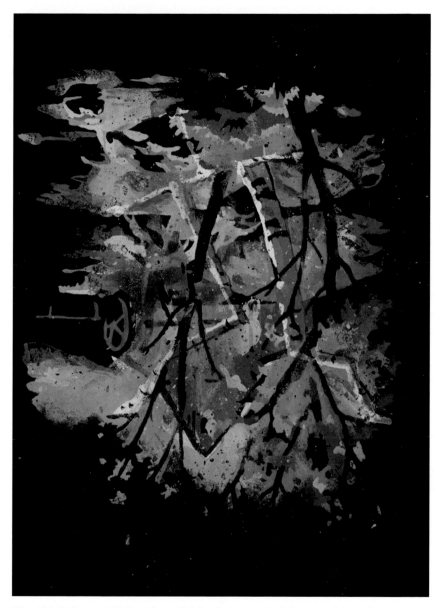

Fig. 194. Bruce Helander, *Stick Figures Walking*, 13 ½ x 9 ½ inches, original acrylic on black velvet board with printed background. (Courtesy Bruce Helander)

interesting, haunting, and thought-provoking addition to his oeuvre; yet it's not without whimsy. By cleverly flipping the mind's and reality's perspective, he morphs nature into supernatural figures in motion.

The petite Curtis Kelly arrived in Palm Beach in 1982 and lived in town until 1991, when she moved across the bridge to West Palm Beach. Kelly, who studied at the Armory Arts Center for many years, exhibited *Candy is Dandy* (fig. 195) at a posh Palm Beach gallery in 2007 and sold it on opening night. Inspired by Ogden Nash's quip "Candy is dandy but liquor is quicker," Kelly created a brilliant study in color contrast with whimsical highlights and subtle sexual overtones. She has since simplified forms towards the abstract but maintains a clever sense of color and a unique approach to the visual arts.

Other local artists include Sam Perry, a renowned teacher at the Armory Arts Center and adjunct professor at Palm Beach Atlantic University. The Art in Public Places program and the Norton Museum of Art are among those organizations that have collected Perry's work. Artist Miroslav Antic has also taught at the Armory Art Center as well as Palm Beach State College. After studying in Belgrade, Yugoslavia, at its Academy of Fine Arts, Antic exhibited on a national basis and has won many fellowships and other awards. Another artist and teacher at the Armory Art Center was Richard Frank, who died too young in April 2014. Frank, who obtained a master of fine arts degree from Temple University's Tyler School of Art, was also the recipient of many prizes, including a New England Foundation for the Arts Fellowship. A curator of education at both the Norton Museum of Art and at the Boca Raton Museum of Art, Frank was also a guest lecturer at The Society of the Four Arts. The Four Arts, Boca Raton Museum of Art, Norton Museum of Art, and some thirty other art institutions hold examples of Frank's work. One can understand why by viewing his masterful *Into the Mystic* (fig. 196), which mixes meticulous realism with surrealism. Yet another artist, Thomas Tribby,

Fig. 195. Curtis Kelly, *Candy is Dandy,* collection of Edward and Deborah Pollack.

who had the honor of exhibiting at the Paris Salon, paints lyrical scenes inspired by South Florida. He has also won the coveted Stars of Design award from the Design Center of the Americas.[9]

An artist with a historical Palm Beach connection is William P. "Billy" Rayner, Emily Rayner's son, whom Alice De Lamar nurtured. After growing up in Palm Beach, Rayner became a fine watercolorist whose worldwide sojourns inspired his art book published in 2013.

From 2000-2015, the number of art collectors in the Palm Beaches has burgeoned beyond description. One of the most significant collections of contemporary art resides in Whitespace, the private museum and gallery within the home of Elayne Mordes. Elayne and her late husband, Marvin, started collecting art in the 1980s. Elayne continued

Fig. 196. Richard Frank, *Into the Mystic.* (Courtesy George Bolge, Museum of Art, Deland, Florida)

her husband's legacy and her own support of art by making their space accessible to art lovers and funding the visual arts through Community Foundation, which has given grants in the area since the 1970s. Another major collector, William Koch, has been one of Palm Beach's most avid art lovers. In 2012, The Society of the Four Arts displayed his impressive collection of western art, which included the only known tintype of Billy the Kid, a Thomas Moran masterpiece (see fig. 197), and the work of Henry F. Farny, the very artist who taught Palm Beach's pioneer illustrator, George Wells Potter. The show was one of the most popular exhibitions in Four Arts history.

Mary Hulitar, Philip Hulitar's widow, carried on the tradition of art philanthropy by her activity as a trustee of The Society of the Four Arts. Additions to the Philip Hulitar Sculpture Garden include *Allies* (fig. 198) by sculptor Lawrence Holofcener, which the Four Arts acquired through a successful fundraising campaign. A realistic piece

Fig. 197. Thomas Moran, *Green River, Wyoming,* 1896, exhibited at The Society of the Four Arts, 2012, former collection of Bill Koch.

portraying Franklin Delano Roosevelt chatting amiably with Winston Churchill, *Allies* is as popular in Palm Beach as its version in London. Holofcener, before exhibiting for the first time at the Gibbes Museum of Art in South Carolina in 1979, was a Broadway and television songwriter, a celebrated actor, and a novelist and poet.[10]

Another beautiful complement to the garden is *The Bond*, 2010 (fig. 199), by David H. Turner, born in 1961. Specializing in wildlife subjects, Turner has worked with his father in creating numerous fine examples from their Virginia studio. *The Bond* is a fresh, tender, and balletic approach to the subject of leaping dolphins

Palm Beach galleries who have joined the venerable Wally

Fig. 199. David H. Turner, *The Bond*, 2010, bronze, the Philip Hulitar Sculpture Garden, The Society of the Four Arts, 2010.1, gift of Zita Hawley Wright. (Photograph by author, courtesy David H. Turner and The Society of the Four Arts, Palm Beach)

Findlay Galleries (led by James Borynack) include Gasiunasen Gallery, Russeck Gallery, Edward and Deborah Pollack Fine Art, Gallery Biba, A. B. Levy Gallery, Taglialatella Galleries, John H. Surovek Gallery, Holden Luntz Gallery, Mark Borghi Fine Art, Gavlak Gallery, Liman Studio Gallery (owned by artist Ellen Liman), Arcature Fine Art, Ashley John Gallery, Brintz Galleries, and DTR Modern. West Palm Beach galleries include Nicole Henry Fine Art, Mary Woerner Fine Arts, Habatat Gallery (specializing in art glass), Suzanne Connors Fine Art, and ArtHouse 429. Critic Jan Sjostrom has carried on the tradition of writers before her to encourage and chronicle the visual arts.

Fig. 198. Lawrence Holofcener, *Allies,* 1992, bronze, the Philip Hulitar Sculpture Garden, The Society of the Four Arts. (Photograph by Paul Kaufman, courtesy Lawrence Holofcener, Sculptor, and The Society of the Four Arts, Palm Beach)

Local artisans include McMow Art Glass studios, who have created jewel-like windows in and around the island of Palm Beach, and the gifted Detra Kay, designer of artistic jewelry (see fig. 200). Kay, who studied art at the University of Florida and Oglethorpe University, has also sculpted dolls and achieved other artistic success. Like Daisy Erb a century before her, Kay's clients include many fashionable women. She shows an aesthetic sensitivity in exotic combinations of subject and materials with a strong nod to the Far East, embraced by so many aesthetes in the nineteenth and early twentieth century. Kay commented: "All my art has always been influenced by Asian art. I've always felt I was an Asian in a previous life. Every art teacher I've ever had has commented on my Asian leaning." Another Palm Beach jewelry designer was Judith "Judy" Murat Grubman, whose daughter Robin Grubman is adept at shell

Fig. 201. John J. Lopinot, *Loggerhead Sea Turtle in a Hurry on the Palm Beach Reef.* (Courtesy John Lopinot Photography LLC, © 2015 John J. Lopinot, www.johnjlopinot.com)

Fig. 200. Detra Kay, magnetic dragonfly brooch. (Courtesy Detra Kay Jewelry Design)

design and has taught this skill at The Society of the Four Arts.[11]

Society photographers working in the early twenty-first century have included Harry Benson, who first came to Palm Beach in the 1970s to photograph socialites for *People* magazine. Benson became hugely successful in Palm Beach, capturing the beautiful and distinguished at their best. Another visual artist with a camera, John J. Lopinot, had a career as a West Palm Beach photojournalist and ever since, when not traveling the world, has let Palm Beach's inspiration guide him to explore the coral reef off its shores and create magical photographs of undersea turtles (see fig. 201). Lopinot has also instructed at The Society of the Four Arts.

Mort Kaye passed away in 2013, but his son, Corby, has continued the Kaye tradition of fine photography. Bob Davidoff's legacy of excellence has remained alive with his son, Daryl. Daryl's photograph of a Palm Beach sunset on Lake Trail portrays the romantic beauty of the day's afterglow (see fig. 202). The peaceful scene is dominated by a majestic kapok tree, planted from seed around 1890 by Palm Beach pioneer Edmund Munger Brelsford, who owned the property. It is just south of Whitehall and just north of where Laura Woodward lived and painted afterglows more than one hundred years ago.[12]

The Garden Club of Palm Beach has continued to devote their extraordinary efforts to beautifying the town through artistry. When Palm Beach celebrated its centennial during the 2010-2011 season, the club presented a colossal living artwork derived from 10,000 plants placed on an 840 square foot wall at the corner of Worth Avenue and County Road (see fig. 203). It is one of the highlights of Palm Beach and reflects contemporary art through a natural medium.[13]

Fig. 202. *Sunset, Palm Beach.* (Davidoff Studios, photograph by Daryl Davidoff)

Fig. 203. The Garden Club of Palm Beach, *Living Wall,* 150 Worth Avenue, Palm Beach. (Photography by author)

Today the visual arts in the Palm Beaches still inspire those from around the world who live in and visit the resort area. Stunning exhibitions occur at The Society of the Four Arts, the Norton Museum of Art, the Cultural Council of Palm Beach County, and the Armory Art Center, as well as in galleries, lively art fairs, and banks. Countless creative people share the color, light, and beauty of Palm Beach in the language of the visual arts. Because of past souls passing the torch of culture to present supporters who will carry it forth, this tropical artistic community will endure.

Fig. 204. Addison Mizner, *Finish,* from Addison Mizner, Oliver Herford, and Ethel Watts Mumford Grant, *The Altogether New Cynic's Calendar of Revised Wisdom for 1907* (San Francisco and New York: Paul Elder, 1907), last page (un-paginated).

Notes

Chapter One

1. Drawing by Potter inscribed "Mechanics Institute, Life Class, November, 1874"; Farny to Potter, June 5, ca. 1873, George Wells Potter Papers, HSPBC; "Mr. H. F. Farny," *Cincinnati Daily Gazette*, October 21, 1872; David Willson, "Putting 135 Years in Perspective," *Palm Beach Daily News,* October 20, 2010, http://cartoonistry.blog.palmbeachdailynews.com/2010/10/20/putting-135-years-in-perspective/, accessed May 30, 2014.

2. James Alexander Henshall, *Camping and Cruising in Florida* (Cincinnati: Robert Clarke, 1884), v.

3. "Mrs. Percy Hadley," Oral History, King Library, The Society of the Four Arts and HSPBC; Deborah C. Pollack, *Laura Woodward: The Artist Behind the Innovator Who Developed Palm Beach* (Palm Beach: Blue Heron Press with the HSPBC, 2009), 170.

4. Richard A. Marconi and Debi Murray with the HSPBC, *Palm Beach* (Charleston: Arcadia, 2009), 18; Frances Gillmor, "Paintings of Palm Beach County Art Club, Display are Admirable in Competence and Technique," *Palm Beach Times,* March 19, 1924.

5. "Charles J. Clarke," *Juno Tropical Sun*, May 24, 1893; Charles John Clarke Jr. to Judge James R. Knott; Clarke's obituary, 1899, Clarke Family Papers, HSPBC.

6. Pollack, *Woodward*, 107, 109, 122-127.

7. Pollack, *Woodward*, 107, 109, 122, 140n126; Gary R. Libby, *Reflections II, Watercolors of Florida 1835-2000 from the Collection of Cici and Hyatt Brown* (Daytona Beach: Museum of Arts and Sciences, 2012), 58-60; The Museum of Arts and Sciences, Daytona Beach, Florida, "Reflections II, Watercolors of Florida 1835-2000 from the Collection of Cici and Hyatt Brown, November 13, 2011-2012," in *Arts and Sciences*, Summer 2011, 27; Museum of Arts & Sciences, Daytona Beach, http://www.moas.org/RII.html (accessed March 2012); watercolor sketch, 1889.

8. Pollack, *Woodward*, 107, 109, 122; Woodward to Winifred Clarke Anthony, July 9, 1918, Clarke Anthony Papers, HSPBC; Frances Gillmor, "History of Palm Beach County Art Club, One of Fascinating Chapters in Annals of the City," *Palm Beach Times,* February 17, 1924; Maybelle Mann, *Art in Florida, 1564-1945* (Sarasota: Pineapple Press, 1999), 123.

9. Deborah C. Pollack, *Visual Art and the Urban Evolution of the New South* (Columbia: University of South Carolina Press, 2015), 251-52; Pollack, *Woodward*, 79, 124, 127, 138n2, 141n40; Mildred Parker Seese, "Artist from Mt. Hope," *Times Herald-Record*, October 29, 1960, Seese Papers, Goshen Historical Society.

10. Pollack, *Woodward*, 83, 92, 96-97, 136.

11. Pollack, *Woodward*, 125, 128; "Local News," *East Coast Advocate*, July 3, 1891; "The Studios," *Tatler*, February 6, 1892; Robert McCormick, "Diary," May 16, 1891, HistoryMiami.

Chapter Two

1. Deborah C. Pollack, *Laura Woodward: The Artist Behind the Innovator Who Developed Palm Beach* (Palm Beach: Blue Heron Press with the HSPBC, 2009), 136; Mildred Parker Seese, "Artist from Mount Hope," *Times Herald-Record*, October 29, 1960, Seese Papers, Goshen Historical Society; "Palm Beach 30 years Ago A Far Cry from that of Today," *Palm Beach Daily News,* February 8, 1920; Daisy Erb, "Data for 'History of Palm Beach County'" (unpublished manuscript), Art and Artists Files, HSPBC; Frances Gillmor, "History of Palm Beach County Art Club, One of Fascinating Chapters in Annals of the City," *Palm Beach Times,* February 17, 1924.

2. Erb, "Data;" Pollack, *Woodward*, 195; Woodward to Winifred Clarke Anthony, July 9, 1918, Clarke Anthony Papers, HSPBC; "Palm Beach Attracts Artists," *Palm Beach Daily News*, March 31, 1936.

3. Enoch Root, Papers, HSPBC; Enoch Root, "Photography as Fine Art," *The Photographic News*, August 18, 1888, 521-22.

4. Edward Ledyard Russell, *Lake Worth* (New York: Ambrotype, 1896); Pollack, *Woodward*, 149; "Russell, Edward L.," *Wellsboro Agitator*, April 16, 1902.

5. M. Thomas & Sons' Galleries, *Catalogue of the Herzog Collection Paintings*, December 5, 6, 7, and 8, 1899; Florence N. Levy, ed., *American Art Annual* (New York: American Art Annual, 1903-4), 36.

6. Charles H. Caffyn, "Some American Sculptors," *The Critic*, April 1905, 337; Erica Donnis, "Pan of Rohallion," *Antiques and Fine Art*, http://www.antiquesandfineart.com/articles/article.cfm?request=362 (accessed November 4, 2014).

7. Caffyn, "Some American Sculptors," 337; Donnis, "Pan of Rohallion"; "Lydia B. Mann and Pan's Garden Honored," *The Preservation Foundation Newsletter*, November 1993, 1-2.

8. "Who We Are," Church of the Transfiguration, http://www.littlechurch.org/#/who-we-are (accessed October 17, 2014); Oral Sumner Coad and Edwin Mims, Jr., *Pageant of America: The American Stage* (New Haven: Yale University Press, 1929), 195-219; Pollack, *Woodward*, 176.

9. Lynn Lasseter Drake and Richard A. Marconi with the HSPBC, *West Palm Beach, 1893-1950* (Mount Pleasant, SC: Arcadia, 2006), 33; Frost to James R. Knott, February 13, 1962, Helen Van Hoy Smith, *Miami Herald*, June 29, 1969; "Tribute to Joseph Jefferson," *Fredericksburg (Virginia) Daily Star*, April 25, 1905; Pollack, *Woodward*, 176, 188.

10. Ernest Histed business card, Histed Papers, HSPBC; "Histed Shows Rare Old Photographs," *Palm Beach Daily News*, January 31, 1934.

11. Richard A. Marconi and Debi Murray with the HSPBC, *Palm Beach* (Charleston: Arcadia, 2009), 66; "The Histed Family," *Beacon News*, June 30, 1966; Histed advertisement, *Palm Beach Daily News*, March 22, 1912; "Histed Shows Rare Old Photographs."

12. "Histed Shows Rare Old Photographs"; "Millionaire J. D. Biddle Weds," *Chicago Daily Inter Ocean*, June 12, 1895; "Wintering at the Seashore," *Palm Beach Daily News*, January 30, 1902; "Catches in the Social Stream," *Palm Beach Daily News*, February 19, 1915.

13. "Richard Resler," State Archives of Florida, Florida Memory, http://www.floridamemory.com/items/show/153287 (accessed November 5, 2014).

14. "The Styx: Removal," and "Thomas Leroy Jefferson," Palm Beach County History Online, HSPBC, http://www.pbchistoryonline.org/page/the-styx (accessed November 5, 2014) and http://www.pbchistoryonline.org/page/thomas-l-jefferson (accessed June 17, 2015); Pollack, *Woodward*, 146, 196-97.

15. Tracy Kamerer, email to author, October 2, 2015.

16. Theodore E. Stebbins, *The Life and Work of Martin Johnson Heade: A Critical Analysis and Catalogue Raisonné* (New Haven: Yale University Press, 2000), 149-50, 194; Deborah C. Pollack, *Felix de Crano: Forgotten Artist of the Flagler Colony* (St. Augustine: Lightner Museum, 2014), 13.

17. Sandra Barghini, *Henry M. Flagler's Paintings Collection: The Taste of a Gilded Age Collector* (Palm Beach: Henry Morrison Flagler Museum, 2002), 17; Kamerer, email to author, October 9, 2015; "Art Notes," *Art Journal*, 1882, 96; Elán M. Ward, "From the University Archives—This Week in UNCW History: 'Young Girl Defending Herself Against Eros' Returns to UNCW, Feb. 12, 2001," University of North Carolina Wilmington, http://library.uncw.edu/archives_special/spotlights/university-archives-week-uncw-history-famous-painting-comes-home-uncw-2001 (accessed November 21, 2014).

18. Denise Allen, "59. William-Adolphe Bouguereau: *Young Girl Defending Herself Against Eros*," in *Masterpieces of Painting in the J. Paul Getty Museum*, 5th ed., J. Paul Getty Museum (Los Angeles: Getty Publications, 2003), 101.

19. Federal Writers' Project of the Work Projects Administration for the State of Florida, *Florida: A Guide to the Southernmost State* (Tallahassee: State of Florida Department of Instruction, 1939), 160.

20. Barghini, *Flagler's Paintings Collection*, 32.

21. Pollack, *Woodward*, 176, 188; "Mrs. Cragin Dies at Jacksonville," *Palm Beach Post*, February 6, 1931; "Music Room," Henry Morrison Flagler Museum, http://www.flaglermuseum.us/music-room (accessed March 31, 2015).

22. Peter H. Falk, ed., "Finney, Harry," *Who was Who in American*

Art: 1564-1975 (Madison, CT: Soundview Press, 1999), 1: 1123; Lois Marie Fink, *American Art at the Nineteenth-Century Paris Salons* (New York: Cambridge University Press, 1990), 342-43.

23. Amelia K. Buckley to HSPBC c/o Flagler Museum, August 1, 1962, Bradley Beach Club Papers, HSPBC; Marconi and Murray, *Palm Beach*, 108-9; Jeff Nillson, "Kentucky Derby," *Saturday Evening Post*, May 2, 2009, http://www.saturdayeveningpost. com/2009/05/02/history/post-perspective/kentucky-derby. html (accessed October 15, 2014).

24. "Exhibit by Daisy E. Erb," *Palm Beach Daily News*, January 20, 1943; Berthe E. Neil, "City Possesses Gifted Artist in Person of Daisy Erb," *Palm Beach Post-Times*, January 6, 1935; clipping, *Palm Beach Post*, May 2, 1925, HSPBC.

25. Joseph Hollenbeck advertisement, *Palm Beach Daily News*, February 10, 1969; "Hollenbeck Studio Open Till June," *Palm Beach Daily News*, April 2, 1947; J. V. Davis, "J. J. Hollenbeck," *Highlights of the Palm Beaches*, 1952; "Catches in the Social Stream," *Palm Beach Daily News*, February 5, 1948; Justine Hartman, "Hollenbeck Paintings are Art for Pure Art's Sake," clipping, March 18, 1961, HSPBC; "Athletic Club to Entertain Palm Beach Organizations With Reception, Exhibition," *Palm Beach Post*, May 2, 1928.

Chapter Three

1. "Exhibit by Daisy E. Erb," *Palm Beach Daily News*, January 30, 1943; Berthe E. Neil, "City Possesses Gifted Artist in Person of Daisy Erb," *Palm Beach Post-Times*, January 6, 1935; "Individuality—A Keynote to a Young Woman's Success," *California's Magazine, Edition Deluxe*, vol. 2 (San Francisco: California's Magazine Co., 1916), 187-89; Don Anderson, email to author, July 28, 2011, regarding John Anderson's entry on "Find a Grave: Daisy Erb," http://www.findagrave.com/cgi-bin/ fg.cgi?page=gr&GRid=49178958, accessed July 28, 2011.

2. "Individuality"; Anderson email.

3. "News and Notes," *Bulletin of Photography*, January 1-25, 1913, 26; Deborah C. Pollack, *Laura Woodward: The Artist Behind the Innovator Who Developed Palm Beach* (Palm Beach: Blue Heron Press with the HSPBC, 2009), 228; "Ben Austrian Dies Suddenly," *Palm Beach Post*, December 14, 1921; "Career of the Late Ben Austrian," *Palm Beach Post*, December 18, 1921.

4. "Our Cover Portrait and the Hall of Fame," *Portrait*, June 1915, 15; "William Louis Koehne," (advertisement), *Palm Beach Daily News*, February 24, 1915.

5. Addison Mizner, undated memoir manuscript, 62, Addison Mizner Papers, HSPBC; Richard A. Marconi and Debi Murray with the HSPBC, *Palm Beach* (Charleston: Arcadia, 2009), 80; "Architects: Mizner in Palm Beach," HSPBC, http://www. pbchistoryonline.org/page/mizner-in-palm-beach (accessed November 2, 2014).

6. Patricia Jobe Pierce, "The Courageous Jane Peterson," *Fine Art Connoisseur*, January-February 2015, http://www. fineartconnoisseur.com/pages/20613959.php?; Pierce, "Jane Peterson," http://wwww.askart.com (accessed July 7, 2015); Meyer Berger, "The Girl Who Came Here in Second-Hand Dresses Now Walks with Princes," *New York Times*, December 12, 1956; "Woman Artist Dares Obscure Turk Hamlets," *Boston Herald*, March 6, 1920.

7. Daisy Erb, "Art in Palm Beach County," *Palm Beach Post*, December 3, 1922; Pollack, *Woodward*, 235; Frances Gillmor, "History of Palm Beach County Art Club, One of Fascinating Chapters in Annals of the City," *Palm Beach Times*, February 17, 1924; Deborah C. Pollack, *Visual Art and the Urban Evolution of the New South* (Columbia: University of South Carolina Press, 2015), 53, 57, 183, 195, 226, 238, 256-57, 262.

8. Thomas Shields Clarke, "An Artist's Florida," *Country Life*, December 1, 1911, 50.

9. French to Clarke, August 19, 1919, Thomas Shields Clarke Letters, 1875-1920, reel AAA 4235 (illegible frame no.), Archives of American Art, Smithsonian Institution; "Cary T. Grayson to T. S. Clarke, October 9, 1919, Cary T. Grayson Papers, Woodrow Wilson Presidential Library and Museum, Staunton, Virginia.

10. "Contemporary Art at the Academy," *American Magazine of Art*, February 18, 1918, 143.

11. "Riter Tableaus Crown Season at Palm Beach," *New York Tribune*, February 23, 1920; Kingore to Whitney, August 3, 1917, Gertrude Vanderbilt Whitney Papers, Archives of American Art, Smithsonian Institution, General Correspondence, Box 6, Folder 58; Chalfin to Whitney, 1911-1942, Whitney Papers, Box 5, Folder 56; Davidson to Whitney, ca. 1919-ca. 1942, Box 5, Folder 56; "Art at Palm Beach," *American Art News*, March 15, 1919, 2; "In

the Galleries," *International Studio*, April 1919, 66; Pollack, *Visual Art*, 259, 268.

12. Kingore to Whitney, August 3, 1917, Gertrude Vanderbilt Whitney Papers, Archives of American Art, Smithsonian Institution, General Correspondence, Box 6, Folder 58; Chalfin to Whitney, 1911-1942, Whitney Papers, Box 5, Folder 56; Davidson to Whitney, ca. 1919-ca. 1942, Box 5, Folder 56; "Art at Palm Beach"; "In the Galleries"; Pollack, *Visual Art*, 259, 268.

13. "Art at Palm Beach."

14. "National Society of Woman Painters and Sculptors Show Art Exhibition at the Woman's Club," clipping, ca. 1920, HSPBC; "Palm Beach Art League Exhibition," *Palm Beach Daily News*, March 24, 1940; Levy, "National Association of Women Painters and Sculptors," *American Art Annual*, 17: 185.

15. Peter H. Falk, ed., "Heaton, Augustus Goodyear," *Who was Who in American Art: 1564-1975 (Madison, CT: Soundview Press, 1999)*, 2: 1512; James T. White et al, eds., "Heaton, Augustus George," *National Cyclopedia of Biography, Volume Five* (New York: J. T. White, 1907), 315; Berthe Elliott Neil, "Did you Know This?" *Palm Beach Post*, July 3, 1921; "Noted Artist Joins Everglades Club," *Palm Beach Post*, March 11, 1919; "Augustus G. Heaton," New York Times, October 12, 1930.

16. "Heaton, Augustus George"; Neil, "Did you Know This?"

17. "Noted Artist Joins Everglades Club"; Neil, "Did you Know This?"; Heaton to Mrs. Walter B. Fraser, postmarked April 23, 1928, Fraser Family Papers, Fraser family, St. Augustine; John W. Fraser, interview with author, January 14, 2015; "Local Artist's Work Purchased for Display," *Palm Beach Post*, February 7, 1929.

18. De Lamar to *Palm Beach Daily News*, January 31, 1980; De Lamar to Judge James R. Knott, July 17, 1975; De Lamar to Edith Taylor, reprinted in Elisa Rolle, "Alice De Lamar & Eva Le Gallienne," http://reviews-and-ramblings.dreamwidth.org/3260459.html (accessed September 2, 2014); Catherine Fleischner (Mary Benson's grandniece), interview with author, June 28, 2014; "J. R. De Lamar," *American Art News*, December 7, 1918, 4; *Dictionary of American Biography*, vol. 3 (New York: MacMillan, 1977), 210-11; American Art Association, *Illustrated Catalogue of Valuable Paintings Collected by the Late Captain J. R. De Lamar* (New York: American Art Association, January 29, 1920), lots 16-18, 26-32, 40-41, 48, 77.

19. Charles Wieland, "Alice De Lamar," Phillips, Son and Neale, Inc., *Property from the Estate of Alice De Lamar* (New York: Phillips, Son and Neale, Inc., April 11, 1984), 6; Donald Curl, "Introduction," *The Architecture of Addison Mizner* (Mineola, NY: Dover), xvi; Elizabeth Spaulding Titus, "Artists All Over the Joint," *Weston Magazine*, Fall, 2011, 45.

20. American Art Association, *Illustrated Catalogue of Valuable Paintings*, lot 77, inscribed "out"; De Lamar to Pavel Tchelitchew and Charles Henri Ford, undated, Pavel Tchelitchew Papers, Harry Ransom Center, University of Texas at Austin; De Lamar to Lanux, March 15 and 17, 1950, April 1 and 5 (no year), Eyre De Lanux Papers, 1865-1995, Box 2, folder 14, Archives of American Art, Smithsonian Institution; De Lamar to Alex Taylor, undated, Otto Kahn Papers, HSPBC; Ernest Samuels, Jayne Samuels, *Bernard Berenson, the Making of a Legend* (Cambridge, MA: Harvard University Press, 1987), 282; Curl, *The Architecture of Addison Mizner*, xiv-xvi; Titus, "The Educator and the Heiress," *Upper East Side Magazine*, Fall 2011; Helen Sheehy, *Eva Le Gallienne: A Biography* (New York: Knopf, 1996), 128; Titus, "Artists All Over The Joint," 42; Nona Footz, "Alice Doesn't Live Here Anymore," *Venu Magazine*, November-December, 2011, 32.

21. De Lamar to Taylor, undated; De Lamar to unknown recipient, San Francisco, 1911; De Lamar to *Palm Beach Post Times*, March 7, 1971; De Lamar to Alva Johnston, March 14, 1948; De Lamar to Knott, October 7, 1975 and March 5, 1981; Alice De Lamar Papers, HSPBC.

22. De Lamar to Lanux, November 24 (no year), Eyre De Lanux papers, 1865-1995, Box 2, Archives of American Art, Smithsonian Institution; De Lamar to Tchelitchew and Ford, November 30, 1947, and De Lamar to Ford, February 18, 1947, Pavel Tchelitchew Papers, Harry Ransom Center, University of Texas at Austin; Suzy Knickerbocker, "Dinny and Andy Phipps are visiting the Rousseaus," *Palm Beach Post*, March 26, 1970.

23. Robert Livingstone, *Caroline van Hook Bean: The Last of the Impressionists* (Cape Cod: Sandy Shores, Kindle Edition, July 1, 2011), 2750-52, 2887, 3188-90; "Caroline Van H. Bean Believes Portrait Should Conform to Sitter's Idea of Himself," *Palm Beach Post*, February 19, 1928; "Studio Gossip," *American Art News*, May 14, 1921, 4.

24. George G. Currie and Josephine Lindley, "The Season's

Greetings from Palm Beach," booklet, George Graham Currie Papers, HSPBC; "Greetings from Palm Beach" (advertisement), *Juno Tropical Sun*, March 4, 1921.

25. Josephine Lindley in Social Security and Florida Death Records, 1920-1940 census, ancestry.com; Lindley to editor, *Palm Beach Post,* July 29, 1933; "Personal Mention," *Tropical Sun*, March 21, 1919; Joe Earman, "Miss Lindley Declines," *Palm Beach Post,* August 25, 1918.

26. Eric D. Walrond, "Augusta Savage Shows Amazing Gift for Sculpture," 1922, reprinted in Tony Martin, ed., *African Fundamentalism: A Literary and Cultural Anthology of Garvey's Harlem Renaissance* (Dover, MA: Majority Press, 1992), 302-5; Cary D. Wintz and Paul Finkelman, eds. "Augusta Savage," *Encyclopedia of the Harlem Renaissance: K-Y* (New York: Routledge, 2004), 1085; Delia Gaze, ed., "Augusta Savage," *Concise Dictionary of Women Artists* (New York: Routledge, 2001), 601; "County Fair Breaks Records," *Palm Beach Post,* March 4, 1921.

27. George Currie, "Recreated," in George Currie, ed., *Songs of Florida* (New York: J. T. White, 1922), 111.

28. Augusta Savage, "Compensation," in *Songs of Florida*, 112-14.

29. Currie, footnote to "Recreated," *Songs of Florida*, 111.

30. Walrond, "Augusta Savage"; Wintz and Finkelman, "Augusta Savage"; Gaze, ed., "Augusta Savage."

31. Amy Schwarz to author, copied from writings by Burt Johnson's brother, Lewis H. Johnson; Amy Schwarz, "Burt W. Johnson (1890-1927)" (unpublished manuscript); Susan Faxon Olney, Barbara Ball Buff, John H. Dryfhout, et al., *A Circle of Friends: Art Colonies of Cornish and Dublin* (Durham: University Art Galleries, University of New Hampshire, 1985), 1, 8, 57; "Palm Beach," *Brooklyn Daily Eagle*, March 5, 1922.

32. Schwarz, "Burt W. Johnson;" "Capt. Dimick Statue to be Erected Soon at West Palm Beach," *Miami Daily Metropolis*, November 19, 1921; "Palm Beach," *Brooklyn Daily Eagle*.

33. Schwarz, "Burt W. Johnson"; "Palm Beach," *Brooklyn Daily Eagle*; State Board of Health of Florida, *Annual Report* (Jacksonville: State Board of Health, 1920), n.p.

Chapter Four

1. Peter H. Falk, ed., "Dietsch, C. Percival," in *Who was Who in American Art: 1564-1975* (Madison, CT: Soundview Press, 1999), 1: 916; "Artist Dietsch Illness is Fatal," *Palm Beach Post,* February 24, 1961.

2. "Mr. Percival Dietsch Arrives in Palm Beach," *Palm Beach Daily News,* December 16, 1946; "Noted Artists Give Exhibits of Work Here," *Palm Beach Post Times,* February 5, 1928; "Artist Dietsch Illness is Fatal"; John Vincent Davis, *Highlights of the Palm Beaches* (New York: Imandt, 1952), 61; Donald Curl, *Mizner's Florida: American Resort Architecture,* Architectural History Foundation American Monography Series (Cambridge: MIT Press, 1987), 58-59, 104.

3. Addison Mizner, "Memoir" (unpublished manuscript), 74-75, Addison Mizner Papers, HSPBC.

4. "Palazzo Davanzati, Museo dell'Antica Casa Fiorentina," Repertorio delle Architetture Civili di Firenze, http://www.palazzospinelli.org/architetture/scheda.asp?offset=1650&ID=712 (accessed September 11, 2014); Caroline Seebohm, *Boca Rococo: How Addison Mizner Invented Florida's Gold Coast* (New York: Clarkson Potter, 2001), 207; "Cottage Colony," *Palm Beach Life,* 1931, 18, clipping, HSPBC; Patricia Lee Rubin, *Images and Identity in Fifteenth-Century Florence* (New Haven: Yale University Press, 2007), 30.

5. *Palm Beach Daily News,* clippings, April 12, 1926, and January 7, 1931; *Palm Beach Life,* clippings, March 11, 1952; "Mizner Plays Host to Party," January 7, 1931, *Palm Beach Daily News,* HSPBC.

6. Alice De Lamar to Alva Johnston, March 14, 1948, Alice De Lamar Papers, HSPBC, 40.

7. De Lamar to Johnston, March 14, 1948, 41, Alice De Lamar Papers, HSPBC; Emilie Keyes, "Achille Angeli is Dead," *Palm Beach Post,* July 19, 1953.

8. Mizner, "Memoir" (unpublished manuscript), 89, Addison Mizner Papers, HSPBC.

9. "Palm Beach, the 'World's Playground' Described by Noted Artist as he Sees It," reprint of *Vogue* article, April 1925, *Palm Beach Times,* May 31, 1925; J. Patrice Marandel, "Appendix 1: Other Works of Art Given by Anna Thomson Dodge or acquired from her Estate" in *The Dodge Collection* (New York: Hudson Hills Press in association with the Detroit Institute of Arts, 1996), 229-33.

10. Andrew Lang, ed., *The Arabian Nights' Entertainments* (New York: Longman's Green, 1898), 155-61; Alva Johnston, "The Palm

Beach Architect: The Boom," *New Yorker,* November 29, 1952, 89.

11. Meryle Secrest, *Duveen: A Life in Art* (Chicago: University of Chicago Press, 2005), 343.

12. Robert Livingstone, *Caroline van Hook Bean: The Last of the Impressionists* (Cape Cod: Sandy Shores, Kindle Edition, July 1, 2011), 2883.

13. Florence N. Levy, ed., *American Art Annual* (New York: American Art Annual, 1903-4), 24: 82; "Catches in the Social Stream," *Palm Beach Daily News,* March 10, 1926; "Artist Will Come Here for a Visit," *Miami Daily Metropolis,* January 13, 1923.

14. "Along the County Road," *Palm Beach Post,* January 24, 1925; "Catches in the Social Stream," *Palm Beach Daily News,* February 20, 1924; "Notes: Palm Beach," *Brooklyn Life,* February 23, 1924.

15. Jethro M. Hurt III, "Bethesda-by-the-Sea: The Spanish Memorial," *The Tustenegee,* HSPBC 4, no. 1 (Spring 2013):14.

16. "Bryan de Grineau," Motoring Art, http://www.motoringart. info/pdf/deGrineauBryan.pdf (accessed April 25, 2014); "Catches in the Social Stream," February 20, 1924.

17. De Lamar to Johnston, March 14, 1948, Alice De Lamar Papers, HSPBC; "Past Season was Largest Ever Here," *Palm Beach Daily News,* March 31, 1925; "Tea at Whitehall a Beautiful Affair," *Palm Beach Daily News,* February 2, 1925; "William van Dresser, Portrait Artist," *Palm Beach Daily News,* January 29, 1945 (obituary).

18. "Beltran-Massés, Federico, *La Maja Marquesa,*" Stair Sainty Gallery, http://www.europeanpaintings.com/paintings/beltran-Massés -federico/la-maja-marquesa-1915/ (accessed July 28, 2014).

19. "Society of Arts Opens Beautifully," *Palm Beach Daily News,* January 17, 1925; José Francés, *El Año Artístico* (Madrid: Mundo Latino, 1915), 1: 101.

20. "Catches in the Social Stream," February 9, 1926; De Lamar to Heller, January 11, 1967, De Lamar Papers, HSPBC.

21. De Lamar to *Palm Beach Daily News,* July 28, 1974.

22. G. Frodl, *Franz Barwig, 1868-1931* (Vienna, Austria: Österreichische Galerie Im Oberen Belvedere, May 23-September 14, 1969), n.p; Donald Curl "Joseph Urban's Palm Beach Architecture," *The Florida Historical Quarterly,* 71, no. 4 (April 1993): 442.

23. Julia Blanshard, "Former Local Resident Tells of Work in World of Painting," undated clipping, Palm Beach County newspaper, HSPBC.

24. "Haratune [*sic*] Michaelyan, Esq." (unpublished essay), Michaelyan Papers, HSPBC; H. Michaelyan business cards, Michaelyan Papers, HSPBC.

25. Blanshard, "Former Local Resident."

26. Eva Le Gallienne, Diary, February 12, 1918, February 14, 1918, February 23, 1918, March 19, 1918, Eva Le Gallienne Papers, Box 1, Folder 2, Library of Congress; Helen Sheehy, *Eva Le Gallienne: A Biography* (New York: Knopf, 1996), 75, 84, 106, 156; "Mary Benson, First Lady of Art," *Palm Beach Life,* January 1962, 50; Pamela Nash Mathews and Susan Sperandeo, telephone interviews with author, May 1, 2014; Eva Le Gallienne, *With a Quiet Heart: An Autobiography* (New York: Viking, 1953), 6.

27. Le Gallienne, Diary, March 19, 1918, September 9, 1918, and December 22, 1918.

28. Mary Duggett, passport application, June 7, 1920 (ancestry. com); Earlene White, "Modern Women," *Lowell Ledger,* August 18, 1938; Leone King, "Party to Close Gallery," *Palm Beach Post,* March 25, 1965; "The Art Galleries," *New Yorker,* December 4, 1937, 115-17; Passenger List, *Olympic,* August 18, 1920 (ancestry. com); Catherine Fleischner, telephone interview with author, May 7, 2014; "Married," *Town and Country,* March 20, 1921; Helen Sheehy, *Eva Le Gallienne: A Biography* (New York: Knopf, 1996), 82, 85, 115, 156.

29. Sheehy, *Le Gallienne,* 140-43, 177.

30. Fleischner, interview with author; "Le Gallienne Aid Seeks Divorce," *Cleveland Plain Dealer,* February 2, 1930.

31. Fleischner, interview with author.

32. "Mary Benson: First Lady of Art."

33. Jo Davidson, *Between Sittings* (New York: Dial, 1971), 193; De Lamar to Taylor, February 10 (no year), Otto Kahn Papers, HSPBC. In an undated letter from De Lamar to Eyre de Lanux, Eyre de Lanux Papers, 1865-1995, Box 2, Archives of American Art, Smithsonian Institution, De Lamar advised de Lanux to make sure to mention Mary Benson's name to Bernard Berenson when de Lanux visited him.

34. Secrest, *Duveen,* 322.

35. Minutes, Friends of the Arts and Crafts, April 1, 1927 and April 6, 1927, Bertha Berdel to Eva Stotesbury, April 10, 1927,

April 15, 1927, and Report of Executive Committee, Art and Artists Files, HSPBC; "Meeting at Mrs. Stotesbury's," *Palm Beach Post,* March-April 1927.

36. Ibid.

37. "Palm Beach, " *St. Petersburg Times,* February 18, 1927; "Private View of Art works Here Feb. 1," *Palm Beach Times,* January 30, 1928.

38. "Association of Artists to Conduct Art Exhibits," *Palm Beach Times,* December 15, 1927.

39. Addison Mizner, inscription beneath Frank E. Geisler photograph, Alice De Lamar Papers, HSPBC; De Lamar to Tchelitchew and Ford, January 9, 26 [1952], Pavel Tchelitchew Papers, Harry Ransom Center, University of Texas at Austin; "Frank E. Geisler," obituary, *The Camera,* July-December 1935, 37; "Frank E. Geisler," obituary, *Palm Beach Times,* February 3, 1935; Frances Gillmor, "Paintings of Palm Beach County Art Club, Display are Admirable in Competence and Technique," *Palm Beach Times,* March 19, 1924.

40. "Mizner Inviting 300 to Exhibit," *Palm Beach Post,* February 27, 1928.

41. Diplomas, Leo Lentelli Papers, reels 108 and 3813, Archives of American Art, Smithsonian Institution; Peter H. Falk, ed., "Lentelli, Leo," *Who was Who in American Art: 1564-1975* (Madison, CT: Soundview Press, 1999), 2: 1996.

42. Letters and postcards to Lentelli from friends in Palm Beach, Leo Lentelli Papers, reel 3813; Falk, "Lentelli, Leo"; Lentelli Scrapbook of artworks, Lentelli Papers, reel 108, frames 27, 430-31, 534; "Worth Avenue Patio Shows Lentelli Work," *Palm Beach Daily News,* February 14, 1946.

43. Lentelli, "Mock up" of a book, "Do and Don't of Drawing," Lentelli Papers, reel 108, frame illegible.

44. "Exhibition of Local Craftsmanship," *Palm Beach Post,* February 22, 1928; "Noted Artists Give Exhibits of Work Here," *Palm Beach Times,* February 5, 1928; Mizner Industries, *Las Manos Pottery,* ca. 1920s (catalogue printed by Tropical Sun Press), Boca Raton Historical Society.

45. "Noted Artist;" "Worth Avenue Gallery Presents MacKinnon Show," *Palm Beach Life,* March 9, 1948, 72; and "Friends of the Arts and Crafts At Exhibition of Rare Paintings," *Palm Beach Post,* January 11, 1928.

46. "Beauties of Florida Lure Artists and Painters Who Declare State their Mecca," *Palm Beach Post,* January 16, 1929.

47. Robert Livingstone, *Caroline van Hook Bean: The Last of the Impressionists* (Cape Cod: Sandy Shores, Kindle Edition, July 1, 2011), 3188-90.

48. De Lamar to Knott, December 10, 1978, De Lamar Papers, HSPBC.

49. Deborah C. Pollack, *Visual Art and the Urban Evolution of the New South* (Columbia: University of South Carolina Press, 2015), 9, 52, 189, 205; "Beach Picks Jury on Art," *Palm Beach Times,* May 16, 1928.

50. "Two More Days of Art Exhibition," *Miami Daily News,* March 18, 1928; "Closing Exhibit of Art Association Features Many Gay Watercolors," *Palm Beach Post,* March 24, 1928; Wilma Spencer, "Renowned Sculptor Visits the Vineta," *Palm Beach Daily News,* March 3, 1965.

51. Valerie Lawson, "Madeleine Parker: Sighs and Whispers," Dancelines, http://dancelines.com.au/madeleine-parker/ (accessed September 16, 2014).

52. "Rapid Progress is being Made on Memorial Fountain," *Palm Beach Daily News,* October 17, 1929; Charles Latham, *The Gardens of Italy* (New York: Scribner's, 1919), 73, Addison Mizner Personal Library, Rare Book Room, Gioconda and Joseph King Library, The Society of the Four Arts; David Rogers, "Addison Mizner-Designed Park: A History of Change," *Palm Beach Daily News,* October 12, 2014, reproducing Davies to Bennett, April 25, 1929, HSPBC.

53. "Rapid Progress," *Palm Beach Daily News*; "Beautiful Memorial Fountain," *Palm Beach Daily News,* January 6, 1930; "August F. Godio" (obituary), *Palm Beach Post,* October 22, 1933; "Ten Years Ago Today," *Palm Beach Daily News,* October 21, 1943; Lynn R. Olson, "Images," *Palm Beach Daily News,* December 23 1982; "Memorial Fountain a Tribute," *Palm Beach Daily News,* September 4, 1983.

Chapter Five

1. "Palm Beach," *Vogue,* March 1930, reprinted in Josephine Ross and Condé Nast, *Society in Vogue: The International Set between the Wars* (New York: Vendome Press, 1992), 83.

2. Constantin Alajalov, "Palm Beach: Village by the Sea," *Vogue,*

March 1936, quoted in Ross and Nast, *Society in Vogue,* 81.

3. Alajalov, "Palm Beach."

4. Cecil Beaton, "Palm Beach History," *Vogue,* February 15, 1937, 6; Frank Greve, "'Amusing' Sir Cecil Still Reigns Supreme," *Miami Herald,* January 5, 1973.

5. Cecil Beaton, *The Glass of Fashion* (New York: Doubleday, 1954; repr., New York: Rizzoli, 2014), 222.

6. Cecil Beaton, "Palm Beach," *Vogue,* April 1, 1931, 2.

7. Beaton, *The Glass of Fashion,* 230.

8. Beaton to Williams, three undated letters, and Alajalov to Micky, Mona Strader Bismark Collection, Filson Historical Society; Rebecca S. Rice, "Mona Strader Bismarck Collection," Filson *Newsmagazine,* Filson Historical Society, vol. 4, no. 3, http://www.filsonhistorical.org/archive/news_v4n3_MonaBismarck.html (accessed August 6, 2014); *Vogue,* February 15, 1937, 46.

9. Beaton, *Glass of Fashion,* 129-30; "Mona Bismarck," Voguepedia, citing "Cristóbal Balenciaga: Perfection Partagée," Paris: Mona Bismarck Foundation, 2006, http://www.vogue.com/voguepedia/Mona_von_Bismarck (accessed July 30, 2014).

10. "Bernard Boutet de Monvel: He Came, He Saw, He Built," *Palm Beach Daily News,* January 12, 1937.

11. Helen Sheehy, *Eva Le Gallienne: A Biography* (New York: Knopf, 1996), 217; "Mary Benson: First Lady of Art," *Palm Beach Life,* January 1962, 51.

12. Parker Tyler, *The Divine Comedy of Pavel Tchelitchew* (New York: Fleet, 1967), 410, 476; Sheehy, *Le Gallienne,* 217, 237; Nona Footz, "Alice Doesn't Live Here Anymore," *Venu Magazine,* November-December, 2011, 32.

13. Catherine Fleischner, interview with author, June 28, 2014; Sheehy, *Le Gallienne,* 206, 224.

14. "Biography of Robert Yarnall Richie," DeGolyer Library, Southern Methodist University, http://www.lib.utexas.edu/taro/smu/00168/smu-00168.html (accessed November 17, 2014).

15. "Local Sculptor Models 'Human Folk' and Not Just Celebrities," *Palm Beach Post,* May 22, 1932; Addison Mizner, undated memoir manuscript, 62, Addison Mizner Papers, HSPBC; "Berberyan Galleries to show Fine Collections," *Palm Beach Daily News,* January 12, 1935; "Munnings Paintings Placed on Exhibition," *Palm Beach Post,* January 22, 1935.

16. Boca Raton Historical Society, *Mizner Industries/Mizner Style* (Boca Raton: Boca Raton Historical Society, December 2009), 21.

17. Emilie Keyes, "Wagner Stone Plant is Another Industry Typical of Palm Beach," *Palm Beach Post,* November 15, 1931.

18. Mignon Roscher (the artist's daughter), "Frederick Roscher," http://www.frederickroscher.com/about.html (accessed July 23, 2014).

19. "The Von Hausen Tradition," *Palm Beach Post,* April 29, 1973.

20. "The Von Hausen Tradition"; Lawrence Dame, "Addison Mizner and F. C. Von Hausen" (unpublished manuscript), ca. 1950s, Art and Artists Files, HSPBC.

21. Palm Beach Art Center, *Catalogue of the Fourth Annual National Exhibition of Paintings, Sculpture, and Etchings, January 30-March 30, 1936*; Jean Wagner Troemel (who exhibited and attended the school at the center), interview with author, December 10, 2014.

22. Pam Sansbury, "Henry Strater," *York County Coast Star,* May 21, 1980, reprinted in "Henry Strater, Ogunquit Artist," *Friends of the Ogunquit Museum Newsletter,* Spring 2014; Ernest Hemingway, *A Moveable Feast: The Restored Edition* (New York: Simon and Schuster, 2009), 209, 234, 236; Nick Strater (Henry Strater's grandson), interview with author, December 30, 2014.

23. Nick Strater, interview with author, December 30, 2014; Betty Chamberlain, "Henry Strater: Form and Adventure through Color," reprint, *American Artist,* May 1972; Frank Rehn Gallery, *Henry Strater: Paintings, 1968-1972, Together with Earlier works, 1920-1967* (New York: Frank Rehn Gallery, 1973), 5-6; Jeffrey Meyers, *Hemingway: A Biography* (New York: Harper & Row, 1985, reprint paperback, Boston: Da Capo, 1999), 74; Gary Schwan, "Palm Beach's Colorful Characters," *Palm Beach Post,* March 16, 1997.

24. Nick Strater, interview with author, July 22, 2014; Beatrice de Holguin, "Tales of Palm Beach, PT. II: The Artists and the Patrons," *Status/Diplomat Magazine,* March 1968, 57; Chris Hunter, "Artist Lauded at 90th Birthday Party," *Palm Beach Daily News,* January 27, 1986.

25. Palm Beach Art Center, *Catalogue*; Deborah C. Pollack, "A Brief History of Fine Art and Artists in Palm Beach, *Palm Beach Jewelry and Antique Show Catalogue,* February 2012, 31; "Things

to Remember" (unpublished manuscript), Society of the Four Arts Papers, King Library, Society of the Four Arts; "Preview Planned for National Art Exhibition," *Palm Beach Daily News,* January 18, 1934.

26. Nancy Whipple Grinnell, *Carrying the Torch: Maud Howe Elliott and the American Renaissance* (Hanover: University Press of New England, 2014), x, xii, 106-8; Susan Faxon Olney, Barbara Ball Buff, John H. Dryfhout, et al., *A Circle of Friends: Art Colonies of Cornish and Dublin* (Durham: University Art Galleries, University of New Hampshire, 1985), 56; "Mrs. Elliott Speaks at Four Arts," *Palm Beach Daily News,* February 8, 1939.

27. H. Barbara Weinberg, "Hassam in East Hampton," in *Childe Hassam: American Impressionist* (New York: Metropolitan Museum of Art, 2004), 236-38, 248.

28. Pollack, "Brief History"; Jean Wagner Troemel, interview with author, December 10, 2014; "Outstanding Painting Awards are Announced," *Palm Beach Post,* March 10, 1936; "Catches in the Social Stream," *Palm Beach Daily News,* March 1, 1936.

29. "Palm Beach Art League Opens Eighteenth Annual Exhibit With Number of Outstanding Pieces," *Palm Beach Post-Times,* March 1936; "Palm Beach Attracts Artists," *Palm Beach Daily News,* March 31, 1936.

30. "Palm Beach Art League Opens," *Palm Beach Post-Times*; "Palm Beach Attracts Artists"; "Four Arts Society Summer Program Starting," *Palm Beach Post-Times,* April 19, 1936; "Things to Remember"; Olivia Gazzam Morrish, "The Early Years of the Four Arts, 1936-1947, Society of Four Arts Papers, King Library; "Worth Avenue Gallery Presents MacKinnon Show," *Palm Beach Life,* March 9, 1948, 72; "Preview Planned for National Art Exhibition," *Palm Beach Daily News,* January 18, 1934; Heidi Roth, Society of the Four Arts, email to author, July 16, 2014.

31. "Alice De Lamar," obituary clipping, Alice De Lamar Papers, HSPBC.

32. Morrish, "The Early Years"; "Catches: The Society of the Four Arts," *Palm Beach Daily News,* January 25, 1936; Ralph Hubbard Norton, "The Donor Speaks," *Art Digest* 23, no. 15 (November 1948): 20; Jan Sjostrom, "Historic Exhibition Marks The Society of the Four Arts' 75th anniversary," *Palm Beach Daily News,* http://www.palmbeachdailynews.com/news/entertainment/arts-theater/historic-exhibition-marks-the-society-of-the-four-/

nMCS3/ (accessed July 23, 2014); William U. Eiland and the Ann Weaver Norton Sculpture Garden, Inc., *Ann Weaver Norton: Sculptor* (West Palm Beach: Ann Weaver Norton Sculpture Garden, Inc., 2000), 31; "Ralph Hubbard Norton," HSPBC, http://www.pbchistoryonline.org/page/ralph-hubbard-norton (accessed June 1, 2015).

33. Morrish, "Early Years"; "Catches: The Society of the Four Arts."

34. The Museum of Modern Art, Press Release, February 20, 1936, MOMA Shared PDFs, https://www.moma.org/momaorg/shared/pdfs/docs/press_archives/313/releases/MOMA_1936_0009_1936-02-20_22036-5.pdf?2010 (accessed July 5, 2014); "New Type of Residence Found in Home of Charles Chadwick," *Palm Beach Post,* January 13, 1932.

35. Thomas C. Clarie, *Memories for the Future: A History of Palm Beach's Royal Poinciana Playhouse* (Portsmouth, NH: Back Channel Press, 2010), 72.

36. Florence N. Levy, "Bache Collection," *Art Annual,* 311; "Mary Benson: First Lady of Art," *Palm Beach Life,* January 1962, 51.

37. Le Gallienne, Diary, November 5, 1937, Box 1, Folder 4; Earlene White, "Modern Women," *Lowell Ledger,* August 18, 1938; Leone King, "Party to Close Gallery," *Palm Beach Post,* March 25, 1965; "The Art Galleries," *The New Yorker,* December 4, 1937, 115-17.

38. Brian H. Peterson, *Form Radiating Life: The Paintings of Charles Rosen* (Philadelphia: University of Pennsylvania Press; Bucks County: James Michener Museum, 2007), 43-44.

39. Peterson, *Rosen,* 43-44; "Culture: Who We Are," The Seminole Tribe of Florida, http://www.semtribe.com/ (accessed September 26, 2014).

40. "Palm Beach Art League Opens Eighteenth Annual Exhibit with a Number of Outstanding Pieces," *Palm Beach Post-Times,* March 15, 1936; "Summer School Courses Ready," *Palm Beach Daily News,* May 19, 1940; Frank Edward Lloyd, World War I draft registration card, 1917-1918, Monroe County, New York (ancestry.com).

41. "Bernard Boutet de Monvel: He Came, He Saw, He Built," *Palm Beach Daily News,* January 12, 1937; "Public Art Gallery for Palm Beach," *Museum News,* May 15, 1938, 2; "Arts Flourish in Florida," *Christian Science Monitor,* January 9, 1938.

42. The Society of the Four Arts, *Collection of Ralph H. and Elizabeth C. Norton and an Exhibition by Invited Paintings for National Exhibition* (Palm Beach: The Society of the Four Arts, 1938); "Four Arts Society Prepares for Number of Exhibitions," *Palm Beach Post-Times,* December 5, 1937; "Art Group Plans for Annual Meet," *Palm Beach Post-Times,* November 11, 1938.

43. "A Sculptor on Worth Avenue," *Palm Beach Daily News,* March 28, 1938.

44. "Hundreds Visit Flower Show," *Palm Beach Daily News,* February 27, 1938.

45. Ruth Butler, *Rodin: The Shape of Genius* (New Haven: Yale University Press, 1993), 104-5, 108-10, 120.

46. "Festival of the Sea at Four Arts Proves Attractive to Youth" and "Nautical Festival Opens at Four Arts with Afternoon Tea," January 25, 1939, clippings, The Society of the Four Arts Scrapbooks.

47. Jeffrey W. Andersen, William Gerdts, and Helen A. Harrison, *En Plein Air: The Art Colonies at East Hampton and Old Lyme, 1880-1930* (Old Lyme, CT: Florence Griswold Museum; East Hampton, New York: Guild Hall Museum, 1989), plate 2, 13, 20, 49-54, 57-58; Grinnell, *Carrying the Torch,* 74, 137; "Four Arts is Given Two Herter Murals by Mrs. Woodhouse," *Palm Beach Post,* March 19, 1939.

48. Charles de Kay, "Albert Herter," *Art and Progress,* February 1914, 130-36; "Herter Looms Revive an Ancient Art," *Fine Arts Journal* 31, no. 5, November 1914: 537-41; Grinnell, *Carrying the Torch,* 137; "Four Arts is Given Two Herter Murals by Mrs. Woodhouse."

49. Grinnell, *Carrying the Torch,* 128, 138, 171.

50. Mrs. Christopher Lindsey, "The Chinese Garden of the Society of the Four Arts" (unpublished manuscript), The Society of the Four Arts Papers, King Library, The Society of the Four Arts; Martin Palmer and Jay Ramsay with Man-ho Kwok, *Kuan Yin: Myths and Revelations of the Chinese Goddess of Compassion* (New York: Thorsons, 1995), 37-38, 50.

51. "The World of Charles Knight," http://www.charlesrknight.com/Biography.htm (accessed July 7, 2012); "Charles Knight Lectures at Four Arts," clipping, The Society of the Four Arts Scrapbooks.

52. National Association of Letter Carriers, AFL-CIO, 2000, *The Postal Record,* December 1985, 20, and April 2000, 11; "Post Office Murals Arrangements Okehed" [*sic*], *Palm Beach Post,* March 23, 1939; Barbara Glass, "Realism Stamps his Art," *Palm Beach Daily News,* December 18, 1976.

53. Ibid.

54. The Society of the Four Arts, "Statement," ca. 1940, The Society of the Four Arts Scrapbooks.

Chapter Six

1. Berthe E. Neil, "City Possesses Gifted Artist in Person of Daisy Erb," *Palm Beach Post-Times,* January 6, 1935; Emilie Keyes, "Palm Beach Art League Opens Most Outstanding Exhibition of Paintings in Its History," *Palm Beach Post-Times,* February 2, 1940; Deborah C. Pollack, *Visual Art and the Urban Evolution of the New South* (Columbia: University of South Carolina Press, 2015), 95; "Southern States Art League" *American Magazine of Art*, June 1922, 186.

2. Ralph Hubbard Norton, "The Donor Speaks," *Art Digest* 23, no. 15 (November 1948): 20-23; Willis F. Woods, introduction to *Paintings and Sculpture: Norton Gallery and School of Art,* by Norton Gallery and School of Art and Palm Beach Art Institute (West Palm Beach: Norton Gallery and School of Art, 1963), 5; Lee Rogers, "Dedicate Norton Art Gallery and School of Art," *Palm Beach Daily News,* February 9, 1941; Pollack, *Visual Art,* 53-54, 144, 198-200; Margaret Martin Burhman, "Treasures of Art," *All Florida Magazine,* January 5, 1958; Jean Wagner Troemel, interview with author, April 19, 2014; Deborah C. Pollack, "A Brief History of Fine Art and Artists in Palm Beach, *Palm Beach Jewelry and Antique Show Catalogue,* February 2012, 29-33; "Daisy Erb Paintings Displayed at Hotel," *Palm Beach Post,* December 19, 1941; Mary E. Aleshire, "Palm Beach Art League Has Interesting History," *Palm Beach Post-Times,* March 31, 1940; E. Robert Hunter, "Norton Gallery of Art: Young, Vital, Attains National Position," *Art Digest* 23, no. 4, November 15, 1948, 13; "Gift of $500,000 Rocks Palm Beach Social Set," *Herald,* 1940 clipping, Norton Museum of Art Papers, HSPBC.

3. Norton, "Donor Speaks."

4. Alexander Sturgis and the National Gallery (Great Britain), *Rebels and Martyrs: The Image of the Artist in the Nineteenth Century* (New Haven: Yale University Press, 2006), 142.

5. Pollack, "A Brief History," 29 33.

6. Gary Schwan, "The Curious Case of the Switched Statues," *Palm Beach Post,* July 24, 1985.

7. Thomas Bulfinch, *Bulfinch's Mythology: The Age of Fable; The Age of Chivalry; Legends of Charlemagne* (New York: Crowell, 1913), 34-35.

8. Wyeth to Norton, June 26, 1940, and July 1, 1940, cited in Schwan, "The Curious Case of the Switched Statues."

9. Wheeler Williams, *Wheeler Williams,* American Sculpture Series (New York: Norton under the auspices of the National Sculpture Society, 1947), 11, 20-21, 24.

10. Ibid., 6, 59.

11. Joy Shepherd Kissam to *Palm Beach Post,* February 5, 1991; Joy Shepherd Kissam, "J. Clinton Shepherd, 1889-1975" (undocumented article), Art and Artists Files, HSPBC.

12. Kissam to *Palm Beach Post;* Kissam, "J. Clinton Shepherd"; "Shepherd Dies Here," *Palm Beach Daily News,* June 29, 1976; "Awards Made for Norton Gallery Exhibit," *Palm Beach Daily News,* March 22, 1941; "This Resort Artist 'Roamed the Range,'" *Palm Beach Daily News,* 75th Anniversary Special, January 1969; "J. Clinton Shepherd New Art School," *Palm Beach Daily News,* December 1942.

13. Lee Rogers, "Jules Bache Praises Contemporary Exhibit," *Palm Beach Daily News,* February 19, 1941.

14. "Exhibit Reviewed by Maud Howe Elliott," *Palm Beach Daily News,* December 18, 1941.

15. Nancy Randolph, "Palm Beach Goes Artistic at Four Arts," *Palm Beach Daily News,* February 9, 1940; Emilie Keyes, "Slightly Off the Record," *Palm Beach Daily News,* January 21, 1940.

16. Chris Romoser, "Photographer Bert Morgan Dies, Funeral Services are Wednesday," *Palm Beach Daily News,* September 21, 1986.

17. "Resort Photographer is Employed by Duke," unidentified clipping, April 29, 1941, HSPBC.

18. Alice De Lamar, "The War Years in Palm Beach" (unpublished manuscript), Alice De Lamar Papers, HSPBC, 1-2; "Four Arts Society Will Show Works with G. I. Slant," *Flight,* February 13, 1943; Helen Van Hoy Smith, "Palm Beach May Expect Bright Season in Homes," *Miami Daily News,* November 29, 1942; "Soldier Art Sells at Palm Beach," *Art Digest,* 17, April 15, 1943: 11.

19. Catherine Fleischner, telephone interview with author, May 7, 2014; *Polk's West Palm Beach Directory* (Richmond, Virginia: R. L. Polk, 1947), 478, ancestry.com; De Lamar, "The War Years," 2-6, 9.

20. Lawrence Dame, "Palm Beach Palette," March 5, 1962, clipping, Art and Artists Files, HSPBC; Elizabeth Vaughan, "Palm Beach . . . A Great Small Art Center," *Palm Beach Daily News,* January 1, 1969; "Mary Benson: First Lady of Art," *Palm Beach Life,* January 1962, 50-51.

21. Agnes Ash, "History," Miami newspaper clipping in the collection of Pamela Nash Mathews; Pamela Nash Mathews and Susan Sperandeo, telephone interviews with author, May 1, 2014; "Mary Benson: First Lady," 50-51; De Lamar to Parsons, November 6, ca. 1968, Betty Parsons Papers, Archives of American Art, Box 23, Folder 27; De Lamar to Romney, "Monday," 1965, Richard Adams Romney Papers, MSS 462 Box 1 f., Beinecke Rare Book and Manuscript Library, Yale University; Leone King, "Party to Close Gallery," *Palm Beach Post,* March 25, 1965.

22. Ash, "History"; "Washington Art Studio," *Palm Beach Daily News,* April 4, 1943.

23. "Mary Benson: First Lady," 50-51; Worth Avenue Gallery flyer, Worth Avenue Gallery Papers, Art and Artists Files, HSPBC.

24. "Mary Benson: First Lady," 51, 75.

25. William U. Eiland and the Ann Weaver Norton Sculpture Garden, Inc., *Ann Weaver Norton: Sculptor* (West Palm Beach: Ann Weaver Norton Sculpture Garden, Inc., 2000), 36.

26. "Story of Ann Weaver Norton," Ann Norton Sculpture Gardens, http://www.ansg.org/page/story-of-ann-weaver-norton (accessed October 24, 2014); "Ann Norton wins Prize at Lowe Gallery Show," *Palm Beach Post,* January 9, 1953; Joel Blackwell, interview with Ann Weaver Norton in "She Strives for 'Inner Spirit' in Sculptures," *Palm Beach Post,* March 7, 1971.

27. Emilie Keyes, "Artist Salvador Dali Would Rather Paint His Wife than Any of Hollywood's Fairest," *Palm Beach Post,* April 21, 1942.

28. Helen Van Hoy Smith, "Two Famous Artists Arrive in Palm Beach for Visit," *Miami Daily News,* April 26, 1942.

29. Ibid.

30. Carol Vogel, "Inside Art," *New York Times,* February 24, 1995.

31. "Palm Beach in Wartime, Florida's Sea-Change," *Vogue,* March 15, 1944, reprinted in Josephine Ross and Condé Nast, *Society in Vogue: The International Set between the Wars* (New York: Vendome Press, 1992), 184; "U.S. Military in Palm Beach," "History Online," HSPBC, http://www.pbchistoryonline.org/page/us-military-in-palm-beach (accessed July 25, 2014); De Lamar, "The War Years," 1-2; untitled clippings, Constantin Alajalov Papers, Archives of American Art, Smithsonian Institution, reel 2091, frames 242 and 243.

32. Worth Avenue Gallery flyer; "There's a Clothesline Out on Worth Avenue," *Palm Beach Daily News,* March 25, 1943; "Artists, Bring Your own Clothesline and Pins!" *Palm Beach Daily News,* March 13, 1946.

33. Worth Avenue Gallery flyer; William Rayner, telephone interview with author, June 9, 2014; Benson to Parsons, February 18, 1947; Worth Avenue Gallery to Parsons, April 15, 1947; Rayner to Parsons, April 15, 1947, box 23, folder 6; Parsons to Rayner, December 3, 1958, box 23, folder 66, Betty Parsons Papers, Archives of American Art, Smithsonian Institution.

34. "Mary Benson: First Lady," 51.

35. "Mary Benson: First Lady," 50-51, 75; Lawrence Dame, "No Room at the Inns for Local Artists," *Palm Beach Post-Times,* January 3, 1971.

36. "Mary Benson: First Lady," 75; Federal Census, 1900, ancestry.com; "Artist Channing Hare Dies at his Palm Beach Home," *Palm Beach Daily News,* February 13, 1976.

37. "Channing Hare Dies"; "Portrait of the Artist," *Palm Beach Post,* March 3, 1972; "There's A PB Game, Says Channing Hare," *Palm Beach Daily News,* December 18, 1970; Gary Schwan, "Palm Beach's Colorful Characters," *Palm Beach Post,* March 16, 1997; "Channing Hare Awarded Prize," *Palm Beach Daily News,* January 17, 1943; "Worth Avenue Gallery," *Palm Beach Life,* March 13, 1945, 28-29; "Society of the Four Arts," *Palm Beach Life,* January 15, 1946, 34-35.

38. Lawrence Dame, "A Most Extraordinary Art Team," *Palm Beach Post,* March 5, 1972; "Channing Hare Dies."

39. Ibid.

40. Mary Benson, Affidavit Under Fictitious Name Statute, no. 6602, April 29, 1946, State of Florida Public Records, Register of Corporation, no. 207309.

41. "Mary Benson: First Lady," 51; Dame, "No Room at the Inns."

42. Christopher Wright and Norton Museum of Art, *Kyril Vassilev: 1908-1987: A Retrospective Exhibition, February 2-March 12, 1989* (West Palm Beach: Norton Gallery of Art, 1989), 68, 73.

43. Wright, *Kyril Vassilev,* 69; Holland Beeber, "Expert to Promote Styles Here," *Miami Daily News,* January 21, 1951; "Kyril P. Vasillev," *New York Times,* June 25, 1987.

44. "Shows Lentelli Work" and "Leo Lentelli, Sculptor," *Palm Beach Life,* clipping, January 14, 1945, 47, Leo Lentelli Papers, Archives of American Art, Smithsonian Institution, reel 3813, frame 424.

45. Ibid.

46. Franz Marc, Annegret Hoberg, Isabelle Jansen, *Franz Marc: The Complete Works: The Oil Paintings* (London: Phillip Wilson, 2004), 152, 334; Gabriella Coslovich, "Art and Atrocity," *The Age,* December 6, 2010, 13.

47. Jack Flam, Katy Rogers, and Tim Clifford, *Robert Motherwell Paintings and Collages: A Catalogue Raisonné 1941–1991* (New Haven: Yale University Press, 2012), vol. 2, 12, 30-32; *Supplementary Works,* Dedalus Foundation, http://dedalusfoundation.org/catalogue_raisonne/paintings_collages/updates_addenda (accessed July 8, 2014).

48. Phylis Brinkman Craig, "Philip Service Brinkman," http://www.philbrinkman.com/phil-brinkman-murals.htm (accessed June 5, 2014); Val Pipps, "Muralist Revisits His Art," *Palm Beach Daily News*, November 18, 1976.

49. "Eric Lundgren," clipping, Art and Artists Files, HSPBC.

50. Draft of De Lamar to *Palm Beach Post-Times*, Palm Beach Chamber of Commerce, and Society of the Four Arts, January 13, 1948, Alice De Lamar Papers, HSPBC; "Capt. Dimick's Statue to Come to Resort," clipping, Art and Artists Files, HSPBC; Emilie Keyes, clipping, Art and Artists Files, HSPBC.

51. "Hiker, by Alice Ruggles Kitson," Art Inventories Catalog, Smithsonian Institution, http://siris-artinventories.si.edu/ (accessed February 24, 2015); Charlotte Rubinstein, *American Women Sculptors: A History of Women Working in Three Dimensions* (Boston: G. K. Hall, 1990), 103–4; "Ruggles, T. A.," birth record, Massachusetts Vital Records, ancestry.com.

52. Emilie Keyes, "Society of Four Arts Celebrates Its 'Coming of Age,'" *Palm Beach Post-Times,* January 11, 1948; "Norton Honors

Donor, Presents New Acquisitions," *Palm Beach Daily News,* December 5, 1948; "Worth Avenue Gallery Climaxes Season of Art with Gay, Colorful Paintings," *Palm Beach Daily News,* March 29, 1949.

Chapter Seven

1. Robert Livingstone, *Caroline van Hook Bean: The Last of the Impressionists* (Cape Cod: Sandy Shores, Kindle Edition, July 1, 2011), 4161; De Lamar to Tchelitchew and Ford, January 9 and 26, 1952, Pavel Tchelitchew Papers, Harry Ransom Center, University of Texas at Austin; Leone King, "Party to Close Gallery," *Palm Beach Post,* March 25, 1965.

2. Edyne Gordon and The Society of the Four Arts, *Ouida George: A Retrospective,* The Society of the Four Arts, 2009; Millie Wolf, "Ouida Wears her Heart on her Canvas," "Palm Beach Galleries Presents Ouida: Biographical Notes," "Ouida George Honored with One-Man Exhibition," clippings, Art and Artists Files, HSPBC; Dan McDonald, "Ouida George's Art is her Life," *Palm Beach Daily News,* March 5, 1982.

3. Hawkins to Pierce, March 1, 1954, Art and Artists Files, HSPBC.

4. Wilma Spencer, "Palm Beach is Home for Noted Artist Zito," *Palm Beach Daily News,* May 14, 1965.

5. Deborah C. Pollack, *Orville Bulman: An Enchanted Life and Fantastic Legacy* (Palm Beach: Blue Heron Press, 2006), 33.

6. Pollack, *Orville Bulman,* 46.

7. Mary Benson, introduction to *Thirty Oils by Orville Bulman,* by the Wilmington Society of the Fine Arts, January 10-31, 1954 (Wilmington: Delaware Art Center, 1954); Pollack, *Orville Bulman,* 95, 126, 148-49.

8. Pollack, *Orville Bulman,* 126, 148-49; Charles House, *The Outrageous Life of Henry Faulkner* (1988, repr., Sarasota: Pub This Press, 2005), 166.

9. Worth Avenue Gallery, *John Franklin Hawkins and Keith Ingermann* (exhibition catalogue), February 5-17, 1951; Worth Avenue Gallery, *Paintings by Keith Ingermann, February 4 through February 16* (undated catalogue).

10. "Worth Avenue Gallery Honors Keith Ingermann in One-Man Show," clipping, February 10, 1953, Art and Artists Files, HSPBC; "Mary Benson: First Lady of Art," *Palm Beach Life,* January 1962, 75; Emilie Keyes, "Young Local Artist Returns from Italy for Exhibition," *Palm Beach Life,* February 12, 1957, 41; "Keith Ingermann Show Opens at the Worth Gallery, *Palm Beach Daily News,* February 5, 1957; "Keith Ingermann Hits High Sales," *Palm Beach Daily News,* November 22, 1962; "Native Returns Home in Triumph," *Palm Beach Post-Times,* February 7, 1971.

11. "Hopkins Hensel, His First Palm Beach Show," *Palm Beach Life,* 1956, 78, clipping, HSPBC; Worth Avenue Gallery, *Hopkins Hensel* (undated catalogue), HSPBC; University of Illinois, "Hensel, Hopkins," *Exhibition of Contemporary American Painting* (Urbana: College of Fine and Applied Art, 1949), n.p.; "Hopkins Hensel and His Paintings," *Palm Beach Life,* March 24, 1960, 41-42.

12. The Society of the Four Arts, *Paul Gauguin: 1848-1903* (exhibition catalogue), 1956, title page; *The Society of the Four Arts, 1956-1957* (handbook); Deborah C. Pollack, *Visual Art and the Urban Evolution of the New South* (Columbia: University of South Carolina Press, 2015), 282.

13. "Sailboats in the Harbor to 'Thistles' are Exhibited," *Palm Beach Daily News,* February 28, 1956; "Mary Benson: First Lady," 50.

14. De Lamar to Romney, "Monday," 1965, Richard Adams Romney Papers, MSS 462 Box 1 f., Beinecke Rare Book and Manuscript Library, Yale University; De Lamar to Tchelitchew and Ford, from Antibes, 1947, Tchelitchew Papers; De Lamar to Lanux (several undated letters), Eyre de Lanux Papers, 1865-1995, Archives of American Art, Smithsonian Institution; Robert A. Schanke, *Shattered Applause: The Lives of Eva Le Gallienne* (Carbondale and Edwardsville, IL: Southern Illinois University Press, 1992), 199; Thomas C. Clarie, *Memories for the Future: A History of Palm Beach's Royal Poinciana Playhouse* (Portsmouth, NH: Back Channel Press, 2010), 352.

15. Pamela Nash Mathews and Susan Sperandeo, telephone interviews with author, May 1, 2014; Catherine Fleischner, interview with author, May 7, 2014; William Rayner, telephone interview with author, June 9, 2014; De Lamar to Tchelitchew and Ford, January 9 [no year, possibly 1956], Tchelitchew Papers.

16. De Lamar to Romney, "Monday"; Leone King, "He Sculpts the Universe," *Palm Beach Post,* March 7, 1965.

17. De Lamar to Romney, "Monday"; Bobbye Smith, telephone interview with author, May 7, 2014.

18. Ibid.

19. Ed Plaisted, "Photo by Ray Howard Means It's a Classic," *Palm Beach Post-Times,* April 6, 1969.

20. Lawrence Dame, "The Critic's Eye," March 4, 1960, unidentified clipping, HSPBC; "The Stone City Art Colony and School 1932-1933," Mount Mercy University, http://projects.mtmercy.edu/stonecity/otherartists/sharp.html (accessed October 8, 2014); Worth Avenue Gallery, *John Sharp* (exhibition catalogue, Palm Beach: Worth Avenue Gallery, n.d.), n.p.; Lawrence Dame, "Palm Beach Palette," March 5, 1962, clipping, Art and Artists Files, HSPBC; "Paul Crosthwaite," Michener Art Museum, http://www.michenermuseum.org/bucksartists/artist.php?artist=61 (accessed October 8, 2014).

21. "Gertrude Schweitzer," Artists and Architects, National Academy of Design, http://www.nationalacademy.org/collections/artists/detail/951/ (accessed July 30, 2014); "Gertrude H. Schweitzer, 79, A Painter and Sculptor," *New York Times,* November 12, 1989; Alfred M. Frankfurter, *Yearbook* (New York: Grand Central Galleries, 1952), 13; "Gertrude Schweitzer's Work Wins Acclaim in Europe," *Palm Beach Post-Times,* January 31, 1954; Norton Gallery and School of Art, et al. *Gertrude Schweitzer: Spring '73 Exhibitions* (New York: Triggs, 1973), n.p.

22. "Gertrude Schweitzer," Artists and Architects; Roger Hurlburt, "Norton Gallery Gets a Notable Picasso," *Sun Sentinel,* February 25, 1988; Leone King, "Palm Beach Notes," *Palm Beach Post-Times,* February 16, 1964.

23. "Schweitzer Art on View Monday at Worth Avenue Gallery, *Palm Beach Post-Times,* February 6, 1955; Register of Corporation, no. 207309, November 4, 1957, State of Florida Public Records; Affidavit Under Fictitious Name Statute, no. 22638, February 2, 1959, State of Florida Public Records.

24. Thomas Hoving, *Making the Mummies Dance: Inside the Metropolitan Museum of Art* (New York: Simon & Schuster, 1993), 90-91; Sophy Burnham, *The Art Crowd* (Bloomington, IN: iUniverse, 2000), 348.

25. William D. Morley, Inc., foreword to *Contents of Playa Riente, Unrestricted Public Auction* (Philadelphia: Wm. D. Morley, 1957), (n.p.); Jane Schermerhorn, "Sad Ending to Fairy Tale," *Detroit News,* March 9, 1957; "N.Y. Dealer Buys 9 Sert Murals for Secret Client," *Detroit News,* March 16, 1957; Helen Van Hoy Smith, "PB Rumor Says Mrs. Dodge to Bestow Sert Murals on Detroit Art Institute," *Miami Herald,* April 7, 1957.

26. Elfrida Simbari, email to author, October 29, 2014; Clarie, *Memories,* 28-29; Rayner, interview with author, June 9, 2014; "Franz Bueb Exhibition Opens at PB Galleries," *Palm Beach Daily News,* March 21, 1971.

27. Clarie, *Memories,* 74; Robert Bushnell Papers, 1943-1944, Archives of American Art, Smithsonian Institution; Everglades Club Files, HSPBC.

28. Justine Hartman, "J. Clinton Shepherd," *Palm Beach Life,* January 12, 1961, 65-67; June S. Shepherd (daughter-in-law of the artist), interview with author, May 31, 2014.

29. Myrna G. Eden, *Energy and Individuality in the Art of Anna Huntington, Sculptor, and Amy Beach, Composer* (Metuchen: Scarecrow Press, 1987), 156-58.

30. Ibid.

31. Jacqueline Francis, "George Bellows," in *The American Collection: Selected Works from the Norton Museum of Art Collection,* by Christina Orr-Cahall (West Palm Beach: Norton Museum of Art, 1994), 55-57.

32. Jacqueline Francis, "Mark Tobey," in *The American Collection: Selected Works from the Norton Museum of Art Collection,* by Christina Orr-Cahall (West Palm Beach: Norton Museum of Art, 1994), 199-201.

33. House, *The Outrageous Life,* 91, 129, 155-56; "Emilie Johnson: Poet and Artist at the Worth Avenue Gallery," *Palm Beach Life,* January 29, 1959, 67-68; John Lahr, *Tennessee Williams: Mad Pilgrimage of the Flesh* (New York: Norton, 2014), 544.

34. House, *The Outrageous Life,* 166; Emilie Keyes, "Henry Lawrence Faulkner Knows Where He Is Going, He Declared," clipping, 1960, Art and Artists Files, HSPBC.

35. House, *The Outrageous Life,* 167-68, 175.

36. "Regarding the Arts," *Palm Beach Illustrated* clipping, 1965, Art and Artists Files, HSPBC.

37. Elfrida Simbari, "The Simbari Diaries: A Fifty Year Adventure," http://www.simbari.co.uk/story_america.php (accessed May 28, 2014).

38. Palm Beach Galleries, file no. 223950, State of Florida Public Records.

Chapter Eight

1. Elfrida Simbari, email to author, October 28, 2014.

2. Simbari email to author, May 29, 2014; Elfrida Simbari, "The Simbari Diaries: A Fifty Year Adventure," http://www.simbari.co.uk/story_america.php (accessed May 28, 2014).

3. Undated, untitled clipping, Bulman Family Papers; Bruce Ward, "Tuesday Night at the Galleries, *Palm Beach Life,* February 1971, 82; "Regarding the Arts," *Palm Beach Illustrated* clipping, 1965, Art and Artists Files, HSPBC; "Palm Beach Galleries to Open its 11th Season," *Palm Beach Daily News,* November 30, 1969.

4. Simbari, emails to author, June 11, 2014, September 3, 2014; Simbari, "The Simbari Diaries."

5. Simbari, email to author, September 3, 2014.

6. Emilie Keyes, "Simbari Matures in Fine Paintings," *Palm Beach Daily News,* February 21, 1962; Simbari, email to author, May 30, 2014; Eugene Walter and Palm Beach Galleries, *Simbari, January 18-31, 1960,* Art and Artists Files, HSPBC; Hervé Bazin, *Simbari* (Paris: Wally Findlay Galleries, 1971), n.p.

7. Emilie Keyes, "Artist Duchamp Decries Routine," *Palm Beach Daily News,* February 15, 1962; "Chester Dale, an Unusual Collector," *Palm Beach Post,* January 20, 1958.

8. "Worth Avenue Gallery Exhibitions: 1959-1960" (advertisement), *Palm Beach Daily News,* November 29, 1959; "The Kennedys Lose Browsing Privacy," *Evening Star* (Washington, DC), December 14, 1960.

9. Deborah C. Pollack, "Thieme, Anthony," in *The New Encyclopedia of Southern Culture,* ed. Judith H. Bonner and Estill Curtis Pennington, vol. 21, *Art and Architecture* (Chapel Hill: University of North Carolina Press, 2013), 438-39.

10. Ibid.

11. "Gala Marks Opening of Findlay Galleries," *Palm Beach Post,* January 27, 1961; Michael Gaeta, "Wally Findlay Celebrates 30 Years in PB," *Palm Beach Daily News,* March 17, 1991.

12. Emilie Keyes, "Tish Massie, Her Shells and Flowers," *Palm Beach Life,* February 20, 1959, Emilie Keyes Papers, HSPBC; David Whitmire, "The Wideners, An American Family," http://www.encyclopedia-titanica.org/documents/the-wideners.pdf (accessed November 20, 2014).

13. "Art Gallery Opens Season with 'Ingenuous' Collection," *Palm Beach Post,* December 13, 1960; Keyes, "Tish Massie"; Whitmire, "The Wideners."

14. "Charles Baskerville Biography" (unpublished manuscript), Charles Baskerville Papers (frame number illegible), reel 577, Archives of American Art, Smithsonian Institution; "Paintings of Charles Baskerville," *Palm Beach Life,* February 23, 1961, 54-56.

15. Maureen O'Sullivan, "Mort Kaye: Dean of Social Photographers," *Palm Beach Illustrated,* March 1997, 85; William Kelly, "Society Photographer Mort Kaye Dies at 97," *Palm Beach Daily News,* September 25, 2013.

16. Michael Price, "Life Behind the Lens," *Palm Beach Daily News,* December 1, 2003; "Corby Kaye follows footsteps of his Father—Legendary Social Photographer Mort Kaye," *Palm Beach Daily News,* June 19, 2010.

17. "Davidoff Biography" (unpublished manuscript), Davidoff Papers, HSPBC; Thom Smith, "He Knew how to Get the Picture," *Palm Beach Post,* October 13, 2004; Shannon Donnelly, "Photographer Davidoff, 78, Dies," *Palm Beach Daily News,* October 12, 2004.

18. Simbari, emails to author, May 26, 2014, May 29, 2014, June 11, 2014, August 31, 2014, and September 2, 2014.

19. Simbari, email to author, May 29, 2014; Emilie Keyes, "Slightly Off the Record," *Palm Beach Daily News,* January 18, 1962; Lawrence Dame, "A Scion of East Africa," *Palm Beach Post-Times,* March 7, 1971; Elizabeth Vaughan, "At the Galleries," *Palm Beach Daily News,* December 16, 1966.

20. Robert S. Hurwitz Loft on the Mile Gallery of Art, *Henry Lawrence Faulkner* (exhibition catalogue, Coral Gables: Robert S. Hurwitz Loft on the Mile Gallery of Art, February 25, no year, ca. 1960s); "Exhibition Opens Monday: Paintings of Cobb and Faulkner to be Previewed at Worth Avenue Galleries," *Palm Beach Daily News,* January 7, 1961.

21. "PB Galleries to Exhibit Work of Cape Cod Pair," *Palm Beach Daily News,* March 24, 1953.

22. "Portrait Artist's Style Captures Personalities," *Palm Beach Daily News,* January 14, 1988; "Biography of Alejo Vidal-Quadras," Alejo Vidal-Quadras Foundation, http://www.alejovidalquadras.com/portraits.htm (accessed September 30, 2014).

23. "The Painter of Three Generations," Vidal-Quadras Foundation, http://www.alejovidalquadras.com/english/ (accessed September 30, 2014).

24. De Lamar to Romney, Monday 1965, MSS 462, Box 1 f.,

Beinecke Rare Book and Manuscript Library, Yale University; "Worth Avenue Gallery has its Final Exhibit," *Palm Beach Daily News,* March 28, 1965.

25. Keyes to De Lamar (copy), March 30, 1965, Emilie Keyes Papers, HSPBC; Emilie Keyes, "Friends Pay Tribute to Gallery Director," *Palm Beach Daily News,* March 31, 1965; Worth Avenue Gallery has its Final Exhibit."

26. Norton Gallery and School of Art, *Paintings and Sculpture from Palm Beach Collections: 25th Anniversary Year, 1941-1966, February 8-March 6, 1966* (West Palm Beach: Norton Gallery and School of Art, 1966), 1-5; Elizabeth Vaughn, "Resort Makes International News as an Art Center," *Palm Beach Daily News,* May 1, 1966.

27. Anne Marie Stein with George Carpozi, Jr., *Three Picassos Before Breakfast* (New York: Hawthorn, 1973), 118-30, 163, 169-70; "Sailors Close Shop, 'Forge' New Life in Jewelry Business," *Palm Beach Daily News,* April 25, 1978.

28. John S. Gray, email to author, September 11, 2014; Ann Genett, "J. Gray: an Artist and his Seascapes," clipping, Art and Artists Files, HSPBC.

29. Helen Sheehy, *Eva Le Gallienne: A Biography* (New York: Knopf, 1996), 378; Catherine Fleischner, interviews with author; De Lamar to Zoning Board, March 7, 1971, Alice De Lamar Papers, HSPBC; De Lamar to National Audubon Society, April 15, 1964, Alice De Lamar Papers, HSPBC.

30. De Lamar to Parsons, November 6, ca. 1968, Betty Parsons Papers, box 23, folder 27, Archives of American Art, Smithsonian Institution.

31. *The Collection of Mrs. John Wintersteen: An Exhibition of Paintings, Drawings and Sculpture* (Palm Beach: The Society of the Four Arts 1969); "Four Arts Shows Draw over 22, 000," clipping, April 6, 1969, The Society of the Four Arts Scrapbooks.

32. *Collection of Mrs. John Wintersteen*; "Four Arts Shows Draw over 22, 000," clipping, April 6, 1969, The Society of the Four Arts scrapbooks.

33. Elizabeth Vaughan, "Palm Beach . . . A Great Small Art Center," *Palm Beach Daily News,* January 1, 1969

Chapter Nine

1. Barbara Marshall, "Norton Museum Director who investigated daring art robbery dies, he was 102," *Palm Beach Post,* July 31, 2011; Elizabeth Vaughan, "What Meets the Eye," *Palm Beach Daily News,* January 15, 1970; "This Week at the Galleries," *Palm Beach Daily News,* January 9, 1972.

2. Cecil Beaton, *The Unexpurgated Beaton: The Cecil Beaton Diaries as He Wrote Them, 1970-1980* (New York: Knopf, 2003), 29, 271; "Hundreds Preview Beaton's Paintings at Gallery, *Palm Beach Daily News,* January 15, 1970; "Sir Cecil Beaton," *The Palm Beacher,* December 19, 1972; and "Lundgren Exhibit."

3. Schweitzer to De Lamar, December 1972, Alice De Lamar Papers, HSPBC.

4. Gary Schwan, "Palm Beach's Colorful Characters," *Palm Beach Post,* March 16, 1997.

5. Lawrence Dame, "The Art Shows in Palm Beach," *Palm Beach Post,* January 15, 1974.

6. "Spaniels Point to Gallery," *Palm Beach Daily News,* December 3, 1972; Marianne Giffin, "For Jimmy Barker success started at a Chinese Wedding Feast," *Nantucket Inquirer and Mirror,* August 12, 1982.

7. "Spaniels Point to Gallery"; Edyne Gordon and The Society of the Four Arts, *Ouida George: A Retrospective,* The Society of the Four Arts, 2009.

8. Steven Gerst, interview with author, November 28, 2014; Jeffrey Rosensweig and Betty Liu, *"Age Smart: Discovering the Fountain of Youth at Midlife and Beyond* (Upper Saddle River, NY: Pearson, 2006), 195-97; Jane Skinner, "Hilde Gerst: An Individual Grace," *Palm Beach Daily News,* December 27, 1971.

9. Jan Sjostrom, "Philip Read Dies at 73," *Palm Beach Daily News,* November 3, 2000; "Alfred Richardson Simson" and "Guy Coheleach" (clippings), Art and Artists Files, HSPBC; Millie Wolff, "Tall Ships Sail Again on his Canvasses," *Palm Beach Daily News,* March 21, 1977.

10. Dominika Glogowski, "Embodied Nature: Isamu Noguchi's *Intetra Fountain,*" in *Meanings of Abstract Art: Between Nature and Theory,* ed. Paul Crowther and Isabel Wünsche (New York: Routledge, 2012), 176-78; "J. James Akston Dies at PB Home," *Palm Beach Daily News,* October 28, 1983.

11. Interview with Eric Donner Grove, June 22, 2015; Georgia Dupuis, "The Present: Eagle Launches Country Into its Third 100 years," *Palm Beach Post,* July 4, 1976; "Statue Site is Pending," *Palm Beach Daily News,* March 12, 1975.

12. William U. Eiland and the Ann Weaver Norton Sculpture Garden, Inc., *Ann Weaver Norton: Sculptor* (West Palm Beach: Ann Weaver Norton Sculpture Garden, Inc., 2000), 70; "Story of Ann Weaver Norton," Ann Norton Sculpture Gardens, http://www.ansg.org/page/story-of-ann-weaver-norton (accessed October 24, 2014); Joel Blackwell, interview with Ann Weaver Norton in "She Strives for 'Inner Spirit' in Sculptures," *Palm Beach Post,* March 7, 1971.

13. "About Edna Hibel," Hibel Museum, http://www.hibel.com/aboutartist.htm (accessed January 13, 2015).

14. Mike Sallah, "Palm Beach Galleries to Close its Doors," *Palm Beach Daily News,* June 7, 1979; Maria Durell Stone, "Huldah Jeffe, A Woman with Recognized Talent," *Palm Beach Daily News.*

15. Elsa Longhauser, "Edward Mitchell, Philadelphia Sculptor, 1915-1980," from Foreword, "Mitchell Retrospective Catalog," 1990, http://www.henrywmitchell.com/About.html (accessed May 14, 2015); "Edward Hoffman 3d, Portrait Sculptor, 74," *New York Times,* September 24, 1991.

16. Helen Sheehy, *Eva Le Gallienne: A Biography* (New York: Knopf, 1996), 449.

17. "About Us," Armory Art Center, http://www.armoryart.org/about-us (accessed September 18, 2015).

18. "Helmut Koller," Helmut Koller Studio, http://www.helmutkoller.com/biography.html (accessed September 20, 2015); "PB Photographer Koller Fetes Egon Schiele with Art," *Palm Beach Daily News,* February 2, 1988.

19. Gary Schwan, "Sitting Pretty," *Palm Beach Post,* January 21, 1990.

Chapter Ten

1. Henry Morrison Flagler Museum, "Bust Returns to Whitehall," *Inside Whitehall,* Spring 2014, 7-8; John Nelander, "Monumental Achievement: Palm Beach on Saturday Dedicates a Statue with Historical Roots to Honor Henry M. Flagler," *Palm Beach Daily News,* December 7, 2010.

2. Barbara Grygutis, email to author, October 9, 2015.

3. "About Marsha," Marsha Montoya Sculpture and Jewelry, http://www.marshamontoya.com/#!about-marsha (accessed September 23, 2015).

4. Sandra Thompson, "Sandra Thompson: Palm Beach Artist" (unpublished manuscript).

5. "Biography," Luis Montoya / Leslie Ortiz, http://luismontoyaleslieortiz.com/biography/ (accessed September 22, 2015).

6. "Biography," Bruce Helander, http://brucehelander.com/biography/ (accessed September 22, 2015).

7. Bruce Helander, email to author, September 30, 2015; "Barbara Joseph Jolly," *Palm Beach Daily News,* May, 1, 2014, http://www.palmbeachdailynews.com/news/lifestyles/barbara-joseph-jolly/nfmCM/ (accessed October 1, 2015); Susan Hall, "Down Palm Beach Way: The Helander House on Historic Root Trail." *South Florida,* September 1993; "About Paul Aho," Paul Aho, http://paul-aho.com/#!/page/122125/bio (accessed October 1, 2015).

8. Helander, email to author.

9. "Sam Perry," Armory Art Center, http://www.armoryart.org/index.cfm?fuseaction=instructors.details&instructorID=14 (accessed October 1, 2015); "Tom Tribby," Thomas L. Tribby, LLC, http://www.tribbyart.com/biography (accessed September 30, 2015); "Richard John Frank," legacy.com, http://www.legacy.com/obituaries/palmbeachpost/obituary.aspx?pid=170912031#sthash.VjAjLvdd.dpuf (accessed September 30, 3015).

10. "Lawrence Holofcener," biography of the artist, http://www.holofcener.com/biography.htm (accessed October 1, 2015).

11. Detra Kay, email to author, October 2, 2015.

12. Interview with David Forrest Dunkle (grandson of Edmund Munger Brelsford), April 12, 2008; untitled published essay in Dunkle's personal papers, 20-22; Town of Palm Beach, *Comprehensive Plan* (Palm Beach: Town of Palm Beach, 1979), 25, http://docserver.townofpalmbeach.com/TownClerkWeblink/1/doc/662655/Page36.aspx (accessed April 8, 2016).

13. Robert Janjigian, "'Living Wall' of lush Tapestry of Plants debuts on Worth Avenue," *Palm Beach Daily News,* November 6, 2010, http://www.palmbeachdailynews.com/news/news/living-wall-of-lush-tapestry-of-plants-debuts-on-w/nMB7T/ (accessed September 29, 2015).

Selected Bibliography

The following are primary documents, books, articles, and other sources studied by the author. The list does not include some primary records found online or other sources that are only cited in the notes, as they would not be of interest for further reading.

Alajalov, Constantin. Papers. Archives of American Art, Smithsonian Institution.

Allen, Denise. "59. William-Adolphe Bouguereau: *Young Girl Defending Herself Against Eros.*" *Masterpieces of Painting in the J. Paul Getty Museum*, 5th ed., J. Paul Getty Museum. Los Angeles: Getty Publications, 2003, 101.

American Art Association. *Illustrated Catalogue of Valuable Paintings Collected by the Late Captain J. R. De Lamar.* New York: American Art Association, January 29, 1920.

American Art Galleries. *Spanish and Persian Rugs: XVI, XVII and XVIII Centuries from the Galleries of Addison Mizner, Palm Beach and Ohan S. Berberyan, New York.* January 1, 1924.

Andersen, Jeffrey W., William Gerdts, and Helen A. Harrison. *En Plein Air: The Art Colonies at East Hampton and Old Lyme, 1880-1930.* Old Lyme, Connecticut: Florence Griswold Museum; East Hampton, New York: Guild Hall Museum, 1989.

Anthony, Clarke. Papers. HSPBC.

"Architects: Mizner in Palm Beach." HSPBC, http://www.pbchistoryonline.org/page/mizner-in-palm-beach (accessed November 2, 2014).

Art and Artists Files. HSPBC.

"Art Galleries." *New Yorker,* December 4, 1937.

"Art at Palm Beach." *American Art News,* March 15, 1919.

Art Institute of Chicago. *Catalogue of Small Bronzes of the National Sculpture Society, October 8 to October 27, 1918.* Chicago: Art Institute, 1918.

"Artist Ricardo Magni Demonstrates Art Can Work for Him in Creating New Home." *Palm Beach Life,* January 21, 1955.

Barghini, Sandra. *Henry M. Flagler's Paintings Collection: The Taste of a Gilded Age Collector.* Palm Beach: Henry Morrison Flagler Museum, 2002.

Baskerville, Charles. Papers. Reel 577, Archives of American Art, Smithsonian Institution.

Bazin, Hervé. *Simbari.* Paris: Wally Findlay Galleries, 1971.

Beaton, Cecil. *The Glass of Fashion.* New York: Rizzoli, 2014. First published 1957 by Doubleday.

———. *The Unexpurgated Beaton: The Cecil Beaton Diaries as He Wrote Them, 1970-1980.* New York: Knopf, 2003.

"Beltran-Massés, Federico, *La Maja Marquesa.*" Stair Sainty Gallery, http://www.europeanpaintings.com/paintings/beltran-Massés-federico/la-maja-marquesa-1915/ (accessed July 28, 2014).

Benson, Mary. Introduction to *Thirty Oils by Orville Bulman,* by Wilmington Society of the Fine Arts, January 10-31, 1954. Wilmington: Delaware Art Center, 1954.

Bingham Family Scrapbook, HSPBC.

"Biography of Alejo Vidal-Quadras." Alejo Vidal-Quadras Foundation, http://www.alejovidalquadras.com/portraits.htm (accessed September 30, 2014).

"Biography of Robert Yarnall Richie." Robert Yarnall Richie Photograph Collection, DeGolyer Library, Southern Methodist University, http://www.lib.utexas.edu/taro/smu/00168/smu-00168.html (accessed November 17, 2014).

Bismarck, Mona Strader. Collection. Filson Historical Society, Louisville, Kentucky.

Boca Raton Historical Society. *Mizner Industries/Mizner Style.* Boca Raton: Boca Raton Historical Society, December 2009.

"Bryan de Grineau," Motoring Art, http://www.motoringart.info/pdf/deGrineauBryan.pdf (accessed April 25, 2014).

Bulfinch, Thomas. *Bulfinch's Mythology: The Age of Fable; The Age of Chivalry; Legends of Charlemagne.* New York: Crowell, 1913.

Burhman, Margaret Martin. "Treasures of Art." *All Florida Magazine,* January 5, 1958.

Burnham, Sophy. *The Art Crowd.* Bloomington, Indiana: iUniverse, 2000.

Bushnell, Robert. Papers, 1943-1944. Archives of American Art, Smithsonian Institution.

Butler, Ruth. *Rodin: The Shape of Genius.* New Haven: Yale University Press, 1993.

Butler, Susan. *East to the Dawn: The Life of Amelia Earhart.* Boston: Da Capo Press, 2009.

Caffyn, Charles H. "Some American Sculptors." *The Critic,* April 1905, 337.

Church of Bethesda-by-the-Sea. *Chronicles: The Church of Bethesda-by-the-Sea, Palm Beach, Florida, 1889-1964.* West Palm Beach: Distinctive Print, 1964.

Clarie, Thomas C. *Memories for the Future: A History of Palm Beach's Royal Poinciana Playhouse.* Portsmouth, New Hampshire: Back Channel Press, 2010.

Clarke Family Papers. HSPBC.

Clarke, Thomas Shields. "An Artist's Florida." *Country Life,* December 1, 1911, 49-55.

———. Letters, 1875-1920. Reel AAA 4235 (illegible frame no.). Archives of American Art, Smithsonian Institution.

Coad, Oral Sumner and Edwin Mims, Jr. *Pageant of America: The American Stage.* New Haven: Yale University Press, 1929.

Collins, Theresa Mary. *Otto Kahn: Art, Money, & Modern Time.* Chapel Hill: University of North Carolina Press, 2002.

"Contemporary Art at the Academy." *American Magazine of Art,* February 18, 1918.

Coslovich, Gabriella. "Art and Atrocity." *The Age.* December 6, 2010.

Craig, Phylis Brinkman. "Philip Service Brinkman," http://www.philbrinkman.com/phil-brinkman-murals.htm (accessed June 5, 2014).

Cummins, Sharon. "Henry Strater's Ogunquit Museum of American Art," Old News Column, May 28, 2009, http://www.someoldnews.com/ (accessed May 2, 2014).

Curl, Donald. "Joseph Urban's Palm Beach Architecture." *The Florida Historical Quarterly,* 71, no. 4 (April 1993): 436-57.

———. *Mizner's Florida: American Resort Architecture.* Architectural History Foundation American Monography Series. Cambridge: MIT Press, 1987.

———. "Tony Biddle and the 'New' Palm Beach." Unpublished manuscript, HSPBC.

Currie, George Graham. Papers. HSPBC.

Dame, Lawrence. "Addison Mizner and F. C. Von Hausen." Art and Artists Papers. HSPBC.

Davidson, Jo. *Between Sittings.* New York: Dial, 1971.

de Kay, Charles. "Albert Herter." *Art and Progress,* February 1914, 130-36.

De Lamar, Alice. Essay re: Addison Mizner to Alva Johnston, March 14, 1948, Alice De Lamar Papers, HSPBC.

———. Papers. HSPBC.

———. "The Everglades Club." Unpublished manuscript, March 14, 1983. Alice De Lamar Papers, HSPBC.

———. "The War Years in Palm Beach." Unpublished manuscript, Alice De Lamar Papers, HSPBC.

de Holguin, Beatrice. "Tales of Palm Beach, PT. II: The Artists and the Patrons." *Status/Diplomat Magazine,* March 1968.

De Lanux, Eyre. Papers, 1865-1995. Archives of American Art, Smithsonian Institution.

Dinse Law Firm, "Dinse, Knapp, & McAndrew, A Short History," http://www.dinse.com/the-firm/history.html (accessed July 24, 2014).

Donnis, Erica. "Pan of Rohallion." *Antiques and Fine Art,* http://www.antiquesandfineart.com/articles/article.cfm?request=362 (accessed November 4, 2014).

Drake, Lynn Lasseter and Richard A. Marconi with the HSPBC. *West Palm Beach, 1893-1950.* Mount Pleasant, South Carolina: Arcadia, 2006.

Eden, Myrna G. *Energy and Individuality in the Art of Anna Huntington, Sculptor, and Amy Beach, Composer.* Metutchen: Scarecrow Press, 1987.

"Edward Ryneal Grove: Biography." Medallic Art Collector, http://medallicartcollector.com/edward-ryneal-grove_biography.html (accessed March 19, 2015).

Eiland, William U. and the Ann Weaver Norton Sculpture Gardens, Inc. *Ann Weaver Norton: Sculptor*. West Palm Beach: Ann Weaver Norton Sculpture Gardens, Inc., 2000.

Erb, Daisy. "Data for 'History of Palm Beach County.'" Unpublished manuscript, Art and Artists Files, HSPBC.

Falk, Peter H., editor. *Who was Who in American Art: 1564-1975*, Madison, Connecticut: Soundview Press, 1999.

Federal Writers' Project of the Work Projects Administration for the State of Florida. *Florida: A Guide to the Southernmost State*. Tallahassee: State of Florida Department of Instruction, 1939.

Ferguson, George. *Signs and Symbols in Christian Art*. New York: Oxford University Press, 1954.

Fink, Lois Marie. *American Art at the Nineteenth-Century Paris Salons*. New York: Cambridge University Press, 1990.

Flam, Jack, Katy Rogers, and Tim Clifford. *Robert Motherwell Paintings and Collages: A Catalogue Raisonné 1941–1991*. New Haven: Yale University Press, 2012.

"Frank E. Geisler." Obituary. *The Camera*, July-December 1935.

Frankfurter, Alfred M. *Yearbook*. New York: Grand Central Art Galleries, 1952.

Frank K. M. Rehn Galleries. *Henry Strater, American Artist, Paintings 1968-1972, together with earlier works, 1920-1927*. New York: Frank Rehn Gallery, 1973.

Fraser Family Papers. Fraser family, St. Augustine.

Frodl, *G. Franz Barwig, 1868-1931*. Vienna, Austria: Österreichische Galerie Im Oberen Belvedere, May 23-September 14, 1969.

Gaze, Delia, ed. "Augusta Savage." *Concise Dictionary of Women Artists*. New York: Routledge, 2001 601.

Gerdts, William H. and Carol Lowrey with Heckscher Museum of Art. *The Golden Age of American Impressionism*. New York: Watson-Guptill, 2003.

"Gertrude Schweitzer," Artists and Architects, National Academy of Design, http://www.nationalacademy.org/collections/artists/detail/951/ (accessed July 30, 2014).

Glogowski, Dominika. "Embodied Nature, Isamu Noguchi's *Intetra Fountain*." In *Meanings of Abstract Art: Between Nature and Theory*, edited by Paul Crowther and Isabel Wünsche, 169-79. New York: Routledge, 2012.

Gold, Arthur and Robert Fizdale. *Misia: The Life of Misia Sert*. New York: Knopf, 1980.

Gordon, Edyne and The Society of the Four Arts. *Ouida George: A Retrospective*. The Society of the Four Arts, 2009.

Grayson, Cary T. Papers. Woodrow Wilson Presidential Library and Museum, Staunton, Virginia.

Grinnell, Nancy Whipple. *Carrying the Torch: Maud Howe Elliott and the American Renaissance*. Hanover: University Press of New England, 2014.

Hall, Susan. "Down Palm Beach Way: The Helander House on Historic Root Trail." *South Florida*, September 1993.

"Haratune [sic] Michaelyan, Esq." Unpublished essay, HSPBC.

Hathaway, Fran. "Paul Riba, Magic Realist," *Palm Beach Life*, January 1973.

"Henry Strater, Ogunquit Artist." *Friends of the Ogunquit Museum Newsletter*, Spring 2014.

Hemingway, Ernest. *A Moveable Feast: The Restored Edition*. New York: Simon and Schuster, 2009.

Henshall, James Alexander. *Camping and Cruising in Florida*. Cincinnati: Robert Clarke, 1884.

Herrera, Hayden. *Listening to Stone: The Art and Life of Isamu Noguchi*. New York: Farrar, Straus and Giroux, 2015.

Herter, Adele McGinnis and Albert Herter. Papers, 1882-1946. Reels 2342-2546, Archives of American Art, Smithsonian Institution.

"Herter Looms Revive an Ancient Art." *Fine Arts Journal* 31, no. 5, November 1914: 537-41.

"Hiker, by Alice Ruggles Kitson." Art Inventories Catalog, Smithsonian Institution, http://siris-artinventories.si.edu/ (accessed February 24, 2015).

Hiss, Anthony. "Miss Caroline Van Hook Bean." *The New Yorker*, April 18, 1970, 34.

Histed Papers. HSPBC.

"History of the Black Mountain Inn," http://www.blackmountaininn.com/history.php (accessed May 18, 2015).

House, Charles. *The Outrageous Life of Henry Faulkner*. Sarasota: Pub This Press, 2005. First published 1988 by University of Tennessee Press.

Hoving, Thomas. *Making the Mummies Dance: Inside the Metropolitan Museum of Art*. New York: Simon & Schuster, 1993.

Hunter, E. Robert. "Norton Gallery of Art: Young, Vital, Attains

National Position." *Art Digest* 23, 4 (November 15, 1948) 12-15.

Hurt, Jethro M. III. "Bethesda-by-the-Sea: The Spanish Memorial." *The Tustenegee,* HSPBC 4, no. 1 (Spring 2013): 10-15.

"Individuality—A Keynote to a Young Woman's Success." *California's Magazine, Edition Deluxe,* vol. 2. San Francisco: California's Magazine Co., 1916.

"In the Galleries." *International Studio,* April 1919.

"In the Quiet of a Palm Beach Loggia." *The Spur,* April 1, 1931.

Johnston, Alva. *The Legendary Mizners.* New York: McMillan, 1953.

———."The Palm Beach Architect: The Boom." *New Yorker,* November 29, 1952.

Joseph, J. Jonathan. *Jane Peterson: An American Artist.* Boston: J. Jonathan Joseph, 1981.

"J. R. De Lamar." *American Art News,* December 7, 1918.

Kahn, Otto. Papers. HSPBC.

Keyes, Emilie. Papers. HSPBC.

———."Tish Massie, Her Shells and Flowers." *Palm Beach Life,* February 20, 1959.

———."Young Local Artist Returns from Italy for Exhibition." *Palm Beach Life,* February 12, 1957.

King, Leone. "Palm Beach Dateline." *Social Pictorial,* March 27, 1972.

Kissam, Joy Shepherd. "J. Clinton Shepherd, 1889-1975." Undocumented article, Art and Artists Papers, HSPBC.

Knott, Judge James R. Papers. HSPBC.

Kuhner, Elizabeth "Betty." Papers. HSPBC.

"La Maja Marquesa." *Federico Beltrán-Masses,* Stair Sainty Gallery. London: Stair Sainty Gallery, 2014, 42-49.

Landmarks Preservation Commission. "The Royal Poinciana Plaza: Designation Report." Palm Beach: Landmarks Preservation Commission, February 21, 2007.

Lahr, John. *Tennessee Williams: Mad Pilgrimage of the Flesh.* New York: Norton, 2014.

Lang, Andrew, editor. *The Arabian Nights' Entertainments.* New York: Longman's Green, 1898.

Latham, Charles. *The Gardens of Italy.* New York: Scribner's, 1919.

Le Gallienne, Eva. Papers. Box 1, Folder 2, Library of Congress.

———.*With a Quiet Heart: An Autobiography.* New York: Viking, 1953.

Lentelli, Leo. Papers. Archives of American Art, Smithsonian Institution.

Levy, Florence N., editor. *American Art Annual.* New York: American Art Annual, 1898-1914; Washington DC: *American Federation of the Arts,* 1903-1947.

Libby, Gary R. *Reflections II, Watercolors of Florida 1835-2000 from the Collection of Cici and Hyatt Brown.* Daytona Beach: Museum of Arts and Sciences, 2012.

Lindsey, Mrs. Christopher. "The Chinese Garden of the Society of the Four Arts." Unpublished manuscript, The Society of the Four Arts Papers, King Library, The Society of the Four Arts.

Livingstone, Robert. *Caroline van Hook Bean: The Last of the Impressionists.* Cape Cod, MA: Sandy Shores, Kindle Edition, July 1, 2011.

"Lydia B. Mann and Pan's Garden Honored." *The Preservation Foundation Newsletter,* November 1993.

Marandel, Patrice J. "Appendix 1: Other Works of Art Given by Anna Thomson Dodge or acquired from her Estate." *The Dodge Collection.* New York: Hudson Hills Press in association with the Detroit Institute of Art, 1996.

Marc, Franz, Annegret Hoberg, Isabelle Jansen. *Franz Marc: The Complete Works: The Oil Paintings.* London: Phillip Wilson, 2004.

Marconi, Richard A. and Debi Murray with the HSPBC. *Palm Beach.* Charleston: Arcadia, 2009.

McCormick, Robert. "Diary," May 16, 1891, HistoryMiami.

Mann, Maybelle. *Art in Florida, 1564-1945.* Sarasota: Pineapple Press, 1999.

"Married." *Town and Country,* March 20, 1921.

"Mary Benson, First Lady of Art." *Palm Beach Life,* January 1962.

Mayhew, Augustus. "Philadelphia in Palm Beach, Part 1." New York Social Diary, http://www.newyorksocialdiary.com/social-history/2011/philadelphia-in-palm-beach-part-i (accessed May 16, 2015).

Mizner, Addison. Papers. HSPBC.

———.Unpublished memoir manuscript, Addison Mizner Papers, HSPBC.

Mizner Industries. Papers. HSPBC.

Mockler, Kim I. *Maurice Fatio: Palm Beach Architect.* Suffolk, UK: Acanthus Press, 2010.

Michaelyan, Harutune. Papers. HSPBC.

"Mona Bismarck." Voguepedia, citing "Cristóbal Balenciaga:

Perfection Partagée." Paris: Mona Bismarck Foundation, 2006, http://www.vogue.com/voguepedia/Mona_von_Bismarck (accessed July 30, 2014).

Morgan, Bert and Richard Morgan. Papers. HSPBC.

Morley, William D., Inc. *Contents of Playa Riente, Unrestricted Public Auction*. Philadelphia: Wm. D. Morley, 1957.

Morrish, Olivia Gazzam. "The Early Years of the Four Arts, 1936-1947. The Society of Four Arts Papers, King Library.

"Mrs. Percy Hadley." Oral History. King Library, The Society of the Four Arts and HSPBC.

Museum of Modern Art. Press Release, February 20, 1936. MOMA Shared PDFs, https://www.moma.org/momaorg/shared/pdfs/docs/press_archives/313/releases/MOMA_1936_0009_1936-02-20_22036-5.pdf?2010 (accessed July 5, 2014).

Musgrove, Martha, "Gertrude Schweitzer: The Artist, the Woman." *Palm Beach Life,* February 1973, 59-62.

Norton Gallery and School of Art and Palm Beach Art Institute. *Paintings and Sculpture from Palm Beach Collections: 25th Anniversary Year, 1941-1966, February 8-March 6, 1966.* West Palm Beach: Norton Gallery and School of Art, 1966.

———.*Paintings and Sculpture: Norton Gallery and School of Art.* West Palm Beach: Norton Gallery and School of Art, 1963.

———.*Gertrude Schweitzer: Spring '73 Exhibitions.* New York: Triggs, 1973.

Norton, Ralph Hubbard. "The Donor Speaks." *Art Digest* 23, no. 15 (November 15, 1948), 20-22.

Olney, Susan Faxon, Barbara Ball Buff, John H. Dryfhout, et al. *A Circle of Friends: Art Colonies of Cornish and Dublin.* Durham: University Art Galleries, University of New Hampshire, 1985.

Orr, Christina. *Addison Mizner: Architect of Dreams and Realities (1872-1933): An Exhibition Organized by the Norton Gallery of Art.* West Palm Beach: Norton Gallery of Art, 1977.

Orr-Cahall, Christina. *The American Collection: Selected Works from the Norton Museum of Art Collection.* West Palm Beach: Norton Museum of Art, 1994.

Österreichische Galerie Belvedere and G. Frodl. *Franz Barwig, 1868-1931.* Translated by E. Baum. Vienna: Österreichische Galerie Belvedere, 1969.

O'Sullivan, Maureen. "Mort Kaye: Dean of Social Photographers." *Palm Beach Illustrated,* March 1997.

"Paintings of Charles Baskerville." *Palm Beach Life,* February 23, 1961, 54-56.

"Palazzo Davanzati, Museo dell'Antica Casa Fiorentina." Repertorio delle Architetture Civili di Firenze, http://www.palazzospinelli.org/architetture/scheda.asp?offset=1650&ID=712 (accessed September 11, 2014).

Palm Beach Art Center. *Catalogue of the Fourth Annual National Exhibition of Paintings, Sculpture, and Etchings, January 30-March 30, 1936.*

Palm Beach Galleries. *DeVries-Patton-Grosperrin.* Gallery Flyer, January 1962, Art and Artists Files, HSPBC.

"Palm Beach: Showplace for Art." *Palm Beach Life,* March 1962, 55.

Palmer, Martin and Jay Ramsay with Man-ho Kwok. *Kuan Yin: Myths and Revelations of the Chinese Goddess of Compassion.* New York: Thorsons, 1995.

Parsons, Betty. Papers. Archives of American Art, Smithsonian Institution, http://www.aaa.si.edu/collections/betty-parsons-gallery-records-and-personal-papers-7211 (accessed May 5, 2014).

"Patricia Massie's Paintings." *Palm Beach Life,* March 9, 1961.

"Paul Crosthwaite," Michener Art Museum, http://www.michenermuseum.org/bucksartists/artist.php?artist=61 (accessed October 8, 2014).

Pennsylvania Academy of the Fine Arts. *Catalogue of the 113th Annual Exhibition, February 3 to March 24, 1918.* Philadelphia: Pennsylvania Academy of the Fine Arts, 1918.

Penny, Nicholas and Karen Serres. "Duveen and the Decorators." *The Burlington Magazine,* June 2007, 400-406.

Peterson, Brian H. *Form Radiating Life: The Paintings of Charles Rosen.* Philadelphia: University of Pennsylvania Press; Bucks County: James Michener Museum, 2007.

Phipps, Lillian Bostwick. *Lillian Phipps Galleries Presents Raoul Dufy January 8-January 21, 1966.* Palm Beach: Lillian Phipps Galleries, 1966.

"Piero Aversa Biography." Piero Aversa Collection, http://www.pieroaversacollection.com/the-artist.htm (accessed October 2, 2014).

Pierce, Patricia Jobe. "The Courageous Jane Peterson." *Fine Art Connoisseur,* January-February 2015, http://www.

fineartconnoisseur.com/pages/20613959.php? (accessed July 7, 2015).

Pollack, Deborah C. "A Brief History of Fine Art and Artists in Palm Beach." *Palm Beach Jewelry and Antique Show Catalogue,* February 2012.

———.*Felix de Crano: Forgotten Artist of the Flagler Colony.* St. Augustine: Lightner Museum, 2014.

———.*Laura Woodward: The Artist Behind the Innovator Who Developed Palm Beach.* Palm Beach: Blue Heron Press with the HSPBC, 2009.

———.*Orville Bulman: An Enchanted Life and Fantastic Legacy.* Palm Beach: Blue Heron Press, 2006.

———."Thieme, Anthony." In *The New Encyclopedia of Southern Culture,* edited by Judith H. Bonner and Estill Curtis Pennington, vol. 21, *Art and Architecture.* Chapel Hill: University of North Carolina Press, 2013.

———.*Visual Art and the Urban Evolution of the New South.* Columbia: University of South Carolina Press, 2015.

"Post Impressionists and their Followers." *Palm Beach Life,* February 8, 1949.

Potter, George Wells. Papers. HSPBC.

Quincey, Sam. Photograph Files. HSPBC.

Rayner, William P. Archive. HSPBC.

"Regarding the Arts." *Palm Beach Illustrated* clipping, 1965, Art and Artist Files, HSPBC.

"Richard Resler." State Archives of Florida, Florida Memory, http://www.floridamemory.com/items/show/153287 (accessed November 5, 2014.

Rice, Rebecca S. "Mona Strader Bismarck Collection." *Filson Newsmagazine.* Filson Historical Society, http://www.filsonhistorical.org/archive/news_v4n3_MonaBismarck.html (accessed August 6, 2014).

Robert S. Hurwitz Loft on the Mile Gallery of Art. *Henry Lawrence Faulkner.* Exhibition catalogue, Coral Gables: Robert S. Hurwitz Loft on the Mile Gallery of Art, February 25, ca. 1960s.

Romney, Richard Adams. Papers. MSS 462 Box 1 f., Beinecke Rare Book and Manuscript Library, Yale University.

Root, Enoch. Papers. HSPBC.

———."Photography as Fine Art." *The Photographic News,* August 18, 1888, 521-22.

Roscher, Mignon. "Frederick Roscher," http://www.frederickroscher.com/about.html (accessed July 23, 2014).

Rosensweig, Jeffrey and Betty Liu, *Age Smart: Discovering the Fountain of Youth at Midlife and Beyond.* Upper Saddle River, New York: Pearson, 2006, 195-97.

Ross, Josephine and Condé Nast. *Society in Vogue: The International Set between the Wars.* New York: Vendome Press, 1992.

Rubinstein, Charlotte. *American Women Sculptors: A History of Women Working in Three Dimensions.* Boston: G. K. Hall, 1990.

Rubin, Patricia Lee. *Images and Identity in Fifteenth-Century Florence.* New Haven: Yale University Press, 2007.

Russell, Edward Ledyard. *Lake Worth.* New York: Ambrotype, 1896.

Salmon, Robin R. *Sculpture of Brookgreen Gardens.* Mt. Pleasant, South Carolina: Arcadia, 2006.

Samuel T. Freeman & Co. *Complete Furnishings of "El Mirasol."* Philadelphia: Samuel T. Freeman & Co., 1947.

Schanke, Robert A. *Shattered Applause: The Lives of Eva Le Gallienne.* Carbondale and Edwardsville, Illinois: Southern Illinois University Press, 1992.

Schwarz, Amy. "Burt W. Johnson (1890-1927)." Unpublished manuscript.

Scrapbooks. The Society of the Four Arts, King Library.

Secrest, Meryle. *Duveen: A Life in Art.* Chicago: University of Chicago Press, 2005.

Seebohm, Caroline. *Boca Rococo: How Addison Mizner Invented Florida's Gold Coast.* New York: Clarkson Potter, 2001.

Sheehy, Helen. *Eva Le Gallienne: A Biography.* New York: Knopf, 1996.

Shippen, Zoe. Papers. HSPBC.

Simbari, Elfrida. "The Simbari Diaries: A Fifty Year Adventure," http://www.simbari.co.uk/story_america.php (accessed May 28, 2014).

Society of the Four Arts. *The Collection of Mrs. John Wintersteen: An Exhibition of Paintings, Drawings and Sculpture.* Palm Beach: The Society of the Four Arts, 1969.

———.*Collection of Ralph H. and Elizabeth C. Norton and an Exhibition by Invited Paintings for National Exhibition.* Palm Beach: The Society of the Four Arts, 1938.

———.*The Society of the Four Arts, 1956-1957* (handbook).

Paul Gauguin, 1848-1903. Exhibition catalogue, 1956.

"Soldier Art Sells at Palm Beach." *Art Digest,* 17, April 15, 1943: 11.

"Southern States Art League." *American Magazine of Art,* June 1922.

Spencer, Wilma Bell. *Palm Beach: A Century of Heritage.* Washington, DC: Mount Vernon, 1975.

State of Florida. State of Florida Public Records, http://www.stateofflorida.com/Portal/DesktopDefault.aspx?tabid=13 (accessed April 12, 2014).

Stebbins, Theodore E. *The Life and Work of Martin Johnson Heade: A Critical Analysis and Catalogue Raisonné.* New Haven: Yale University Press, 2000.

Stein, Anne Marie with George Carpozi, Jr. *Three Picassos Before Breakfast.* New York: Hawthorn, 1973.

"Stone City Art Colony and School 1932-1933," Mount Mercy University, http://projects.mtmercy.edu/stonecity/otherartists/sharp.html (accessed October 8, 2014).

Strater, Henry. Papers. Reel 3465, Archives of American Art, Smithsonian Institution.

"Studio Gossip." *American Art News,* May 14, 1921.

Sturgis, Alexander and the National Gallery (Great Britain). *Rebels and Martyrs: The Image of the Artist in the Nineteenth Century.* New Haven: Yale University Press, 2006.

"Styx: Removal." Palm Beach County History Online, HSPBC, http://www.pbchistoryonline.org/page/the-styx (accessed November 5, 2014).

Tchelitchew, Pavel. Papers. Harry Ransom Center, University of Texas at Austin.

"Things to Remember." Unpublished manuscript, Society of the Four Arts Papers, King Library, Society of the Four Arts.

"Thomas Shields Clarke." Obituary. *American Art News,* November 20, 1920.

Thompson, David R. and Sandra Thompson. *Palm Beach from the Other Side of the Lake.* New York: Vantage Press, 1992.

Thompson, Sandra. "Sandra Thompson: Palm Beach Artist." Unpublished manuscript.

Troemel, Jean Wagner. Scrapbook. Personal documents.

Town of Palm Beach. *Comprehensive Plan* (Palm Beach: Town of Palm Beach, 1979), 25, http://docserver.townofpalmbeach.com/TownClerkWeblink/1/doc/662655/Page36.aspx (accessed April 8, 2016).

Trosby Galleries. *Impressionist and Modern Paintings, Drawings, and Sculpture in the Collection of Mr. and Mrs. Edgardo Acosta.* Palm Beach: Trosby Galleries, 1966.

Turgeon, Frank. Papers. HSPBC.

Tyler, Parker. *The Divine Comedy of Pavel Tchelitchew.* New York: Fleet, 1967.

United States Department of the Interior, National Park Service. "National Register of Historic Places Continuation Sheet," http://pdfhost.focus.nps.gov/docs/NRHP/Text/64500748.pdf (accessed February 24, 2015).

"U.S. Military in Palm Beach." "History Online," HSPBC, http://www.pbchistoryonline.org/page/us-military-in-palm-beach (accessed July 25, 2014).

Villa, Emilio, Raymond Charmet, and Stuart Preston. *The Simbari Collection, 1950-1983.* St. Helier, Jersey, Channel Islands: Selene, 1983.

Walrond, Eric D. "Augusta Savage Shows Amazing Gift for Sculpture," 1922. Reprinted in Tony Martin, ed., *African Fundamentalism: A Literary and Cultural Anthology of Garvey's Harlem Renaissance.* Dover, Massachusetts: Majority Press, 1992.

Walter, Eugene and Palm Beach Galleries. *Simbari, January 18-31, 1960.* Palm Beach Galleries, Art and Artists Files, HSPBC.

Ward, Bruce. "Tuesday Night at the Galleries. *Palm Beach Life,* February 1971.

Ward, Elán M. "From the University Archives—This Week in UNCW History: 'Young Girl Defending Herself Against Eros' Returns to UNCW, Feb. 12, 2001." University of North Carolina Wilmington, http://library.uncw.edu/archives_special/spotlights/university-archives-week-uncw-history-famous-painting-comes-home-uncw-2001 (accessed November 21, 2014).

Weinberg, H. Barbara. "Hassam in East Hampton." *Childe Hassam: American Impressionist.* New York: Metropolitan Museum of Art, 2004, 231-52.

White, James T. et al, editors. "Heaton, Augustus George." *National Cyclopedia of Biography, Volume Five,* New York: J. T. White, 1907.

Wildenstein & Co. *A Loan Exhibition of Degas for the Benefit of the Citizen's Committee for Children of New York, Inc., April 7-May 7, 1960.* New York: Wildenstein, 1960.

Williams, Wheeler. *Wheeler Williams.* American Sculpture Series. New York: Norton under the auspices of the National Sculpture Society, 1947.

Wintz, Cary D. and Paul Finkelman, eds. "Augusta Savage." *Encyclopedia of the Harlem Renaissance: K-Y.* New York: Routledge, 2004.

Witkowski, Quinn. Zoe (Jewett) Shippen." AskArt discussion board, http://www.askart.com/AskART/artists/bulletin.as px?searchtype=DISCUSS&artist=100087 (accessed June 28, 2014).

"World of Charles Knight," http://www.charlesrknight.com/ Biography.htm (accessed July 7, 2012).

"Worth Avenue Gallery." *Palm Beach Life,* January 1948.

Worth Avenue Gallery. Papers. Art and Artists Files, HSPBC.

———.*John Franklin Hawkins and Keith Ingermann.* Exhibition catalogue, February 5-17, 1951.

———.*John Sharp.* Undated catalogue.

———.*Orville Bulman, Recent Paintings.* March 16-28, 1952, March 14-27, 1955.

———.*Paintings by Keith Ingermann, February 4-16.* Undated catalogue.

Wright, Christopher and Norton Museum of Art. *Kyril Vassilev: 1908-1987: A Retrospective Exhibition, February 2-March 12, 1989.* West Palm Beach: Norton Gallery of Art, 1989.

Zito, Vincenzo. "Eighty Superb Celebrity Caricatures . . ." Sketchbook of Celebrities, *RR Auction Catalogue,* 267, January 23, 2014, http://issuu.com/rrauction/docs/423vc (accessed October 28, 2014).

Index

Erickson, Alfred, 54, 75
Ernst, Max, 145
Escuela Nacional de Pintura, Escultura y Grabado, 109
Everglades Club, 30, 33, 37, 41, 44, 49, 51, 63, 90, 124, 128

Fahs-Smith, Mrs. Neville, 101
Farny, Henry F., 13, 159
Fatio, Maurice, 55, 63, 66, 69, 75, 77
Faulkner, Henry, 126-28, 136
Ferargil Galleries, 59
Findlay, Walstein "Wally," 131, 136, 143
Fini, Leonor, 115
Fink, Denman, 73
Flagler, Henry Morrison, 9, 14, 16-17, 21, 23-26, 29, 41, 61, 70, 151, 154
Flagler, Mary Lily Kenan, 24, 154
Flair Galleries, 145
Florida Artists Hall of Fame, 17, 157
Florida Federation of Art, 77
Florida Watercolor Society, 90
Flushing, New York, 39
Fortnightly Club, 26
Fountain of Youth, 34, 42, 88
Fountain of Youth Archaeological Park, 34
Frank, Richard, 158
Fraser, James Earle, 39-40
Fraser, Walter, 34
French, Daniel Chester, 32, 107
Friends of the Arts and Crafts, 55-56, 58-59, 72, 74
Frishmuth, Harriet Whitney, 47, 60

Gainsborough, Thomas, 75, 151
Galerie Jean Tiroche, 145
Galerie Juarez, 145
Galerie Montmarte, 145
Galerie Trianon, 139
Gallery Biba, 160
Gallery Gemini, 144
Garden Club of Palm Beach, 20, 59
Gardner, Isabella Stewart, 35
Gasiunasen Gallery, 160
Gauguin, Paul, 86, 114
Gavlak Gallery, 160

Geisler, Frank E., 56
Geldzahler, Henry, 157
George, Ouida, 109-10, 144
Gérôme, Jean-Léon, 34
Gerst, Hilde, 144
Geske, Erich John, 73
Getty Museum, 25
Gibbes Museum of Art, 160
Gilded Age, 22, 25
Gimenez y Martin, Juan, 25
Gioconda and Joseph King Library, Society of the Four Arts, 49, 77, 82, 103
Godio, August, 61
Goldman, Albert, 144
Gonzalez, Xavier, 113
Goodrich, Lloyd, 79
Goya, Francisco, 75
Grace, Princess of Monaco, 136, 151
Grand Duchess Serge of Russia (Federovna, Elizabeth), 22
Grand Rapids Museum of Art, 124
Gray, Jack Lorimer, 140-41, 144
Green, Roe, 155
Gris, Juan, 107
Grove, Edward Ryneal, 147
Grubman, Judith, 161
Grubman, Robin, 161
Grygutis, Barbara, 155
Gubelmann, Mrs. Walter, 110, 136
Gubelmann, Walter, 110
Guest, Amy Phipps, 9, 41, 56, 59, 60, 72, 74, 77, 93, 100, 115
Guest, C. Z., 115
Guggenheim, Peggy, 115, 145

Habatat Gallery, 160
Halpert, Edith, 97
Hamilton, Carl, 35
Hammerstein, Dorothy, 142
Hanke, G. F. Robert, 154
Hanson, Duane, 157
Hare, Channing Weir, 97-98, 118, 151
Harlem Renaissance, 39
Hartford, Huntington, 121
Hartley, Jonathan Scott, 59